DEPARTURE STORIES

DEPARTURE STORIES

Betty Crocker Made Matzoh Balls (and other lies)

—⁓—

ELISA BERNICK

INDIANA UNIVERSITY PRESS

This book is a publication of

Indiana University Press
Office of Scholarly Publishing
Herman B Wells Library 350
1320 East 10th Street
Bloomington, Indiana 47405 USA

iupress.indiana.edu

Manufactured in the United States of America
Disclaimer: This book is a memoir. It reflects the author's present recollections of experiences over time. Some names and characteristics have been changed, some events have been compressed, and some dialogue has been recreated.

Permission Credit Lines:
Excerpt(s) from *A Field Guide to Getting Lost* by Rebecca Solnit, copyright © 2005 by Rebecca Solnit. Used by permission of Viking Books, an imprint of Penguin Publishing Group, a division of Penguin Random House LLC. All rights reserved.
Excerpt from *Sister Outsider: Essays and Speeches* by Audre Lord, copyright © 1984 by Crossing Press.
Excerpt from *Hiroshima in the Morning* by Rahna Reiko Rizzuto. Reprinted with the permission of The Permissions Company, LLC on behalf of The Feminist Press, www.feministpress.org.
Excerpt from *Revolution from Within: A Book of Self-Esteem* by Gloria Steinem, copyright © 1992. Reprinted by permission of Little, Brown & Company, an imprint of Hachette Book Group, Inc.
Excerpt from *Betty Crocker's Picture Cookbook 1956, Second Edition*, used with permission of General Mills Marketing, Inc.

First printing 2022

Cataloging information is available from the Library of Congress.

ISBN 978-0-253-06406-6 (hdbk.)
ISBN 978-0-253-06407-3 (pbk.)
ISBN 978-0-253-06408-0 (web PDF)

With my love,
Past, present, and future

Arlene Defren, December 11, 1937–March 3, 2017
Lori Bernick Tellez, June 4, 1965–August 18, 2018

Mrs. Bernick with Danny, 5, and Elisa, 3
Flowers on clothes chest match curtains.
Minnesota Historical Society, *Minneapolis Tribune* photo by Donald Black, April 27,
1964

CONTENTS

AUTHOR'S NOTE

Departure
1. the act of leaving a place
2. a variation that deviates from the standard or norm
—*Merriam-Webster Dictionary*

The two central definitions of *departure*—leaving and deviating from the norm—aptly describe the history and character of my family, the Jews, and my experience of growing up Jewish in the White Christian Minnesota suburbs. They also describe my mother, whose various departures (from sanity, from her marriage, from her children, and, eventually, from Minnesota) drove the plot line in my family's story.

This book examines my family's narrative through the broader lens of Minnesota history, in particular the cultural shifts that swept the country during the 1960s and 1970s. Many of these tales will feel familiar to anyone, Jewish or not, who grew up during this tumultuous period when marital expectations, parental duties, and women's growing independence were in conflict.

These stories are rooted in Minnesota's antisemitism and its unique relationship to "difference." My family was one of only a handful of Jewish families living in the Minneapolis suburb of New Hope at this time. Among the humorous anecdotes of latkes and lutefisk, you'll find tales of Jews as insiders/outsiders—tolerated but not quite welcome. It's a different perspective of Minnesota's particular brand of "Nice."

DEPARTURE STORIES

PART ONE

Arrivals

Arrival in the world is really a departure and that, which we call departure, is only a return.

—Dejan Stojanovic, *The Sun Watches the Sun*

In portaging from one river to another, Wabanakis had to carry their canoes and all other possessions. Everyone knew the value of traveling light and understood that it required leaving some things behind. Nothing encumbered movement more than fear, which was often the most difficult burden to surrender.

—Bunny McBride, *Women of the Dawn*

—✺—

THE BERNICK FAMILY SURVIVAL RELAY

To Baby
"Miracle that is daily with us."
Bringer of joy,
Disturber of the peace—and of complacency
Intrepid explorer—beloved of family and friends
Welcomed by the whole household of Israel.

"Our Baby—A Record Book for the Jewish Child," the National
Women's League of the United Synagogue of America

I KNEW FROM THE START that departure was my salvation. From my earliest breaths, I was on the run, trying to find the exits.

"You came out squirming and twisting so much, Dr. Sinykin almost dropped you right on the floor," my mom always said about my birth. "Your little legs were going so fast. You were like a bloody little eggbeater."

I loved this gory detail. It was both horrifying and thrilling.

Even though my mom was unconscious during all four of her children's births, suspended in the 1950s and 1960s "twilight sleep" of general anesthesia, she claimed she was able to narrate the details of our births with "one hundred percent accuracy."

"The nurses called you 'Speedy Gonzales,'" she said. "It's like you came out running and never stopped. Look in your baby book if you don't believe me."

My baby book is entitled "Our Baby—A Record Book for the Jewish Child." It had been distributed by the National Women's League of the United Synagogue of America. My mom had dutifully filled out the parchment-colored pages in her perfect cursive. Under the heading "A Child Is Born to Us," she wrote,

Elisa Rae Bernick. Born: October 30, 1960. 9:26 p.m. Mount Sinai Hospital, Mpls. MN. 6lb. 14oz. Hebrew name: Etau.

On the page entitled "Congratulations and Gifts," my mom had pasted this newspaper clipping:

Look Who's Here
Girls
Mr and Mrs:
Sam Bernick, 7625 N. 30th Av., Crystal
Ralph G. Blossom, 6866 NE. Madison, Fridley
Kenneth E. Christian, 2400 W. Jones Pl., Bloomington
Ralph G. Cummens, 4125 W. 21st

The last entry is cut off, along with the names of all the other fathers of little girls born in Minneapolis on my birthday. Notice how invisible the mothers of those newborns are—only the fathers receive names. My dad's name is first on the list. The invisibility of females in the 1960s feels startling today, but it's a good reminder of what life was like for women back then.

On a page called "The Naming of a Daughter," there is a second newspaper clipping, this one from the *Jewish World*. It reports that "Mr. and Mrs. Samuel Bernick" participated in a baby blessing ceremony at the Beth El Synagogue. Once again, my mother is invisible. Despite the many differences between Christians and Jews in the 1960s, the lowly status of women was a belief they shared.

If you skip past "A Son Enters the Covenant," "Covenant of Circumcision," and "Pidyon Haben," a special Jewish ceremony for a firstborn son (all hail the firstborn son), you eventually come to a page called "Little by Little, Step by Step."

In the lower right-hand corner, next to a wisp of my dark baby hair attached by a yellowing strip of scotch tape, underneath a photo of me asleep in a hospital bassinet, tightly swaddled, undoubtedly to keep me from dashing out the door, my mom had written this: "First Nicknames: Speedy Gonzales and Road Runner."

I owe my speed, in part, to my mother's red hair. It was the outward manifestation of her inner ire. Her hair looked like someone had lit her head on fire; oranges, reds, and yellows all ablaze. She was a female suburban Samson whose explosive temper regularly shook the walls of our family until it ultimately collapsed. But when I was young, before I had any curiosity about the source of her powerful anger, I assumed it was her flaming red hair.

Later in life, my mother told me I was her only "wanted" child, but I didn't sense this as I was growing up. There was no evidence of my special status—no hugs, goodnight kisses, or words of comfort. No pats on the back or ready smiles. My mom had a caustic tongue and a bruising slap—with her hand, a belt, and a wooden spoon. She came from the "Stop crying or I'll give you something to cry about" school of parenting. My father followed her lead in this and nearly everything else.

I remember the moment I realized how unusual her hair color was. It was right after my fifth birthday. I was sitting at the kitchen table with a new box of forty-eight Crayola crayons, drawing her portrait. She wore her hair in an elaborately teased bouffant that wobbled whenever she got mad, which was all the time. My dad called her "a firecracker" and said, "Redheads have a short fuse."

He said this a lot.

The words *firecracker* and *fuse* gave me a brilliant idea. I grabbed the orange red, orange yellow, and red orange crayons and started hitting the ends of them on top of her paper head. "Sparks," I thought, feeling clever. My mom's hair was the color of sparks! I hit the paper harder and harder, imagining her head exploding and all the swear words inside it shooting straight out the top.

"Elisa, what in the hell are you doing out there?" my mom yelled from the kitchen.

She was making Cherry Top Hats for the New Hope Jaycees' "Magic Muffins" contest. I had been helping her until I used too much filling, and she told me to find something else to do besides bother her.

"I thought you were coloring a picture!"

"I am."

"Since when does coloring make so much goddamn noise?"

The sparking nature of my mom's hair did not make her one of the popular moms on Zealand Avenue in New Hope. My dad said she was a "a real hot tamale" who "shot from the hip." When she was mad, he told her to calm down because "the veins were sticking out of her neck."

This only made her madder, of course.

Given my mom's *challenging personality*, is it any surprise I ran away a lot as a kid?

"I got so sick of chasing after you, I decided if you got hit by a car, so be it."

I thought she was joking the first time she said this. The second time, I wasn't so sure.

"Your little legs were going so fast you'd have thought you'd grow up to break the world's record in some kind of race."

She was not wrong about this. The name of the race was the Bernick Family Survival Relay, and I didn't need a baton to tell me when to head out the door.

Neighbors found me on their swing sets at seven in the morning and nine at night. When I was four, I ran away from my mom in the Red Owl produce section. I ran right past a man pushing a big cart of bananas through the long hanging plastic strips back to where the workers were unloading trucks. I kept running straight out the back door and down the loading dock steps. An hour later the police found me eating a doughnut in the break room of Polanski's bakery two blocks away.

"Oh sure, run away," she always yelled when I headed out the door. "A fat lot of good that will do you!"

She was right, of course. She was still there when I got back, but what else could I do? I went to bed each night wishing for Glinda the Good Witch, but the Wicked Witch of the West called me to breakfast.

Running away was my best (and only) option.

I remember another morning when I was five. My mom's head exploded because my brother Danny, who was seven at the time, made a mess of his school clothes after he painted a Malt-O-Meal beard and mustache on his face instead of eating it. I couldn't help giggling, which was the last straw, according to my mom.

"You think this is funny?" she asked me, slapping Danny on the top of the head, while wrestling his shirt off him. "We'll see how funny it is when I get back."

The moment she dragged Danny out the back door, I headed out the front. It was raining, so I leaped over puddles with raindrops pelting the top of my head, wondering where I could go in the rain. Should I hide in the old refrigerator box in the Millers' garage or hunker down under the Westlunds' deck? Anything was better than seeing the veins stick out of my mom's neck when she got back from Danny's bus stop.

The word *bus stop* gave me an idea. I could go to the bus stop where I waited for the city bus with Aunt Freda when we went downtown to the art museum. I had never run away on the city bus before. Maybe it would take me so far away my mom would never find me.

At the bus stop I hid behind a tree and pressed my cheek against the moist, rough bark. People were waiting underneath umbrellas, and nobody noticed me. When the bus pulled up, the big door whooshed warmth into the damp chill as I slipped in line between a man wearing a black raincoat and a woman holding another little girl's hand. Kids rode free, so nobody questioned me.

For nearly two hours I basked in the good will of other riders, who assumed I was someone else's charge. Finally, the bus emptied out and the bus driver noticed me near the back of the bus, swinging my legs and staring out the rain-speckled window.

"Hey, kid!" he called back, while looking at me in the overhead mirror. "Are ya lost?"

"Nope," I called back, not lost in the least.

He raised a mirrored eyebrow and picked up the walkie-talkie.

At 9:50 a.m. the bus roared up Zealand Avenue and stopped in front of our house with me as its only passenger. My mom was standing in the driveway out in the rain, and I knew I was in serious trouble. My heart thudded in my ears as I waved goodbye to Mac the bus driver, and my mom dragged me down the bus steps toward the house by the elbow.

"Elisa Rae Bernick, do you know how much trouble you're in?"

I had never seen my mom so mad.

"I was scared to death!"

Her voice was tight and low.

"I had no idea where you were! I called the police!"

She pinched my arm hard, and I started crying.

"Stop crying right now, Goddamn it, or I'll really give you something to cry about!"

I slipped on the wet pavement, and she dragged me to standing without pausing.

"I'm sick to death of you running away, Elisa! I mean it!"

We were almost to the house, and I tried to pull out of her viselike grip. I saw Mrs. Miller standing on her steps, watching us from across the street.

"I won't run away anymore. I promise!"

She pushed me through the front door and slammed it shut behind us.

"Stop lying, Elisa!"

I heard the danger in her voice and saw the flat look in her eyes. I knew what was coming next. I started to scream and kick, doing my best to dodge her hand, but she pulled me down hard to the floor. She smashed my cheek into the nubby blue carpet and yanked my underpants down right there in front of the door.

"No, Mom, please. I won't run away anymore. I promise!"

"Goddamn it, Elisa!"

"Ow!"

"I'm sick to death of you running away!"

"Mommy, stop!"

"When are you gonna learn your goddamn lesson?"

"No, Mommy! No!"

"Why . . . (smack!) won't you stop (smack!) . . . running . . . away (smack!)."

I closed my eyes and kept screaming. It's only when her voice got hoarse and my screams turned to silent shudders that she stopped hitting me.

I lay on my side shaking silently. My thin white legs quaked in the pink-hemmed underwear still down around my knees.

"I . . . Elisa . . . please stop running away from me. I'm sorry."

I barely heard her apology over the words of comfort I was whispering to myself. I was already moving away from my small, bruised body, flying upward through the ceiling like a bird. I flew higher and higher, breaking through the gray, bulging clouds to the fluffy blue sky above. The sandpaper-gray rooftops of Zealand Avenue were a shapeless blur beneath me as I hurtled through space. I was an arrow of blue light streaking away from my mom's cracked and stormy heart, looking for a sunny place where I was loved.

MEMORY IS A SLIPPERY FISH

> She was the keeper of the family stories and photographs, though they served less as buttresses of a stable sense of the past than phantasms and fictions that metamorphose continually in accordance with the needs of the present.
>
> —Rebecca Solnit, *A Field Guide to Getting Lost*

LET'S TAKE A MOMENT TO talk about memories, because that's what this book is built on.

My own memory of running away on the city bus and then being punished by my mom certainly feels true to me. But given the slippery nature of memory, can I be sure it's the truth?

No. And neither can you.

Although we rely on our memories to establish the facts of our lives and identities, science has soundly disproven their "factual" nature. We don't store memories in orderly files and call them up as static snapshots of moments in time. Instead, selectivity, trauma, and time alter the way we remember significant events. Memory and imagination fuse together. Each time we call up a memory, we depart from an earlier version and record something different. Rather than remembering the actual event, we remember the last time we recalled the memory, and we tweak it a little before tucking it back into its synaptic brain bed.

Cognitive scientists like to say that *using memory changes memory.*

When I remember that rainy day when I was five, I'm guessing at some of the details. Maybe I was younger or older. Maybe I didn't ride the bus for two hours. Or maybe I made the whole thing up without knowing it.

I'm not saying I did, but it's possible. In addition to editing, distorting, exaggerating, and embellishing memories, we constantly "remember" things that

9

aren't true. In study after study, people believe they've visited places they haven't and believe they've done things they never did. Psychologists can easily convince people they've committed armed robbery and worse. Researchers at MIT have even successfully planted false memories in mice.

"Even memories which are detailed and vivid and held with 100 percent conviction can be completely false," says University of London professor Chris French.

As a writer and a journalist, I've been recording my childhood memories for thirty years in one form or another. I'm convinced of their emotional truth, but I'm less certain about the accuracy of the details. I know I ran away a lot as a kid, and punishment at the hands of my mom was often brutal. But did I really run away on the city bus?

My sister Lori isn't convinced. She thinks it was our aunt who ran away on the city bus when she was young. But I swear it was me. Did I make this up? Did I insert myself into a story I'd heard around the dinner table and make it my own? Even odder, I've written stories I swear are fiction that Lori says are completely true. Like the one about me hitchhiking to the airport in Los Angeles when I was thirteen.

"You don't remember hitchhiking that night?" Lori asked, after reading the story.

No, I really don't. I remember being at the airport, but I have no idea how I got there. How could I possibly forget something like that?

A few years ago, after writer Elizabeth McCracken reread Beverly Cleary's Ramona Quimby books as an adult, she tweeted, "87% of my kindergarten memories are in fact plagiarized from *Ramona the Pest*." Not only is this hilarious, but I suspect it's the way most of us remember our childhoods. Not like Ramona Quimby's, necessarily (mine sure wasn't), but as stories embroidered with tidbits from books, movies, television shows, song lyrics, photo albums, family lore, and fantasies.

There's a lot of handwringing among nonfiction writers about the "truth" of our memories and how to present them authentically. The consensus is that we should seek their emotional truth, while acknowledging that they may contain elements of invention and imagination. We're not supposed to intentionally mislead our readers, but instead do something that writing instructors Brenda Miller and Suzanne Paola describe as "plumping the skeletal facts with the flesh of the imagination."

You will find intentional plumping in these pages. There are moments when I wonder aloud about my accurate recall of a memory or a past event. But what of my unintentional plumping? It is not my intention to mislead you, but the research makes it clear that our memories are flexible by design. The reason we continually "plump," adjust, and even reinvent our memories is that it allows us to adapt to our changing environments.

It's a survival mechanism.

Looked at in this way, the very act of remembering is a continual departure from one constructed memory to its new construction. Every time I roll that rainy-day memory around in my brain, tonguing it like some psychological jawbreaker, I alter it a little. I flavor it with something from this present-day moment, before my brain "encodes" it and it slips into the invisible matter of my cells.

This ability to adjust our memories keeps them relevant and helps us navigate our constantly shifting circumstances. I'm a great-granddaughter of Jewish refugees in Minnesota, and the "shifting circumstances" of my ancestors meant continually abandoning belongings, businesses, and the bones of children to run from pitchforks and paranoia, trying to find escape routes to survival.

I carry some of these memories in my cells, as did my parents, as do my children. They include the taste of fear and panic as my ancestors were chased into smaller and smaller containers. *Shtetl*, ghetto, train car. Starved, set on fire, gassed. These memories are sodden artifacts of departures and survival: the flotsam and jetsam of my ancestors' brief sense of belonging to the in-group, cast off again and again, to reveal a stark sense of "otherness" and "difference"—all still floating in the murky soup of my soul.

Perhaps the memory of running from my mother in the rain keeps my survival instincts honed.

The question, then, is, Does relying on my own and my family members' imperfect memories make my investigation of the past less truthful? What about the census records, newspaper articles, scrapbook notations, and archival materials I scoured, many of which are included in these pages? How "true" are these historical documents if history itself is in part a collective memory?

"History is never a 'given'; it is always a 'creation,'" says Annette Atkins in her book *Creating Minnesota: A History from the Inside Out*. She reminds us that history, like memory, is a flexible construct that becomes the dominant narrative and is something that usually serves the dominant group.

For the peripatetic Jews, our survival is rooted in memories that travel within our bodies and stories. The means of departure may change—on foot or horseback, on train or ship, through imagination or assimilation—but the goal has always been to flee and survive our shifting circumstances. And despite centuries of determined persecution, it's clear that Jews are survivors. If epigenetic research is correct, my ancestors' collective pool of memories—their shared history of flight and survival as "the other"—is actually hardwired in my genes. My very existence relies on these invisible memories: shifting stories that trace the flight path of my Jewish ancestors all the way from the shtetl to the Minnesota suburban prairie and beyond.

Our memories are the stories we tell ourselves about the future.

"THE GREAT JEWISH INVASION"

When Russia swallowed large chunks of Poland, one population was found to
be indigestible—the Jews.

—Linda Mack Schloff, *And Prairie Dogs Weren't Kosher*

MY FAMILY'S DEPARTURE STORY IS part of Minnesota's White immigration
history, which began nearly 175 years ago when it became the Minnesota Terri-
tory in 1849 and the thirty-second US state in 1858. Before and after the American
Civil War and the Dakota War of 1862, nonnative people were intent on removing
"obstacles" to their domination by clear-cutting trees as well as the indigenous
populations of the Anishinaabe (Chippewa, Ojibwe) and Dakota (Sioux). The
state's White economy, built on the back of this cultural genocide, started to
develop when natural resources were tapped for logging and farming.

The first major wave of immigration came in the 1860s and 1870s. These people
were mostly sensible, hardworking German, Norwegian, and Swedish farmers,
who came from harsh climates and weren't surprised by more of the same. They
were lured by inexpensive farmland and glowing missives from recent immigrants
extolling Minnesota's jobs, open spaces, and religious and political freedom (for
Whites), things that were sorely lacking in the countries they left behind. The
Irish came next, driven by religious persecution and the potato famine.

By the 1900s, Minnesota's population topped 1.3 million. At the time, the
foreign-born population in the United States was only 15 percent, but in Minnesota, 40 percent were foreign-born, and a third of all the Norwegians in the
country called Minnesota home. By combining forces with the Swedes, these

Nordic immigrants exerted an oversized influence on state politics and on civic and religious sensibilities.

In 1903, when my great-uncle Haim Berniker arrived in St. Paul, he wasn't coming for the weather, the land, or the Lutheran piety. He was a refugee fleeing the poverty and pogroms of Jewish life in Tzarist Russia. Soon after his arrival, *McClure's*, a popular US magazine, ran an article with the headline "The Great Jewish Invasion." Of Russian Jews like my great-uncle, it said, "No people have had a more inadequate preparation, educational and economic, for American citizenship."

Welcome to America.

A decade later, my great-grandfather, Shmuel Berniker, joined his brother in St. Paul just before the onset of World War I. He left the stench of the tannery in a shtetl called Derechin for a job as a mattress maker in Minnesota. He left my grandfather Itze (Isadore, Izzy), his oldest child, to care for his pregnant wife Chana and their five younger children. By the time Shmuel Berniker, now calling himself Samuel Bernick, had saved up enough money to send for his family, it was 1921, and his infant daughter Rochel had suffered through World War I and died of malnutrition without his ever meeting her.

I picture my Grandpa Izzy back then—a skinny twenty-one-year-old shepherding his mother and younger siblings to America. Broke, starved, and exhausted, clutching his family's papers, climbing in and out of wagons, finding his way to train stations, and finally, surviving the weeks at sea in the bowels of ship's steerage. Is it any wonder he never parted with a plastic bag or pencil stub later in life? He lived his entire life with the memories of those years of deprivation. He was grateful that America opened its doors to him, but he was always ready for those doors to be slammed in his face.

Exile was his default setting.

When Grandpa Izzy arrived in St. Paul, 99 percent of Minnesotans were Catholic or Lutheran—mostly Lutheran. Minnesota's history books refer to a "mass migration" of Jews to Minnesota between the 1880s and the 1920s, but the facts don't bear this out. Before 1880, there were fewer than one thousand Jews in Minnesota. By the 1920s, before immigration quotas stemmed the flow (my grandpa made it in just under the wire), there were approximately forty thousand Jews in the state, most of them from Poland, Ukraine, White Russia (Belarus), the Baltic provinces, and Romania.

According to the US census of 1937, the year my mom was born, there were 43,700 Jews in Minnesota—31,560 of them in Minneapolis where my mom grew up, 11,000 in St. Paul where my dad grew up, and 1,000 in Duluth. That leaves 140

Jews wandering around the prairie. All told, Jews represented a minuscule 0.9 percent of the state's total population and 1.7 percent of the Twin Cities' population. That's about the same percentage of Jews living in Minnesota today—hardly what you'd call a "mass migration." It does, however, give you a sense of how Jews have been perceived by the state's non-Jewish inhabitants from the very beginning.

THREE JEWISH JOKES

AN ANTISEMITE IS DRINKING IN a bar. He notices a Jew sitting at a table nearby and doesn't like it.

"Bartender! A round of the good stuff for everyone except him! It's on me."

Everyone except the Jewish man receives a glass of premium Scotch.

The antisemite looks over at the Jew with a smug grin.

The Jew smiles back.

The antisemite loses his satisfied expression.

"Bartender! Give everyone a drink of your finest, and a burger! It's on me."

He looks directly at the Jew and adds, "Everyone except the Jew."

The Jewish man looks at the antisemite and smiles again.

Furious, the antisemite says to the bartender, "Is that Jew just stupid or pretending to be?"

"Oh no, sir, he's the owner."

A WOMAN ON A TRAIN walks up to a man. "Excuse me," she says, "but are you Jewish?"

"No," replies the man.

A few minutes later the woman returns. "Excuse me," she says again, "are you sure you're not Jewish?"

"I'm sure," says the man.

A few minutes later, she approaches a third time. "Are you absolutely sure you're not Jewish?"

"All right, all right," the man says. "Yes, I'm Jewish."

"That's funny," says the woman. "You don't look Jewish."

IN A SMALL VILLAGE IN Poland, a terrifying rumor is spreading: A Christian girl has been found murdered.

Fearing retaliation, the Jewish community gathers in the shul to plan whatever defensive actions are possible under the circumstances.

Just as the emergency meeting is being called to order, in runs the president of the synagogue, out of breath and all excited.

"Brothers," he cries out. "I have wonderful news! The murdered girl is Jewish!"

—∭—

THREE MINNESOTA JOKES

LARS: "OLE, STAND IN FRONNA my car and tell me if da turn signals are vorking."

Ole: "Ya, No, Ya, No, Ya, No, Ya, No. . . ."

OLE DIED, SO LENA WENT to the local paper to put a notice in the obituaries. The gentleman at the counter offered his condolences and asked Lena what she would like to say about Ole.

Lena said, "You yust put 'Ole died.'"

The gentleman, somewhat perplexed, said, "That's it? Just 'Ole died'? Surely, there must be something more you'd like to say about Ole. If it's money you're concerned about, the first five words are free. We must say something more."

So, Lena thought about it for a few minutes and finally said, "OK. You put 'Ole died. Boat for sale.'"

"DID 'JA HEAR THE ONE about the Swedish [or Norwegian or German] farmer who loved his wife so much he almost told her?"

A DEPARTURE FROM "MINNESOTA NICE"

The white people here like to think of themselves as nice people. The idea that they actually might not be such nice people is so antithetical to their self-image, one feels their brains might actually explode if they even begin to contemplate such a negative notion.

—David Mura, *A Good Time for the Truth: Race in Minnesota*

IMPLICIT IN THE IDEA OF *departure* is "a departure from," or "difference." Difference is a challenging concept for Minnesotans, thanks, in part, to the state's immigration history. Along with a bootstrapping tradition of hard work and civility, those early Nordic settlers brought with them an enduring cultural expectation of quiet conformity. This is a central tenet of "Minnesota Nice."

In the 2016 book of essays *A Good Time for the Truth: Race in Minnesota*, sixteen contributors from a variety of races and ethnicities, none of them Jewish, discuss the gap in experience between Minnesota Nice and the reality of the outsider "non-White" experience in this state. In his essay "People Like Us," David Lawrence Grant says Minnesota Nice has two faces: "Outwardly, Minnesota Nice is about being courteous, respectful, and polite—to anyone and everyone—helpful and welcoming to strangers. . . . It's also marked by a high degree of reserve; an aversion to confrontation and outward "unpleasantness"; a certain amount of self-deprecation, paired with a strong disinclination to stand out or appear different from the norm; a marked discomfort with strong displays of feeling or emotion."

Minnesotans are uncomfortable with things that appear different from the norm, and for the past 175 years, that norm has overwhelmingly been White and Christian.

How Christian?

Here are the results of a 2008 survey by the Pew Forum on Religion & Public Life in Minnesota:

32 percent Mainline Protestant
28 percent Roman Catholic
21 percent Evangelical Protestant
13 percent Unaffiliated
1 percent Jewish
1 percent Muslim
4 percent Other faiths

Today, the statistics from the World Population Review aren't much different: 74 percent Christian, 5 percent non-Christian, and 20 percent unaffiliated.

Fifty years ago, when I was growing up in New Hope, a suburb twelve miles northwest of Minneapolis, you can bet the number of "unaffiliated" Minnesotans and those of "other faiths" was even lower. There were so many Christian churches in New Hope that my mom called them "the 31 flavors of Christian-Robbins ice cream." (She didn't know the Baskin-Robbins ice cream chain was founded by two Jewish brothers-in-law in 1945.)

In 1960, the year I was born, New Hope had 3,552 residents. By 1970 there were 23,180—more than 500 percent growth—and almost every one of them was a White well-educated Christian. Thanks to redlining, the Chinese Exclusion Act, and a raft of economic policies that prevented non-Whites from living in the suburbs, there were no Black people or Asians in my suburban schools or neighborhood. No Korean adoptees. There were no Hmong people, no Somalis. No American Indians.

Just White Christians.

And my family.

The only Jews in New Hope.

You wouldn't immediately think our family would stick out that much. We had a brand-new four-bedroom split-level like everyone else, with central air conditioning, a two-car garage, Schwinn Sting-Rays in the driveway, and Better Boy tomatoes in the garden. We were White like everyone else, too. My younger brother and sister were blond, and we didn't walk around in kippahs or have side curls. But given the dense wall of Christianity around us, our differences were easy to spot.

Our neighbors noticed we didn't put up Christmas lights or have a Christmas tree. They noticed we didn't go to one of the many, *many* suburban churches. My older brother and I brought the Hanukkah menorah to school each December to talk about why we didn't celebrate Christmas. We missed school during the

High Holidays when we went to the synagogue, and we brought peanut butter and jelly sandwiches on matzoh for lunch during Passover. Living in New Hope, we were Jews in a sea of gentiles—"herring in a sea of sharks," as my father put it. We ate gefilte fish while our neighbors ate lutefisk. Just these small differences were enough to set us apart.

Of course, under the norms of Minnesota Nice, it's not polite to *acknowledge* difference. It's considered rude, like staring at someone who's in a wheelchair. Difference makes Minnesotans uncomfortable, and the word itself is a common Minnesota pejorative—a not-so-secret code that politely expresses your discomfort with something outside of your White Christian experience.

"Oh," someone might say about a new colleague who is another color, religion, ethnicity, (fill in the blank) . . . "She's a little . . . different."

Even as a five-year-old I knew different was a problem. When people said something was different it meant they didn't like it. I could tell by the little pause they threw in.

"Well, that's . . . different," said Mrs. Miller when I told her I didn't eat pork.

"Oh, that's . . . different," said Mrs. Schoonover, my Brownie troop leader, when I told her we didn't have a Christmas tree to hang my glitter and Popsicle stick Christmas ornament on.

At school bake sales, my mother's blue- and white-frosted dreidel and menorah cookies provoked a nervous "Huh, that's . . . different," before the commenter moved on to the safety of Mrs. Johnson's Christmas tree cutouts and Mrs. Olson's Candy Cane Crumbles. Calling something or someone "different," or its common variant . . . "interesting," is a Minnesota Nice way of dismissing and diminishing something's value without being "rude." Nobody wants to be rude. So, difference is best left unacknowledged, overlooked, and ignored. Not seeing difference renders it invisible, which makes it disappear and leaves the comfortable inner circle of White Christians intact.

Given the Jews' long history of being singled out and slaughtered, you might wonder why the invisibility I experienced growing up was problematic. Isn't it better, my non-Jewish husband wondered after the 2018 Tree of Life Synagogue massacre, to have your difference overlooked rather than to be persecuted or killed? My husband is a thoughtful, White midwesterner who doesn't see malicious intent in a phrase I heard frequently growing up in Minnesota: "Really? You don't look Jewish."

But no matter how you pick this phrase apart, it's not a positive and it's not neutral. Although it's usually meant as a compliment, it implies that I should be thankful that I don't "look Jewish" because obviously *that's different and undesirable.*

Given the dominant White Christian culture, growing up Jewish presented me with a handful of choices: I could thank people for telling me that I didn't look like what I was; I could "out" my difference and have Minnesota Nice erase me; or I could "blend in" and erase myself.

Which type of invisibility would you choose?

Now, you might be tempted to think, "People weren't being negative, they just didn't know anything about Jewish people." Hmmm. Maybe. But Minnesota is a state with a particularly odious history of antisemitism. Minneapolis was considered the most antisemitic city *in the country* in the 1940s. Many people are surprised by this.

Really? Right here in Minnesota?

Ya, you betcha. (In the appendix, see the "Jews (and My Family) in Minnesota, 1840–1962" Timeline for more information on this.)

By the time I grew up in the 1960s suburbs, antisemitism was more nuanced. There were, of course, a few unabashed antisemites among our neighbors (Hello, Mrs. Swanson). Antisemitism is rife in the world, and it would be nearly impossible to grow up anywhere without encountering it. But the antisemitism I felt was mostly hidden.

If my neighbors thought about Jews at all, it was either as concentration camp victims, "Christ-killers," or the Jews from the 1956 biblical epic *The Ten Commandments* with the inspired casting of Charleston Heston as Moses.

Funny, he doesn't look Jewish.

Our neighbors expected Jews to walk around with either flowing caftans or jackets labeled with yellow stars. Since our family had regular winter coats, boots, and hats like everybody else, when people found out we were Jewish they were confused and wary. One Hanukkah when I was eight, I remember coming out of the Red Owl grocery store and wishing two smiling Salvation Army bell ringers in Santa Claus hats "Happy Hanukkah" instead of "Merry Christmas." They stopped ringing their bells and stared at me suspiciously, like I was trying to pick a fight or trick them somehow.

Jews.

"They're a little ... different."

—⚡︎—

A STORY TOLD TO ME BY GRANDPA IZZY

(In his thick Polish/Russian accent)

"MY YOUNGER BROTHER ABIE WAS the smartest person I ever knew."

(Points to his temple and winks.)

"When the Germans came to our village, he was maybe ten or eleven. We had one cow. We were lucky to have this cow. But we were also unlucky to have this cow because the Germans would come every morning at 5:00 and force us to milk the cow while they watched, and then we had to give all the milk to the soldiers with nothing left for ourselves."

(His eyes get misty.)

"But Abie outsmarted them all."

(Winks again.)

"Abie got up at 4:00 every morning. It was dark and terrible cold, but he milked the cow once before the soldiers arrived and then again when they were there. That way . . ."

(Pauses for the punchline.)

". . . we got the cream and they got what was left."

(Laughs uproariously at the cleverness of his brother outwitting the Germans.)

—un—

ALIENS FROM "DEE OLT COUNTREE"

You're traveling through another dimension, a dimension not only of sight and sound but of mind; a journey into a wondrous land whose boundaries are that of imagination. That's the signpost up ahead—your next stop, the Twilight Zone.

—Rod Serling

MY DAD'S RELATIVES WERE FROM "dee olt countree," and growing up, I was sure "dee olt countree" was populated by aliens from *The Twilight Zone*.

Every Sunday morning my dad made us go to my Grandpa Izzy's house in St. Paul's Highland Park to clean. Even though his house was only twenty-nine miles from New Hope, it felt like we entered a time machine and landed in "dee olt countree" twenty-nine thousand miles away.

The moment we drove across the Mississippi River bridge that connects Minneapolis to St. Paul, Rod Serling's ominous baritone thrummed inside my head: "You've just crossed over . . . into the Twilight Zone."

The Mississippi River was the dividing line between normal and weird.

I suspect my dad's childhood was like that episode of *The Twilight Zone* where the boy finds out his whole family has been replaced by aliens disguised as humans. At first, the boy isn't sure what's wrong with his family, he just knows something is *different*. Eventually he discovers that underneath their human masks, his parents are giant cockroaches. Except my dad's family wasn't wearing masks. Grandpa Izzy, Grandma Rose, and Uncle Norman were all *really different*.

The most direct route to Grandpa Izzy's was down Cretin Avenue, which meant my older brother Danny called me a cretin every Sunday morning of my childhood. We drove past the Town and Country Golf Club (Jews not welcome) beneath the outstretched limbs of one-hundred-year-old elms.

Block after block, past the College of St. Thomas (Jews not welcome), a towering canopy of green leaves blinkered crazy patterns of sun and shadows overhead. The flickering light felt like a strange Morse code from the natural world. I wondered if the trees were trying to tell me something important. Something about my grandparents. It made my head hurt, so I closed my eyes and watched their secret signals through the squiggly veins behind my eyelids.

Even with my eyes closed I knew we'd reached my grandparents' street because my dad made the exact same sound at the exact same spot every Sunday morning: a sigh that sounded like air coming out of a deflating balloon. I didn't open my eyes until we pulled up to the curb and the time machine had officially landed in the odiferous "Olt Countree."

My grandparent's house was a dingy white stucco bungalow that looked like it should have been condemned years before. There were six crumbling concrete steps leading up to the front door, with a single rusty iron banister that tilted dangerously to one side. Both Danny and I had learned the hard way not to touch the banister unless you wanted rusty metal splinters in your hand.

The top step was framed by a narrow stucco archway supported by two columns. Each column had a rusty, flaking metal bulldog nailed to it. Before I was born, the dogs held shiny house numbers in their mouths, but the numbers had rusted away a long time ago. Now the bulldogs looked like they were peeing rust stains down the pitted stucco walls.

Isadore Bernick, a.k.a Grandpa Izzy, had been a tailor all his life. But by the time I met him, he was old and going blind from glaucoma. He looked like a life-size Mongolian Kewpie doll with his cloudy slanted eyes, giant bald head, barrel chest, and skinny arms and legs. My dad told me that when Grandpa Izzy came to America, he considered changing his name from "Bernick" to "Berns" to make it more "American" sounding. But when he learned it cost twenty-five dollars to make the change, he decided that Bernick was fine after all.

I'm not surprised Grandpa Izzy didn't want to spend the money; his frugality, like my father's, was legendary. I'm surprised he ever wanted to be more American. He seemed perfectly content to live in St. Paul like he was still living in "dee olt countree."

Entering my grandparents' house took serious mental preparation. I'm not sure which smelled worse: Grandpa's breath, since he ate onions like apples, or his dank, malodorous house. The shades and windows were always closed, even in the summertime, and liverwurst and onion smells drifted through the rooms tinged with mold and eau de moth balls. When we visited, I tasted all the smells in the back of my throat.

It wasn't only the smells and rundown condition of the house that bothered me, it was the dirt. Even though we cleaned each Sunday, it felt like the house was moldering into the earth. Like "olt countree" dirt was worming its way up through the horsehair backing of the thirty-year-old carpeting. Danny and I kept our shoes on at Grandpa Izzy's.

Grandpa lived with Grandma Rose and Uncle Norman, but for all the house-keeping help he got from those two, he might as well have been living alone. Grandma Rose was short and round and wore a lot of rouge, lipstick, and stinky-sweet perfume she squeezed from an old-fashioned atomizer on her bedroom dresser. She had oily gray-black hair, and breasts so large and saggy that when she hugged me, I felt like a piece of liverwurst stuck inside a smelly bosom sandwich.

Danny avoided Grandma Rose's hugs entirely, but I felt like it was my duty. Something was wrong with her, and I didn't know what. She didn't really talk. She just smiled a lot and said, "Hi, hi, hi, hi, hi" before she wrapped you in that overpowering hug.

When I asked my mom why Grandma Rose never talked, she just shook her head.

"Oy, your poor Grandma Rose. It's not her fault she was born with a low IQ. Her father had some money, and he paid your Grandpa Izzy to marry her."

"Grandpa Izzy was *paid* to marry Grandma Rose?"

I was amazed something like that could happen in America.

"I know it sounds crazy, but people did things like that back then. And then she had Uncle Norman, and she was in and out of hospitals, shock therapy, problem after problem. What a life she's had, poor thing."

She shook her finger at me.

"Just treat your Grandma Rose nice and don't upset her."

I couldn't imagine *anything* upsetting Grandma Rose. Every Sunday she sat on the couch and watched us clean. I had no idea what she was thinking behind her shiny black cat-eye glasses. Did Grandpa Izzy really get paid to marry her? It seemed possible. I knew Grandpa Izzy liked a good deal. Maybe Grandma Rose's father made him an offer he couldn't refuse.

The third alien of the household was Uncle Norman, my dad's brother. Uncle Norman was only five years older than my dad, but he looked as old as Grandpa Izzy. He had a huge bald head, a long, horsey face, and he wore old-man pants belted up to his armpits. Most of the time he stood hunched in a corner rubbing his hands together while saying "Yesssssssss" over and over.

My dad didn't say much about Uncle Norman. He acted like it was perfectly normal for someone to stand in the corner and rub his hands together all day long. When I finally asked him why Uncle Norman was so weird, he seemed surprised by the question.

"You think he acts weird?"

I wasn't sure if my dad was kidding or not.

"When your Uncle Norman was born, the doctor used some big tongs called forceps to help him come out. The doctor made a mistake and Uncle Norman's brain was damaged, so that's why he still acts like a little boy. But he'll never hurt you, if that's what you're worried about."

I tried to imagine Uncle Norman being born and having his grapefruit-sized head squeezed between metal clamps. Sometimes I searched his giant bald head for evidence of the crime, but I didn't see any squashy indentations in his pale, yellow flesh.

"That's a complete lie," my mom said, after she heard my dad's explanation.

"Your Grandma Rose dropped your Uncle Norman on his head when he was a baby, and that's why he has brain damage, but no one wants to admit it was her fault, poor thing."

I didn't know what to believe about Uncle Norman. Danny and I just made sure we were never alone in a room with him.

Can you imagine being my dad and growing up with creepy parents and a brother like this? I swear I am not exaggerating. Nobody would believe you if you told them you had these people as relatives, but it's all true. My brother remembers it exactly the same way. (Please refer to the chapter "Memory Is a Slippery Fish.")

Danny and I never told *anybody* where we went on Sunday mornings. Our neighbors thought we went to our "Jewish church." Thankfully, our St. Paul relatives rarely came to New Hope. Our neighbors already thought we were *interesting* enough.

Whenever I wonder why my dad married my mom, all I have to do is imagine him growing up in St. Paul with Grandpa Izzy, Uncle Norman, and Grandma Rose. If you'd been living inside a *Twilight Zone* episode your whole life, I guess even my mom would seem like an improvement.

"Goddamn it, Dad, I told you to throw these envelopes out! You can't use them again. They're already postmarked! Throw them out, for Chrissake!"

Every Sunday my dad yelled at Grandpa Izzy about throwing stuff out, but it never did any good. Grandpa Izzy was a collector. That's how I thought of it, even though my mom used words like *tightwad, hoarder, packrat,* and *skinflint*.

"He's just too damn cheap to throw anything away," she said, whenever she came with us to clean.

"You'd probably be like that too, if you'd gone through the Depression," my dad countered, stuffing five years' worth of used bread bags into the garbage can.

Some of Grandpa Izzy's collections:

Six cigar boxes stacked inside the rolltop desk in the dining room filled with
    unsharpened pencils, pencil stubs with no erasers, and lots of pens, some
    of which worked
Twelve paper bags on the back porch filled with used envelopes and
    shoehorns
Three plastic bread bags in the pantry closet full of twist ties
Seven rusty coffee cans under the kitchen sink filled with small pink and
    white packets of sugar and saccharin pilfered from cheap restaurants and
    Bar Mitzvah coffee trays
Ten shoeboxes down in the basement sewing room filled with used zippers,
    sewing machine attachments, and loose and carded buttons. These
    included black and gray suit buttons, red and coral dress buttons, plastic
    and bone buttons, steel and shell buttons, and fabric-covered buttons with
    loose threads still attached (He hadn't worked as a tailor for decades.)
Two heavy wooden ironing boards mounded with ripped-out pockets,
    yellowed shoulder pads, worn belts, and leftover suit coat linings
Eight wooden shelves in the basement piled high with mildewed fabrics
    wrapped in plastic and paper; these included silks and damasks, worsteds
    and plaids
Two giant musty-smelling leather trunks from "dee olt countree" stacked
    with flat cardboard boxes filled with elastic trim, seam binding, and lace
Six metal buckets heaped with belt buckles, rusty washers, presser feet, and
    a Zippo lighter that Danny once used to light my hair on fire.

I think my dad had a little "olt countree" in him, too. He yelled at my mom if she bought something from Red Owl that wasn't on the grocery list or if she bought the good kind of chocolate chip cookies. She was supposed to buy the off-brand even though the tiny "chocolate chips" tasted like soap. For my dad, the only thing that mattered was how much something cost.

At home, we had a secret room under our steps where my dad stockpiled cans of tomato soup and boxes of saltine crackers on rickety metal shelves. You had to walk crouched over so you didn't hit your head. I guess if the world suddenly went haywire, we were going to creep down there and eat cold tomato soup with stale saltine crackers and have soapy-tasting chocolate chip cookies for dessert.

—꿈—

DECAMPING TO THE SUBURBS

Though still not as assimilated into mainstream Minnesota culture as other European immigrant groups, Minnesota Jews were beginning to benefit from aspects of White privilege in Minnesota for the first time, leaving their former African American neighbors, and much of their urban immigrant identity behind as they began to organize their community in a suburban setting.

—Jacob Cohn, Maggie Goldberger, and Maya Margolis, "Religious Diversity in Minnesota Initiative" at Carlton College, Northfield, Minnesota

—m—

INTERESTING DEMOGRAPHICS

ACCORDING TO THE 1978 *GYRE*, my suburban Armstrong Senior High School yearbook, my graduating class of 649 students included:

Seventeen Johnsons
Seventeen Andersons
Nine Olsons
Seven Nelsons
Five Petersons
Three Olsens
Three Larsons
Three Hansons

Also,

Six Jewish students (possibly seven; I'm not sure about one boy)
Four Black students (one boy and three girls)
Two Asian students (one was a Japanese exchange student)
One Hispanic student (boy)

—ɯ—

EMIGRATION TO ASSIMILATION

Like a one-two punch, assimilation reinforces the damage done by anti-Semitism, robbing us of our rich heritage, shoving Jews into WASP conformity, inviting us to loathe who we really are.

—Penny Rosenwasser, *Hope into Practice:*
Jewish Women Choosing Justice Despite Our Fears

DEPARTURES OFTEN INVOLVE A TRADE-OFF. You give up something in return for getting something else. This, according to *Merriam-Webster*, requires finding a balance "between two desirable but incompatible features." For my parents, emigrating to the promised land of assimilation meant finding a balance between retaining their identities as Jews while raising a family and becoming successful middle-class Americans. This turned out to be more complicated than they imagined.

I don't remember the exact day we moved to New Hope, but I do have a clear memory of being almost five and tightrope-walking along the foundation walls of our new house as it was being built. It was the fall of 1965. The walleye had just been named the state fish (news flash!) and my family had just moved to this brand-new suburban development.

New Hope is a six-square-mile parcel, one of the many rapidly growing suburbs ringing Minneapolis at the time. It had almost no sidewalks and little bus service. The wide driveways and attached double garages were an important design feature. In the suburbs, if you wanted to get anywhere, you had to drive.

The timing of my dad's graduation from the University of Minnesota in 1958 with a civil engineering degree, and the unprecedented infusion of government funding for freeways across the country coincided perfectly. He was hired straight out of college by the Hennepin County Highway Department, and his office was a ten-minute drive from our house in New Hope. My parents were in their late twenties. They'd been married for eight years, and this was already the second suburban house they'd owned; the first was in neighboring Crystal.

The 1950s and 1960s were an optimistic time for my parents and thousands of young, White, well-educated families who were still riding the tsunami of suburban development fueled by housing shortages and the financing options made possible by the US government after World War II. According to the US census, between 1950 and 1960 suburban populations around the country increased by 60 percent while central city populations increased by just over 3 percent. Non-Whites, as I mentioned earlier, were prevented from boarding the ship to suburban success thanks to housing covenants and social and economic policies that made it impossible for them to own their own homes or leave the inner cities. The Twin Cities is living with the consequences of this disgraceful legacy today.

Moving to the suburbs required my parents to make trade-offs both large and small. Although raised in an Orthodox Jewish family, my dad followed my mom's lead and switched to Conservative Judaism. This dispensed with the Orthodox requirement of keeping kosher and allowed travel to and from the synagogue by car on the Sabbath—a critical component for Jews living in the suburbs. I don't know if my parents decided this together, or whether my mom decided and my dad just went along. Probably the latter.

When my parents moved to New Hope, the only Twin Cities suburb with more than a handful of Jews was St. Louis Park, aka "St. Jewish Park." My dad claims he was initially concerned about moving to New Hope because it had so few Jews. He wanted a Jewish education for his kids, and he knew the Talmud Torah bus in St. Louis Park wouldn't come the fifteen miles to New Hope to pick us up for Hebrew school.

But my mom was already comfortable in the northwest suburbs. She wanted to remain in proximity to her extended family in Robbinsdale, and she wanted an excellent education for her children, something the Robbinsdale school district was known for. Perhaps the name itself, "New Hope," inspired a flush of uncharacteristic optimism, and my mother was too busy imagining her future successes to worry about the steeples, crucifixes, and bell towers lined up along Winnetka Avenue.

For my father, the son of a poor Russian refugee, the opportunity to build a four-bedroom split-level with central air conditioning on a large lot for $28,000 vied mightily with the desire for his kids to have a solid Jewish identity. Ultimately, the good deal won out.

Historians see the Jewish population's move to the suburbs as something that both diluted Jewish identity and required Jewish families to be more intentional about their Jewish lives. In my parents' compacted Jewish neighborhoods of North Minneapolis and St. Paul's Highland Park, Jewish identity was reinforced by their environments. They shopped at Jewish businesses and socialized with Jewish neighbors. But out in suburbia, Jewish identity had to be consciously created and nurtured. New Hope didn't have kosher butchers, The Red Owl didn't sell matzoh, and the closest synagogue was a fifteen-mile schlepp to St. Louis Park.

Young suburban Jews like my parents had to make hard choices about what being Jewish would mean for their families. If my parents had been readers or intellectuals (they were neither), they might have had books by the celebrated Jewish writer Phillip Roth on their bookshelves.

Roth's novels reflected many of the central questions facing my parents' generation of Jews. "There was a book for every facet of this quandary," writes Taffy Brodesser-Akner in the 2018 *New York Times* article "What Philip Roth Taught Me about Being an American Jew." She cites his novels *Goodbye, Columbus* for interclass tensions, *The Human Stain* and *American Pastoral* for the perils of passing as White and Christian, and *Indignation* for assimilation and intermarriage:

> Roth's books answered the question of how all this Jewish education I was getting would translate into the real world, should I survive the ordeal of childhood. What did it mean to be Jewish in America? Were we supposed to convey pride in our religion and our culture? Were we the punch lines to a joke that was constantly being made? Were the jokes at least funny? And such small portions? Was being Jewish a bad thing? Were we proud? Were we embarrassed? Did we still have to watch our backs? How should a modern Jew behave in the world? How should a modern Jew assert his or her Jewishness? Were we white? You're kidding yourself if you think we're white! Do the goyim like us, or do they simply tolerate us? You're kidding yourself if you think they tolerate us! How to act, how to assimilate but not too much, how to remind them about the Holocaust when they got uppity about Jewish privilege. How to not break into laughter when someone used the phrase 'Jewish privilege.'

My parents claim they didn't feel antisemitism in New Hope, but they both admit there were incidents during my childhood when we were singled out as Jews. I remember my mom feeling the weekly slight of never being invited to the Tuesday morning Zealand Avenue Coffee Klatch.

"You call that Minnesota Nice?" my mom complained each Tuesday, as she stood at the kitchen window watching the neighbor ladies carry their tins of cookies and bars to Glenda Thompson's.

I can imagine the confusion of those nice Christian suburban ladies meeting my mom in 1965. Not only was she a flaming redhead and *Jewish*, she was blunt, loud, abrasive, emotional, and dramatic, and she spoke over people, something linguist Deborah Tannen says is common among Eastern European Jewish transplants. Tannen describes this way of speaking as "high-involvement" and "cooperative overlapping."

I bet our neighbors on Zealand Avenue described it differently.

I'm sure my mom's "emotionality" was disconcerting for the more restrained Swedes, Danes, Germans, and Norwegians in our new neighborhood. They came from cultures that listened when others spoke. Where it's considered polite to remain silent when your opinion isn't shared by the group, except of course to say, "That's . . . interesting."

My mom found their behavior rude.

"Even though I have tried to be neighborly, your precious neighbors have never been interested in welcoming us," she would say each Tuesday from her perch at the sink. "Shirley Miller made that quite clear from the start."

She loved to tell the story about how Mrs. Miller walked across the street with a tray of ham sandwiches the day we moved in. Linda Miller was my best friend, but my mom didn't like Mrs. Miller because she had six kids ("They breed like rabbits," she would say), and also because Mrs. Miller was Catholic.

"It's not because she's Catholic. It's her holier-than-thou attitude I don't like."

My mom and I had this same conversation every time she told the story. Looking back, I suspect some of her resentment stemmed from the fact that even though Mrs. Miller was one of the only Catholics on the block, she was embraced by the Zealand Avenue Lutheran sisterhood, and my mom was not.

The history of Catholics and Lutherans in Minnesota includes long-simmering tensions over allegiances to parish and priest and the right to establish moral authority. But suburban car culture and cheap financing made it possible for (White) Catholics to live almost anywhere and still remain an active part of their parochial communities.

It must have gnawed at my mom that even as my brother and I trooped to the public school bus stop each morning with everyone else, while the Miller kids flapped around their front yard like blue jays in their blue and white checkered Catholic school uniforms, Shirley Miller was invited to the Zealand Avenue Coffee Klatch, and my mom remained an outcast.

"Mrs. Miller didn't know we don't eat ham, Mom."

"It wasn't about the ham, Elisa. Or Glenda Thompson's lemon bars."

I could see the ham making her uncomfortable, but I have no idea what she had against Mrs. Thompson's lemon bars. They were delicious.

"Oy, that Glenda Thompson! With those new drapes that matched her Gold Harvest range and refrigerator. Those gold tassels were the ugliest thing I'd ever seen. They were just plain tacky."

"But, Mom, if you've never been invited inside Mrs. Thompson's house, how do you know what her kitchen looks like?"

She looked at me like I'd shot her.

"That has nothing whatsoever to do with this story, Elisa. If you're not interested in what happened that first Tuesday morning after we moved in, then I won't tell you about it."

I made an elaborate zipping motion across my lips. My mom's stories were one of her best qualities. I never questioned the veracity of her tales. I just accepted the fact that she could tell you with 100 percent accuracy what happened that first Tuesday at the Zealand Avenue Neighborhood Coffee Klatch (even though she wasn't there).

"There they were. All sitting around Glenda Thompson's kitchen table with their coffee and cinnamon swirl coffee cake. We'd just moved in, remember?"

I was five, so I don't really remember.

"Did they waste any time making nicey-nice about us? Oh no. Shirley Miller was the one who started the whole thing off."

My mom wrinkled her nose.

"Catholics always feel it's their God-given right to point out the error of everyone else's ways without examining any of their own."

She shook her head.

"That damn Shirley Miller. She didn't even wait until the coffee was poured."

THE FIRST COFFEE KLATCH

(Told with one hundred percent accuracy by Arlene Bernick and reported by Elisa Bernick, neither of whom was actually there.)

"You should have seen the nasty look that new neighbor gave me when I handed her those sandwiches," Shirley Miller said that morning with a sniff. "That was a Corn King ham and you know how tasty that is."

She patted an errant curl into place near the crown of her new Eva Gabor wig.

"She was so ungrateful."

"Well, she seemed to like my lemon bars well enough," Glenda Thompson said, as she filled the ladies' cups with freshly percolated Butternut coffee.

"And the plate was perfectly clean when she returned it. But they do seem a bit . . . *different* somehow."

"I saw a little boy out in the front yard this morning," Doris Christensen said. "Cute as a button. Couldn't be more than six or seven."

She helped herself to a piece of coffee cake from the plate in the middle of the gold-flecked Formica table and lit a cigarette.

"And the wife, what's her name . . . Irene? Maybe she's feeling out of sorts with the heat and unpacking and two little ones? And you know how redheads are. Emotional."

Eleanor Anderson wiped her lips delicately and leaned forward, dropping her voice to a whisper. "Mike says they're a different persuasion from the rest of us."

"What do you mean? They're not Mormons, are they?" Glenda Thompson looked horror-stricken.

"Even worse," Eleanor Anderson said.

She pulled up the ruffled bottom of the white lace curtain to peek out the window.

"They're *Jewish*."

36

All the women's heads cranked in unison toward the window. Jewish! Not a one of them had even *met* a Jewish person before. And now, an entire *family* of Jews had moved to the block. The kitchen clock ticked loudly, and the gold tassels bounced cheerily at the bottom of Glenda Thompson's new curtains as the ladies stared in silence at the shiny black shutters and white aluminum siding of the house across the street.

NOW, YOU MIGHT BE WONDERING, is this a "true" story or am I making this up? Yes.

Haven't we already discussed the fuzzy nature of truth and memory? I'll admit to "plumping" the details, but given what I remember about our neighbors and the stories my mom told, I suspect I'm not too far off.

What I find interesting about this weekly snub is that my mom claimed to have been bothered more by its "unneighborliness" than its antisemitism.

I don't think my mom and dad could afford to acknowledge the antisemitism they experienced, intent as they were on climbing out of their poor, dysfunctional Jewish families into the privileged White middle class. Unlike their own parents, Sam and Arlene Bernick felt like Americans. Who were also Jews. The challenge was to figure out a way to balance those identities, or at least allow for them to coexist. During the early years of their marriage, my parents did this by driving us to and from St. Louis Park to attend the Beth El Synagogue for Friday night services, Hebrew school, and Sunday school.

We weren't religious per se. The most frequent mention of God in our house was my mother yelling "Goddamn it!" But our family celebrated all of the Jewish holidays and only Jewish holidays. We observed Shabbat for a while, and although we didn't keep kosher once we moved to New Hope, we didn't eat pork or shellfish. I didn't even *smell* bacon until I was at a sleepover when I was nine. According to one study, by the end of World War I, only 20 percent of US Jews kept kosher. By 1967, it was down to 5 percent. We were just part of the larger trend.

For American Jews after World War II, the Holocaust and the emerging state of Israel were the primary touchstones of Jewish identity. The Holocaust fed Jewish nightmares, but it was a monster kept mostly under the bed. Growing up, I remember the Holocaust being discussed openly only once a year at the Beth El Synagogue—on Yom HaShoah, Holocaust Remembrance Day.

To mark the anniversary, we spent a grisly morning of religious school in "Holocaust education," which started when I was six. We listened to elderly Holocaust survivors tell terrible stories about the Warsaw Ghetto and Auschwitz, and then we walked past their outstretched arms and touched the faded blue tattooed numbers on their withered skin. Afterward, we marched down to the gymnasium and sat in folding chairs set up in front of a small film screen in the chilly, darkened room.

It was completely silent except for the tick . . . tick . . . tick . . . of the film sprockets in the projector as the films unwound horrifying images in the flickering light.

For fifteen minutes we watched shrunken, misshapen bodies being tossed and rolled into deep pits of other emaciated bodies; layers upon layers of dead and broken bodies. Grim, ghastly reminders of what the world did to Jews as bodies tumbled into deep pits. And then we walked back to class in stunned silence.

The experience was, of course, traumatizing. After watching those horrifying images in the dark, I felt them imprinted on the *inside* of my skin, just like those faded tattoos, which of course, was the point—to ensure that Jews *never forget*.

Israel was something easier to rally around. I remember dropping quarters into Tu Bishvat collection tins to be sent away to "plant trees in Israel," and the fun of dressing up in blue and white and parading through the synagogue hallways each May waving Israeli flags to celebrate Israeli Independence Day.

Given the importance of these touchstones, anthropologist Karen Brodkin points out in her book *How Jews Became White Folks* that no matter how "White" Jews became, no matter how eagerly they welcomed assimilation, "Both the Holocaust and Israel gave Jews a degree of critical distance from the mainstream American whiteness, a sense of otherness even in the midst of being ardently embraced by the mainstream."

The suburban diaspora from the "old neighborhoods" was also an important factor in the breakdown of generational connections. Unlike other immigrant groups, young Jews were willing to leave their family enclaves to live independent, middle-class lives—which allowed them to achieve a higher social status, but also had a negative impact on family solidarity.

This was a trade-off my mom and dad welcomed. They couldn't wait to escape their oppressive homelives. As my siblings and I grew up, our visits with extended family happened less and less. We cleaned Grandpa Izzy's house on Sunday mornings, and we saw my mom's volatile family for Shabbat a couple times a month. We celebrated Passover and birthdays at my Uncle Harvey (my mom's brother) and Aunt Sharon's house with our cousins David and Jeff. But by the time I was nine, most of my mom's Robbinsdale relatives had migrated to California, and by that time, our family was in free fall.

Even though my dad was happy to leave behind that claustrophobic house and its strange trio of occupants in Highland Park, he had an uneasy relationship with assimilation. He didn't want us to hide our Jewishness, but he didn't want antisemitism to prevent us from enjoying the benefits available to middle-class Christian Americans. He was embarrassed by Grandpa Izzy's thick "olt countree" accent and his eternally closed window shades, but he also understood the reality of his father's brutal childhood and the long history of the Jews as convenient scapegoats and worse.

My dad's approach wasn't to retreat—our shades were kept open—but his attitude toward assimilation was rooted in the same fear as my grandfather's. If they know you're Jewish, they might turn on you. Keep a low profile and don't draw attention to your difference. Yes, we're Jewish, but don't make a big deal about it. I heard that message loud and clear growing up (reinforced by the larger culture). I internalized it. You're Jewish, but people think there's something wrong with that. Don't shine a light on it. Hide it.

My mom was more comfortable with her Judaism. Maybe it's because she already had experience living among Christians in the suburbs and had developed a different relationship to her Jewish identity. She actively cultivated our family's connections to the Beth El and Talmud Torah Hebrew school, just as her mother had done for her while she and her siblings were the only Jews at their schools in suburban Robbinsdale. Not only were the shades of our house kept open, my mom taped Hanukkah decorations to the living room windows.

Jewish historians discuss the new suburban American Jewish identity as a primary driver in the transformation of gender roles for Jewish women. This was playing out during a time when women's roles in general were undergoing a significant transformation. Unlike in the Orthodox Jewish community, Conservative Jewish women took on leadership roles at the synagogue, and my mom was a natural leader. She was part of the Beth El Synagogue Women's League, the primary fundraising arm for the synagogue's religious school, nursery school, and library. The Women's League sponsored rummage sales, bake sales, theatrical events, and style shows. My mom loved every bit of it.

In the meticulously detailed scrapbook my mother kept of her many domestic accomplishments in the mid-1960s, there's a *Minneapolis Tribune* newspaper article about the synagogue's activities. I'm guessing the reporter, Eileen Chapman, was Jewish, because why else would the *Minneapolis Tribune* have any interest in the Beth El? The article discusses a play being presented by the synagogue's Mr. and Mrs. Club called *Let Me Go, Lityak*. My mom and dad are both quoted.

SYNAGOGUE GROUP GETS HUSBANDS INTO THE ACT

> Beth El Synagogue matrons have found a way to maintain a happy husband along with an active social schedule away from home—put hubby in the act, too.
>
> "I got roped in," pretended Sam Bernick, then he quickly added, "But, I'm liking it."
>
> "I brought him along because he said he didn't see enough of me last year," explained Mrs. Bernick.

Notice that my mom doesn't get a first name in the article. None of the wives do. Also notice that she was already spending significant time away from home. This would become a pattern in my parents' marriage.

The synagogue was my mom's primary method of socializing. Despite her desire to be a successful suburban housewife, she felt more comfortable around other Jews. And even at the synagogue, cultivating friendships didn't come naturally to her. My dad, on the other hand, was a go-along-get-along kind of guy and an athlete. He certainly had Jewish friends—his best friends throughout his life were the guys he met in AZA (Aleph Zadik Aleph), a Jewish teen group—but he also bowled and coached athletics. He found plenty of ways to socialize out in New Hope, while my mom, snubbed by the neighbors and socially awkward, felt lonely and friendless much of the time.

Living in New Hope was her choice, but it meant living further from her religious community. Eventually the distance, assimilation, the fledgling women's movement, and changing marital expectations would all provoke an unmooring. The trade-offs my parents made to buy that cheap house in New Hope would ultimately cost our family a great deal.

WAIKIKI MEATBALLS (RECIPE)

WAIKIKI MEATBALLS

"Tasty all-beef meatballs in a sweet-sour sauce."
(*BETTY CROCKER COOKBOOK*, 1965)

1 1/2 pounds ground beef
2/3 cup cracker crumbs
1/3 cup minced onion
1 egg
1 1/2 teaspoons salt
1/4 teaspoon ginger
1/4 cup milk
1 tablespoon shortening
2 tablespoons cornstarch
1/2 cup brown sugar (packed)
1 can (13 1/2 ounces) pineapple tidbits, drained (reserve syrup)
1/3 cup vinegar
1 tablespoon soy sauce
1/3 cup chopped green pepper

Mix thoroughly beef, crumbs, onion, egg, salt, ginger, and milk. Shape mixture by rounded tablespoonfuls into balls. Melt shortening in a large skillet: brown and cook meatballs. Remove meatballs; keep warm. Pour fat from skillet.

Mix cornstarch and sugar. Stir in reserved pineapple syrup, vinegar, and soy sauce until smooth. Pour into skillet; cook over medium heat, stirring constantly, until mixture thickens and boils. Boil and stir 1 minute. Add meatballs, pineapple tidbits, and green pepper; heat through. 6 servings.

—ᴍ—

ARLENE WANTS NICE LAMPS—1965

Every morning before breakfast, comb hair, apply makeup, a dash of cologne and perhaps some simple earrings: Does wonders for your morale! . . . Harbor pleasant thoughts while working. It'll make every task lighter and pleasanter. . . . Notice humorous and interesting incidents to relate at dinner time when family is together.

—"Special Helps," *Betty Crocker's Picture Cookbook,* 1956

THERE'S NO DOUBT MY MOM had a "difficult" personality, but living with my dad couldn't have been easy. Each week he gave her an allowance for groceries, and with this she tried to work her Betty Crocker magic. Inside each of the kitchen cabinets, my dad taped lists of the number of canned goods and other groceries she was allowed to buy on her weekly shopping trips to the Red Owl. Buying something "not on the list" invited an uncomfortable discussion (a big fight). This was a typical dinner table conversation:

"Do you see how dark it is in the living room, Sam?"

My mom wasted no time on small talk at the dinner table. It didn't occur to her to ask how my father's day was.

"For the umpteenth time," she said. "Could we please get some lamps in the living room? It's so dark in there you can't read the newspaper after 4:00 in the afternoon."

"So read it in the morning."

"Sam!"

My dad sighed loudly.

"Why do we need lamps? We got the ceiling light."

"I hate that overhead light. I'm talking nice lamps with shades. For next to the couch. With real fabric shades. Like nice families have."

"Who you trying to impress? *If* we get new lamps, plastic shades are going to be fine."

"They may be fine for a cheap *schmuck* like you, but they're not fine for me. I want quality."

My dad rolled his eyes at her.

"Oh, never mind," my mom said, swatting the air with her spoon. "Forget about the lamps, Mr. Cheapskate. I'll buy some flashlights, and we'll sit on the couch and read by flashlight."

"You're a real comedian, Arlene," my dad said.

My mom pointed to a steaming bowl of meatballs in yellow gravy on the table.

"Go ahead and start. You've got bowling tonight."

"What is it?" He nodded at the thick concoction.

"Dinner."

"I know it's dinner. But what is it?"

"Waikiki Meatballs."

"What's in it?"

My dad dipped his finger into the meatball sauce, licked it, and recoiled in surprise.

"It's sweet! What's in this stuff?"

"It's pineapple. Ever heard of it?"

"Pineapple? From Hawaii?"

"Well, I didn't have to go all the way there for it."

These two should play the Catskills.

My mom pushed a bowl of rice toward him.

"It's pineapple from a can. You're supposed to put it over the rice. Just try it."

He spooned some rice onto his plate and followed it with some meatballs, pineapple chunks, and gravy. He speared a meatball and took a suspicious bite as we all watched.

"So?" she asked. "What do you think?"

He finished chewing and speared a chunk of pineapple.

"It's good. How much was the pineapple?"

My mom rolled her eyes.

"It doesn't matter."

"Yes, Arlene, it does. You want new lamps? We're not made of money. So. How much was the pineapple?"

My mom ignored him and started spooning some of the rice onto our plates.

"I asked you a simple question. How much was the pineapple?"

She glared at him across the table.

"Fine, Sam. It was expensive. I won't buy it again. You want cheap, we'll eat cheap. Liver and tongue, the cheapest meats around. I hope you like onions, because that's what you'll be eating. Liver, tongue, and onions. Like a good Jew. The neighbors will smell you coming a mile away. What's that smell? Oh, it's only the cheap Jew from next door."

"What a mouth you have on you, Arlene."

"Do you deny you're cheap?"

"There's nothing wrong with being frugal and getting a good deal on something. It gives me a lot of satisfaction."

"Fine already, Mr. Frugal. Let's go shopping for cheap lamps."

"I've got bowling tonight, remember? And anyway . . ."

He picked up the bowl of meatballs and speared a couple more chunks of pineapple.

"When I'm done paying off the pineapple, we'll go shopping for lamps."

We ate liver and onions every Wednesday during my childhood, and tongue on Thursdays. I have no doubt those Waikiki Meatballs were the reason why.

—⚍—

MAKING A BETTY CROCKER BREAK FOR IT

Betty Crocker, who taught my Central American mother how to cook like a
United Statesian, lived in Minnesota. And to get my childhood imaginative
dreamland simmering before bedtime, my mother read tales of Minnesota and
beyond from *Little House on the Prairie*. Minnesota: land of Laura Ingalls Wilder
running down the hills with huge smiles of possibility.
Happy people everywhere!

—Robert Farid Karimi, "Songlines for Future Culturewalkers," in
A Good Time for the Truth: Race in Minnesota

IN THE 1950S AND EARLY 1960S, success for my mom and many other American
women was epitomized by Betty Crocker. Minnesotans claim Betty Crocker as
one of their own. In the land of ten thousand lakes, one of the busiest freeways in
the state takes you past Betty Crocker Drive near the General Mills headquarters
in Golden Valley, a suburb just outside of Minneapolis and not far from New
Hope.

Despite being a fictitious character, Betty Crocker was a national icon for
forty years. In the 1940s, she was the second most popular woman in America;
Eleanor Roosevelt was the first. Her popularity continued well into the 1960s,
until her star began to dim once Jackie Kennedy and Gloria Steinem appeared
on the scene.

A look at Betty's "official portraits" over the years provides some insight into
the evolution of a large swath of women, including my mother. Betty's first portrait was painted in 1936, the year before my mom was born. It shows a motherly
brunette wearing a red top with an upright ruffled white collar. She has a weary,
determined expression—perfect for getting American women through the end

of the Great Depression and on through the war years. She looks, frankly, a little pinched and tired.

For nearly twenty years she looks tired. Finally, in 1955, her official portrait gets an update. America's future looks brighter and so does Betty. Living in the post–World War II bubble of American prosperity, Betty Crocker still appears "motherly," but she also looks calm and well rested. Her white collar is now open, exposing a small triangle of flesh well above the V of her red jacket. She seems cheerful and ready to greet the day.

In 1955, Arlene Defren (my mom) was an eighteen-year-old college student in the University of Minnesota's two-year dental hygiene program. The way she tells it, she graduated with terrible grades because she wasn't really interested in dental hygiene. Her only other career options were secretarial school and teaching, but she hated typing and didn't care for children in large doses, so dental hygiene it was.

That same year, she met Sam Bernick (my dad) at a dance sponsored by the U of M's Jewish fraternity Sigma Alpha Mu. She immediately liked his long eyelashes, brown eyes, and athletic build. He was a little serious and responsible for her taste, but he was cute and willing to put up with her father's strict rules about dating, so she said yes when he asked her out the following weekend.

Their courtship was complicated by the fact that they both lived at home while in college. Arlene lived way out in Robbinsdale in a crowded, quarrelsome house with her mom, dad, three siblings, two aunts, and an uncle. Arlene's siblings included her fraternal twin sister, Elaine, a quiet, bookish brunette who was considered "odd" and "the smart one." Arlene's competitive nature and low self-esteem was exacerbated by her twin's acuity, her red-haired younger sister's proximity, her father's neglect, her mother's verbal and physical abuse, her aunts' and uncle's constant arguing, and an overall lack of empathy, attachment, and emotional intelligence: all family traits.

Arlene felt overlooked and deprived of opportunities and attention. There was never any money for new clothes, shoes, after-school parties, or any fun at all. The only bright spots were sewing (she sewed all her own clothes) and a borrowed French horn that allowed her to march in the school band. But she was constantly dogged by her mother's insistence that she drag her reserved twin sister along to every event. Arlene was never allowed to shine on her own, or have her own friends, and her resentment created a blinding ambition to succeed.

She competed to win at sports, at school, and at home. Every contest was an attempt to prove her worth and escape her family's oppressive emotional and economic poverty. This dynamic deepened when a shocking event tumbled the family into further dysfunction: Elaine had a stroke and died the year she and Arlene turned twenty. Given the resentment she'd felt toward Elaine during their childhood, Arlene was unable to process her complicated emotions surrounding her sister's death. Elaine's name was rarely brought up again by anyone in the family, including Arlene.

Arlene's mother Goldie was a foul-mouthed tyrant, and her father Phillip was a narcissistic SOB (Goldie's description) who was rarely present and did almost nothing to support the family, so they relied on her aunts and uncle to survive. Arlene's parents did nothing but fight, mostly over the fact that her dad never brought home money from his job as a milkman. Many years later, Arlene and her siblings would discover that their father's money was going to support his other wives and children—two wives in New York and several others right there in Minnesota. And yes, he really was a milkman.

A couple of years after Arlene graduated from dental school and married Sam, Goldie divorced Phillip. Arlene didn't know why her mother divorced her father. All she knew was that her mother criticized her constantly. Goldie hit Arlene whenever she said something her mother didn't like, which seemed to be all the time. Arlene knew she should probably shut up, but she couldn't.

She just couldn't.

Sam (my dad) was wowed by Arlene in every way. He liked her lightly freckled skin, brassy red hair, large breasts, and forceful personality. He had little experience with women, and he told his friends she was a real "hot tamale." Sam graduated with a degree in civil engineering, which was not his first career choice. He was an American boy, and his lifelong dream was to play professional baseball. He was a star of his high school baseball team, and he thought he might have a shot at the pros, but his father (Grandpa Izzy) wanted him to be a rabbi. They compromised on Sam becoming a doctor (of course). Unfortunately, he wasn't cut out for medical school. The smell of formaldehyde made him faint. He was good at math, so he switched to engineering.

Sam and Arlene dated for two years. He borrowed his dad's car every Friday night and made the twenty-nine-mile trek from St. Paul to Robbinsdale. In 1955 that was a long drive—the freeways were still a few years away—so he spent weekends in Robbinsdale and headed back to St. Paul on Sunday nights.

If Arlene's dad was around, he made Sam do three hours of hard labor around the house and yard before each of their dates, but according to my dad, it was worth it. Escaping to Robbinsdale each weekend was better than being home with his awful family. As an added bonus, Arlene snuck down to the basement where he slept at night so they could fool around a little.

My mom was a hot tamale all right!

They got married in 1957 when Arlene was twenty and Sam was twenty-two. Arlene's poorly fitting diaphragm yielded Danny in 1958, Elisa in 1960, Lori in 1965, and David in 1968. But being a wife and mother was only mildly interesting. What Arlene really wanted was to be Betty Crocker.

My mother's journey in the 1950s, 1960s, and early 1970s closely mirrored Betty Crocker's transformation from homemaker to "modern" woman determined to take on new challenges outside the home. Like Betty, my mom excelled at the "domestic arts," but she was also competitive, ambitious, and creative. She was determined to find financial success for herself and our family. Even relative to other Jews at the time, my mom was different in this regard. Jewish mothers rarely worked outside the home, but my mother worked part-time as a dental hygienist from the time I was born in 1960. Even in 1971, only 1 percent of Jewish mothers in the US held jobs outside the home, while nationally, more than half of all mothers did.

My mom was a go-getter with few places to go. As a young Jewish mother in the 1960s midwestern suburbs, her options were limited to a vaguely unsatisfactory marriage, a vaguely unsatisfactory part-time job, four kids, and a four-bedroom split-level. For a while, that was enough—until it wasn't. Like many other college-educated women of that period, my mother started wondering, *Is this all there is?*

By the late 1960s, the notion that a woman should feel "fulfilled" by marriage, kids, and Beanie-Weenie hotdish became untenable, and my mom started spinning away from our family. But in 1964, when she was twenty-six, the only prize available to her was Betty's domestic goddess crown, and my mom wanted to wear it. She wanted to be a winner. Someone who mattered. Her younger sister Berta, now teaching and attending graduate school in Milwaukee, Wisconsin, had just been named one of twelve finalists in the Miss Milwaukee contest.

A contest? One of my mom's favorite things! And given her competitive nature, it probably felt like Berta had thrown down a gauntlet that required an answer. My mother felt *compelled* to compete with her sister. Indeed, she was determined to *best* her. So, just a few months before our family moved from Crystal to New Hope, my mom competed as one of seventeen contestants in the 1964 Mrs. Minnesota contest.

Ya, you betcha. My mom went for the gold.

—ɷ—

MRS. MINNESOTA 1964

CRYSTAL WOMAN ONE OF 17 FINALISTS IN
ANNUAL MRS. MINNESOTA CONTEST

Mrs. Samuel Bernick of 7625 30th Ave. N., Crystal, is one of 17 Minnesota
  homemakers who have been named as finalists in the annual Mrs. Minnesota
  contest held in conjunction with the Northwest Builders Show from March 15–17.
Mrs. Bernick and the other 16 finalists were selected on the basis of their
  community service record and on recipes and menus submitted to the
  committee.
At the state finals competition scheduled for Minneapolis on March 15, 16 and
  17 at the Northwest Builders Show, the 18 [sic] homemakers will demonstrate
  their skill in several homemaking arts including meal preparation, baking,
  table setting, and menu planning. Although the competition, now in its 25th
  year, is not a beauty contest, each of the finalists will be judged on her poise
  and personality.
The new Minnesota winner will receive a charm school course, courtesy of
  the Estelle Compton Models Inst., a television set from WTCN, a stereo set
  from the Northwest Builders Show, 50 gallons of Fairmont milk, Swift meat
  products, a bread tray from Fleischmann Yeast, a "Pampered in Pink" weekend
  at the Northstar Inn, and $100 worth of grocery products from Red Owl.
Mrs. Minnesota and her husband will also receive a 10-day all-expense paid
  vacation trip to St. Petersburg, Fla. in April where she will represent the State
  in the 1964 Mrs. America pageant. In addition, finalists will receive gifts and
  prizes including baskets of Red Owl groceries.

—*Minnesota Tribune*, 1964

The seventeen Mrs. Minnesota contest finalists and the retiring queen taken at the studios of WTCN-TV, Minneapolis, immediately after the crowning of the 1964 Mrs. Minnesota.
Mrs. Samuel (Arlene) Bernick is seated in the center row, third from the left. Mrs. Jay (Beverly) Babcock, the 1964 winner, is seated in the center row, fourth from the left. The retiring winner, Mrs. Theodore (Virginia) Firnschild, is standing in the back row, fourth from the left. WTCN-TV, Minneapolis, Photo by R. C. Mickelson

ONE LOOK AT THE YELLOWED cardboard scrapbook my mom kept during the spring of 1964 makes it clear that the Mrs. Minnesota contest was a big deal—not only for her but for the entire state. The 1964 contest was the twenty-fifth year of the state competition, and, given the amount of publicity it received, you can tell it captured the public's imagination. Winning the state competition was the only way to qualify for the popular nationally televised Mrs. America pageant—and my mom was determined to go all the way.

In the 1960s, the Mrs. America pageant celebrated the "Leave It to Beaver" family model of perfect suburban domestic bliss, which is certainly what my mom was aiming for in those early years. It's hard for me to imagine my dad being gung ho about this project given the outlay of money it would have required in terms of outfits, makeup, food costs, and so on. I suspect he was ultimately won over by the chance to win a television set, as well as my mom's unwillingness to take no for an answer.

She could be very persistent.

—ɯ—

MRS. JEWISH MINNESOTA 1964

"I'm going to enter the Mrs. Minnesota contest," my mom announced on a chilly October evening over a dinner of meatloaf, tater tots, and canned corn.

"The what?" my dad asked.

"The Mrs. Minnesota contest. It's being held at the Minneapolis Auditorium in March. I'm going to show the judges why I'm the best mother and homemaker in the state. And . . ."—she paused dramatically—"I'm going to win prizes and a trip to Florida to compete in the Mrs. America Pageant! I could win $10,000!"

My mom smiled. She didn't smile very often, so this was notable.

"There's a hairstyling competition, a cooking contest, sewing, and some other things. You have to be sponsored by a business in the community, and I already talked to Jerry Olsen down at the bank."

"What?" my dad said through a mouthful of tater tot. "You talked to Jerry about this?"

"He's thinking it over. And I've already got some great recipe ideas!"

"Number one . . . ," my dad pointed his fork at my mom. "Stop talking about this with Jerry. Number two, tell me exactly what you can win. And number three, how much is it going to cost me?"

"For once in your life, Sam, think about something besides money. Think about what it's going to mean to our family when I win. We can go on a trip to Florida!"

"*If* you win," my dad said. "How do you know you're going to win? It's a state-wide thing, right?" He pointed his fork at her again. "There's gonna be a lot of other wives . . ."

"Don't worry, I'm gonna win."

She waved away his doubts with a shake of her napkin and then leaned across the table and grabbed Danny's hand out of the tater tot bowl.

"No more tater tots, Mister, until you eat some more corn. You too, Elisa. Stop pushing the corn around, and put some in your mouth."

"You really think they're going to let a Jew win the Mrs. Minnesota contest?" my dad asked.

My mom rolled her eyes at him.

"What's that got to do with anything?"

"C'mon, Arlene, think about it. Has a Jew ever been elected president of the United States?"

"What the hell does that have to do with the Mrs. Minnesota contest?"

My dad shook his head, unconvinced.

"All I'm saying is I think you're biting off more than you can chew. And you still haven't told me how much it's going to cost me. Before you go any further with this crazy idea, I want to know exactly how much it's going to cost."

"This is not a crazy idea!"

My mom grabbed Danny's plate and started spooning corn onto it, striking the spoon hard against the plate each time.

"Maybe, maybe not," my dad said. "But think about it. A Jewish Mrs. Minnesota? Whaddya gonna do if they ask for your *lefse* recipe? Give 'em your *latke* recipe instead?"

He laughed while my mom glared at him.

—m—

MRS. SAMUEL BERNICK REACHES FOR
THE CROWN

MRS. BERNICK IS FINALIST IN CONTEST

Mrs. Arlene Bernick, wife of engineering aid [*sic*] Sam Bernick, has been
selected as one of twelve finalists [*sic*] in the Mrs. Minnesota contest. The
contest is for the statewide title, leading to the national Mrs. America pageant to
be held later this spring in Florida. The finals of the Minnesota contest will be
held March 15–17. The final evening of judging, incidentally, will be on local TV.
Although this is not necessarily a beauty contest, this writer can say without
fear of contradiction that the red-haired Arlene would rate highly if it were.
The *Bugle* congratulates Sam on his selection of a queen for a wife and wishes
Arlene success in the finals.

—M. L. Kruschke, in *The Bugle*, the Hennepin County
Highway Department newsletter

INCIDENTALLY, THE OTHER STORIES IN that issue of *The Bugle*, the official
newspaper of my dad's employer, included seasonal road restriction notices and
bowling scores from the Highway Department's company bowling league, the
"Dead Ends." My dad was part of the team.

Although *The Bugle* article says the competition wasn't "necessarily a beauty
contest," in the earliest years of the Mrs. America pageant, contestants were
judged solely on their looks and personality. In 1953, *Billboard* magazine called
it "a cheesecake parade." But in 1954, the whole thing was reincarnated as something less of a beauty pageant and more of a domestic goddess talent show. According to the rules, contestants were graded on cooking, sewing, ironing, party

preparation, *family psychology* (italics mine), grooming, poise, personality, and "general attractiveness."

The pageant offered notoriety, approbation, and prizes for things my mom was good at. Back then, being publicly lauded, much less financially rewarded, for household work was a rarity. I can certainly understand why my mom, who relished proving her worth in every way possible to the wider world, would have been interested.

Most of the articles about the Minnesota competition listed the contestants' address, age, height, weight, husband's occupation, list of hobbies, church group, civic participation, and number of children. My mom was among the youngest, and the only one to list a non-Christian church affiliation. Here are some typical entries:

> Mrs. Clarence D. Anderson, age 54, from Dassel, is married to an evangelical minister and has two children ages 23 and 27. She is five feet, 6 inches and weighs 155 pounds. She is a member of the Minnesota Branch of American Pen Women and her hobbies are art, crafts, photography, sewing, refinishing furniture and millinery.

> Mrs. Clark Tufte, Fergus Falls, age 26, graduate of Concordia College, Moorhead, with majors in business education, sociology, psychology. Her husband is an elementary school supervisor. She has two children ages 5 and 2. She belongs to the American Lutheran Church Women and a square dancing club.

> Mrs. Jay Babcock from Minneapolis, age 32, has three children ages 2, 5 and 7, and her husband is a chief clerk in the Great Northern Railroad transportation department. Five feet, 8 inches and 139 pounds. She is also vice president of TOPS (Take Off Pounds Sensibly), assists with a Blue Bird group, enjoys knitting, training and showing the family dog, swimming, bowling, skating and sewing and is active at church.

> Mrs. Samuel Bernick, age 26, University of Minnesota graduate of dental hygiene and part-time dental hygienist is a room mother at school, past president of the Beth El Women's League, and likes sewing, knitting, baking, piano playing, bowling, designing clothes and amateur theatricals. Her husband is a draftsman for the Hennepin County Highway Department. She is mother to two children ages 3 and 5. Five feet, 3 inches and 104 pounds.

In 1964, feminism was on the rise. Betty Friedan's *The Feminine Mystique* had been released just a year earlier. The state competitions for the Mrs. America pageant attracted contestants who were actively participating in civic women's groups and religious organizations—arenas where they were allowed to be leaders.

Although it was also the era of civil rights, there were no women of color in the 1964 Mrs. Minnesota contest. It wasn't until 1968 that the first Black woman competed in the national pageant. And despite my mom's certainty about winning the state contest and getting a chance at the national crown, my dad's skepticism about whether the judges would pick a Jewish Mrs. Minnesota seems reasonable. All the contestants listed some sort of church affiliation. Did the entry form require a religious affiliation? Is that why my mom felt compelled to list the Beth El? Did she actually feel comfortable revealing her Jewish status? Was she concerned about it? I have no idea, but I'm sure she was aware that all of the other contestants were likely to be Christians.

—∿—

"HUSBANDS OF CONTESTANTS
WASH DISHES"

Sam Bernick not only washed dishes but he was one of the bus drivers for
the contestants during the three-day contest. Bernick, a draftsman for the
Hennepin County Highway Department, helped his wife shop and carry
groceries....

The 17 homemakers competing through today for the Mrs. Minnesota crown
range in age from 26 to 51, have an average of four children and participate in
hobbies varying from amateur acting to writing poetry.

Most of them are Minnesota natives and have received post-high school
training of some kind. Their favorite household tasks are likely to be cooking
and baking, with cleaning their least favorite.

The 17 contestants, the largest number to compete in the annual contest, are
demonstrating skills in meal preparation, table setting, hair styling and
menu-planning at the Northwest Builders show, Minneapolis Auditorium.
They will shop for groceries, change their hair styles and participate in many
homemaking quizzes. They also will cook a meal, bake sweet rolls and fix
hors d'oeuvres trays in model kitchens both afternoons and tonight.

The new Mrs. Minnesota will be announced during a WTCN-TV show of the
Mrs. Minnesota pageant at 8 p.m. today.

—Mary Hart, *Minneapolis Morning Tribune*, Tuesday, March 17, 1964

A QUICK ANALYSIS OF THE Mrs. Minnesota contest entries shows that the
average candidate was thirty-five years old, weighed 128 pounds, and had brown
hair and blue eyes. Amazingly, almost no blondes!

Given the conflicting dates in the articles, it's hard to tell if the actual competition was held over two days or three, but either way, it meant my dad had to take time off work so my mom could compete.

Since I wasn't even four at the time of the contest, my own memories of this event are pretty sketchy. But luckily, thanks to my mother's detailed scrapbook, her stories, and my astounding ability to know what my mom was thinking at all times, I can tell you with "one hundred percent accuracy" exactly what happened the night they announced the winner.

—⚋—

PAGEANT NIGHT—MRS. MINNESOTA 1964

(Told from Arlene's POV with one hundred percent
accuracy by Elisa Bernick, who was
only three at the time.)

ON THE FINAL NIGHT OF the 1964 Mrs. Minnesota contest, Arlene Bernick felt cool as a cucumber. She felt radiant. Like a winner. She flashed the audience a smile as she strolled down the catwalk, did an expert pivot, and then sashayed to center stage for her interview. Her hair was teased into a lofty red crown, and the rhinestones she'd sewn around the collar of her sleeveless lime-green blouse sparkled and flashed beneath the spotlights. Draped across her right shoulder, the white satin sash that read "Crystal Savings and Loan!" fluttered against the waistband of her white faux leather hot pants as she moved.

When she reached the microphone, she calmly recited a list of all the activities she did at home that qualified her to be the next Mrs. Minnesota. When she had finished, she nodded at Dave Lee, the tuxedoed master of ceremonies, who stood beside her on the stage in the cavernous Minneapolis Auditorium.

"That's a very impressive list of activities, Mrs. Burnick," Dave Lee said into the microphone.

"Very impressive."

His deep voice reverberated through the room.

"It certainly sounds like your husband and children are lucky to have you looking after them."

Dave Lee was a local television personality and star of the afternoon children's show *Popeye & Pete*. Although Arlene found him irritating on television, she thought he looked almost handsome in his tux without that ugly penguin puppet on the end of his arm.

On the risers behind her, she could hear the other contestants fidgeting in various states of nervousness. Not her. She was reveling in her moment beneath the spotlights.

"Don't you agree?"

Dave Lee turned to the audience.

"Isn't Mrs. Burnick's family lucky to have her?"

Arlene pivoted on her shiny satin lime-green high heels to acknowledge the smattering of applause that ricocheted through the room. She stole a glance at the section reserved for contestants' families.

Oy vey.

There was Sam with the Kodak smiling like the cat who ate the canary. As if he had anything to do with her being up here on stage. She'd had to plead with him for the costume money, and even then, he'd only given her half of what she needed. She'd had to use grocery money to cover the rest.

That cheap son of a bitch. Forcing her to steal food from the kids.

If Sam knew how much she'd spent on the rhinestones, he'd throw up.

Arlene saw Elisa and Danny sitting in the row with the rest of her relatives. Her mom, Goldie, Aunt Freda, and Uncle Leo sat stone-faced next to her brother Harvey, his wife Sharon, and her nephews David and Jeff.

Danny put two fingers in his mouth and whistled loudly.

Arlene smiled and waved.

"Mrs. Burnick."

Dave Lee consulted the notecard in his hand.

"What do you like to do in your spare time?"

Arlene pivoted back toward him in one graceful motion, setting her white satin sash aflutter.

"In my spare time I like to sew and compete in baking competitions. I play the piano and French horn, and I like to volunteer as a reader in my children's classrooms. I am also very active at my family's place of worship and in the Boy and Girl Scouts of America organizations."

Arlene smiled fetchingly at the tuxedoed men sitting at the judges table in front of the stage. Her rhinestones winked and beckoned. She was going to win this pageant. She was going to spend an entire year riding in parades wearing a jeweled crown and a sash that said "Mrs. Minnesota—Best Mother and Home-maker." She was going to travel to Florida and compete against all the other winners from around the country.

She was going all the way.

Arlene waved at the judges. She'd been practicing her parade wave for months.

"Thank you, Mrs. Burnick. I see you have listed as your place of worship the Beth El . . . Synagogue . . ."

Dave Lee stumbled over the words.

"That's . . . *interesting.*"

She saw him exchange a look with the judges.

Oh boy, she thought. *Here we go. One goddamn thing after another.*

First, they spelled her name wrong in the program. Burnick instead of Ber-nick. And, predictably, all the stage decorations had an Easter theme. There were goddamn cardboard Easter eggs and potted Easter lilies all over the stage, and there was a giant Easter basket filled with gifts for the winners near the judges table.

And now this.

Arlene ignored Dave Lee and forced herself to continue smiling at the line of sweaty, tuxedoed judges. Who the hell were these guys anyway? From where she was standing she could read a few of their name cards. Robert Walsh, *Seven Corners Hardware.* William Hamm Jr., *Hamms Brewery.* Larry Platt Jr., *Midwest Lumber.*

Every one of them a goy for sure.

Dave Lee nodded to her.

"Thank you, Mrs. Burnick. We look forward to learning more about you during the sewing competition."

"I didn't know you played the French horn, Mom. What's a French horn?"

"Danny, please don't ask me any questions right now. We're on next."

Arlene stood backstage behind the blue velvet curtain with Danny, Elisa, and her nephews. Danny and Elisa wore Hansel and Gretel costumes, and David and Jeff were dressed as Laurel and Hardy.

"Okay, kids, pay attention. Danny, you're the leader. I want you to walk in a big circle around the stage, and then stop right in front of the judges while I talk about what you're wearing. Elisa, you go next. Make sure the braids stay in front, and stop scratching! Danny!"

She thumped Danny on the back of his head.

"Stop throwing the confetti. Save it until you're onstage, and don't toss it. Pretend you're sprinkling breadcrumbs. David, where's your cane?"

"Danny stole it."

She thumped Danny's head again.

"Goddamn it, Danny, give David his cane. David, you and Jeff follow Elisa, but leave a little space between you. Walk slowly so I don't have to rush what I'm saying."

Arlene held up her compact and checked the new red fall that sat high on her head. She looked good, Arlene thought, and boy-oh-boy she'd better. This getup had cost a fortune. Along with the new fall, Arlene had changed into a sleeveless rose-colored minidress with rhinestones sewed around the collar and the hem. She had on bright pink lipstick, sheer nylons, and hot pink high heels. She was also wearing dangle earrings with pink rhinestone-covered balls at the bottom that gleamed in the dim light.

"OK you guys, follow me. And no pushing. Danny, Goddamn it, I said stop throwing that confetti!"

They were right behind the center curtain now, and Arlene held her finger to her lips for silence.

"And now, here is Mrs. Samuel Burnick representing Crystal as she presents enchanting children's costumes that she designed and sewed herself. Mrs. Burnick..."

Obviously, given how young I was, I can't remember exactly what happened backstage that night or once we got home that evening. I know my mom invited her relatives to our house for Shabbat dinner to celebrate her pageant victory. Unfortunately, it turned out to be a postmortem of her defeat. She was named "Fifth Runner-Up" and won a year's supply of Gold Medal flour and twenty-five boxes of Betty Crocker cake mix (mixed varieties).

But having lived through years of Shabbat dinners with my Grandma Goldie, Aunt Freda, and Uncle Leo (my mom's mother and siblings), I have a pretty good idea of what happened the night my mom lost the 1964 Mrs. Minnesota contest.

"If my last name wasn't Bernick, I'd have won!"

My mom stabbed a fork into the hot gray mound of brisket sitting in a roasting pan on the counter. She started hacking into the meat with a large knife, as she complained to Grandma Goldie, who was taking a challah out of the oven.

"And look who they picked for the winner. Beverly Babcock. Beverly—Mrs. blue-eyed Minnesota Lutheran—Babcock. She couldn't cook a box of macaroni to save her life!"

"Well," Grandma Goldie said, without a trace of sympathy behind her blue cat-eye glasses, "she scored a lot higher than you did in the hairstyling competition."

"She did three hairstyles, and they all looked exactly the same. She looked like goddamn Jackie Kennedy in all three! She just changed her hats!"

My mom gestured violently with the knife and flicked a piece of brisket onto the floor.

"I told you they'd never let a Jew win," Grandma Goldie said, shaking her head as she leaned down to retrieve the meat.

My mom ignored her as Danny and I raced around the kitchen locked in a *Bonanza*-style shootout.

"Ya got me!" Danny said and tumbled over onto the floor. "Aaaargggghhhh ...!"
He lay writhing on the linoleum as I wielded a toy pistol above him.
"Knock it off, you two!"
My mom nudged Danny's head hard with her shoe.
"Your father just pulled into the driveway. Danny, go pick up the toys on the
landing like I asked you, and tell your Uncle Leo and Aunt Freda to come up.
Elisa! So *nu*? Put the napkins on the table."
Danny aimed his gun at me and took another shot.
"Got ya!"
Grandma Goldie leaned over and grabbed his ear.
"OW!"
"Stop fooling around and listen to your mother! Now!"

My mom spent the meal staring at her plate and pressing geometric patterns
into the mashed potatoes with her fork.
OK, I can't be sure we had mashed potatoes that night (if we did, they were
probably Potato Buds, remember those?). But I'm one hundred percent sure we
endured the nonstop bickering of Grandma Goldie, Uncle Leo, and Aunt Freda.
They still lived together in that house in Robbinsdale, and it's amazing to me
they didn't kill each other. All they did was argue. They fought about everything.
Everything.
Since I can't remember the exact conversation from this particular evening,
I'm going to give you an example of one of their dinner table fights that happened
when I was six or seven. I've confirmed this with my brother Dan, and he, too,
remembers it clearly.
The fight was about *lettuce*, and it was all my fault.
"Please pass the salad," I asked during a lull in the bickering. I should have
kept my mouth shut.
"Iceberg lettuce has no nutritional value," Grandma Goldie said.
"What are you talking about?" Uncle Leo growled from across the table.
His bald head glistened beneath the dining room chandelier.
"You talk, talk, talk, Goldie, and you don't know what you're talking about."
"I certainly do know what I'm talking about, Leo. I read an article about it in
the newspaper. Iceberg lettuce has almost no vitamins."
"It may not have vitamins, but it's good roughage," Aunt Freda chimed in. "And
there's certainly a lot of value to that."
My mom rolled her eyes. She did this whenever Aunt Freda talked about food.
Aunt Freda had a humped back and terrible teeth, and she ate almost nothing

because she had a "delicate" stomach. She always brought her own food to Shabbat dinner, packed in baby food jars.

"Neither of you know what you're talking about," Uncle Leo said, his already loud voice getting louder. "Let her have the lettuce, for god's sake. Lettuce is a vegetable, and vegetables have vitamins."

"Iceberg lettuce was developed because it ships well and stays fresh for a long time in grocery stores," Grandma Goldie said. "Not because it has vitamins. Elisa would be better off having the beans or some more potatoes."

"Potatoes aren't that good for you," Aunt Freda said softly. "They're mostly starch."

Uncle Leo picked up the bowl of potatoes and gestured toward me.

"Potatoes have been eaten for thousands of years . . ."

"Actually . . ."

Grandma Goldie took the bowl from him and set it down in front of me.

". . . potatoes are from the New World. They weren't introduced to Europe until the 1500s. Go ahead, Elisa. Or have some more meat. Pass her the roast, Freda."

"I don't want . . . ," I started to say.

"The roast is full of fat. She doesn't need more fat," Aunt Freda said.

"Have some more beans. Or would you like to have some applesauce? Hand her the bowl."

"Stop interfering, Freda. For god's sakes! She doesn't want the applesauce! She doesn't want the beans. She wants the salad. Give her the goddamn salad!"

Uncle Leo pushed his chair back, stood up, and walked around to where the salad bowl sat in front of Aunt Freda. He picked it up with two hands and carried it over and set it down hard in front of me.

"There you go, Elisa. Now have some salad."

In the silence that followed, all of my relatives sat glaring at me. The idea of eating more salad filled me with dread, and I wasn't sure what to do. My mom and dad exchanged a look across the table.

"Elisa," my dad said. "Go ahead and take a little salad."

I forked one piece of iceberg lettuce and one withered tomato from the bowl and set them on my plate.

"Thank you," I said softly.

Danny smirked at me across the table. He aimed his fork and mouthed, "You're dead."

"Danny!" My mom glared at him.

Nobody said anything for a minute as they watched me eat my lettuce and tomato.

"Can you believe the new Mrs. Minnesota won because she looks like Jackie Kennedy?" my mom asked, looking around the table. "I mean, what the hell kind of homemaking talent is that?"

There was another moment of silence as the table considered her question. My dad shook his head and said nothing. He didn't have to. From the start he'd thought the whole pageant was a complete waste of money, and he only let my mom do it because the bank paid the seventy-five-dollar entry fee. He was never going to let her forget about the fifty bucks he spent on her outfits and all those rhinestones.

My mom stared at his pinched mouth across the table, and I knew exactly what she was thinking.

Cheap son of a bitch.

"Arlene!" Uncle Leo banged the table with his fist. "Will you shut up already about that goddamn pageant!"

He glared at her across the table, challenging her to say another word about it.

"You lost already, now forget about it!"

My mom glared back at him. Then she glared at Grandma Goldie. And then at my dad. And my Aunt Freda. And finally at me and Danny. She didn't say anything, but she didn't have to. We could read her expression loud and clear.

Damn the whole goddamn unsympathetic lot of you.

WINNERS AND LOSERS

MINNEAPOLIS WOMAN WINS MRS. MINNESOTA '64 CROWN

Mrs. Jay (Beverly) Babcock weighed 157 pounds a year ago, and lost enough
weight the past months to win the crown of Mrs. Minnesota Tuesday night. . . .
Mrs. Babcock's description of a representative homemaker: "A woman who is
active in the interests of her husband and children, a woman who does her part
in working for her church and community, supports her political beliefs with
physical efforts and yet takes the time and effort to keep her home and herself
attractive."

—Minneapolis Tribune

ALAS, IT'S TRUE. MY MOM gave it her all, but she did not win the 1964 Mrs. Minnesota contest. She didn't win the baking contest (Mrs. Clarence D. Anderson),
the hors d'oeuvre tray (Mrs. Lincoln Poupore), or the menu planning (same).
She didn't win for table setting (Mrs. Clark Tufte), or even for the sewing and
crafts (Mrs. Conrad Hoff). The new Mrs. Minnesota was Mrs. Jay (Beverly)
Babcock. You will notice the article above finally gives the poor woman a first
name—but in parentheses, like a pat on the head!

Beverly Babcock won first place in the hairstyling competition, "in which
contestants were asked to fix their hair in three different styles without outside
help." The runner-up in the state contest was Mrs. Jerry D. Kline, who took first
place in meal preparation and a "living pleasure" quiz.

My mom placed fifth overall, so not a terrible showing. And it's impossible to
sense her disappointment from her scrapbook. There are several photos of my
mom and others taken during the competition, with captions like this:

"Wielding rollers in the hairstyling competition . . ."
(The photo shows my mom and two others sitting in front of small mirrors at a table, putting their hair in rollers.)
  "In the baking contest, Mrs. Samuel Bernick whipped up a batter . . ."
(The photo shows my mom stirring something in the "test kitchen.")

After the Mrs. Minnesota contest ended, several of the contestants continued to receive media attention, including Mrs. Hoff, the fourth-place winner. The *St. Paul Dispatch*'s "News for WOMEN" section included an article that called Mrs. Hoff a "candidate for busiest homemaker." Her activities included planning food service for twelve hundred at a local church, coordinating an international program "for 300 members attending a homemakers holiday event," teaching sewing classes, AND hosting a weekly daytime television program called *Tea at Three*. What couldn't Mrs. Hoff do?

The article, which was accompanied by a photo of Mrs. Hoff adjusting her six-year-old daughter's Easter dress, described Mrs. Hoff's Easter plans and included several of her favorite recipes for using ham leftovers. I know you're dying to know what Mrs. Hoff served for Easter dinner, so here is her menu:

Baked Ham with Mustard Sauce
Stuffed Baked Potatoes
Honey Glazed Carrots
Grapefruit Ginger Salad
Hot Rolls
Lemon Angel Pie
Milk and Coffee

On the second-to-last page in my mother's scrapbook there is a letter dated March 26, 1964. It's from Robert N. Benham, the manager of public relations for Red Owl Stores, Inc.

Mrs. Samuel Bernick
7625 30th Avenue North
Crystal, Minnesota

Dear Mrs. Bernick:
  Just a reminder to send me your transportation expenses to and from the Mrs. Minnesota Contest so that we may reimburse you. Also, please send me copies of any publicity about the Contest that has appeared in your area. If you only have one newspaper clipping available, we will reproduce it and return the original to you.

Some of the contestants have asked for the names and addresses of the judges, sponsoring firms, and other contestants. We are now in the process of putting together a brochure for you with this information in it. You should receive a copy within a few days.

We would like to have you and your family be our guest for an Easter ham or some other Red Owl Holiday item. We hope you will accept the attached merchandise certificate which may be redeemed at any Red Owl food store.

Very truly yours,
RED OWL STORES, INC.
Robert N. Benham

I can well imagine what my mother thought of the offer of a free Easter ham or other "Red Owl Holiday" item. In 1964, Easter was the only possible spring holiday acknowledged by suburban grocery stores. My mom certainly wasn't going to find boxes of matzoh or jars of gefilte fish stocked among the holiday hams, Peeps, and jelly beans. Instead, we ate the spoils of her Mrs. Minnesota contest defeat for Passover that year after she convinced the store manager at our local Red Owl to let her redeem her merchandise certificate for a "holiday" brisket.

—∭—

JEWISHNOTCHRISTIAN

This was my first clue about internalized antisemitism—the way so many of us, as Jewish girls, got the (ridiculous, toxic) message that something was wrong with us. That we just didn't fit the white Protestant mold this country valorized. . . . Disdaining Jewishness is often the lesson of a Christian-centric society; it's what assimilation teaches.

—Penny Rosenwasser, *Hope into Practice:*
Jewish Women Choosing Justice Despite Our Fears

I'M NOT ACTUALLY CERTAIN WHETHER antisemitism played a role in the 1964 Mrs. Minnesota contest, but if it did, my parents wouldn't have been surprised. Their Jewish identities were defined by the overt antisemitism around them. My mom was nine and my dad was eleven in 1946 when journalist Carey McWilliams described Minneapolis as "the capital of anti-Semitism in the United States" in *Common Ground* magazine. My parents' sense of self was rooted in a Jewish community that absorbed and ameliorated the dominant culture's potent rejection. Their insular Jewish neighborhoods, schools, and synagogues allowed them to navigate their assimilation into White, middle-class, suburban Minnesota America with their Jewish identities solidly intact. The Christian waters might threaten to drown them, but their Jewish life jackets were securely fastened.

I, on the other hand, grew up an assimilated Jew in New Hope, Minnesota, and my Jewish life jacket fit differently. I didn't feel the same buoyancy, nor did I feel the need to have it strapped on so tight. When I started kindergarten in the mid-1960s, antisemitism still lurked beneath the cool blue waters of the New Hope swimming pool, but it surfaced only on rare occasions. My parents' efforts to assimilate were so successful that in many ways I felt the same as everyone else around me. I learned the same things in school, I watched the same TV programs, I had the same friends as everyone else in my neighborhood, and I was part of the in-group.

Almost.

I wasn't a Christian, and this was an important difference. Christianity was the only religion acknowledged. No exceptions. There weren't any Muslims or atheists, God forbid. There were just different flavors of Christian. And yes, Catholics are Christian.

I was certainly Jewish, but it wasn't the same kind of Jewish as my parents. I was certainly White, suburban, and middle-class, but it wasn't the same kind of White, suburban, and middle-class as my Christian friends. I was *somethingnotsomething*. I was *JewishNotChristian*—a departure from both my parents and my friends.

The confusing thing was that thanks to Minnesota Nice, unless I brought up my Jewish difference, neither my religion nor my difference existed. I was the same as all the other White Minnesotans around me. Insider–outsider status confers both difference and invisibility, belonging and not belonging, at the exact same time.

Back then I didn't understand the consequences of never having my Jewish identity acknowledged positively (or at all) by the dominant culture. I didn't sense that a core part of me was constantly being erased and diminished, or that I was actively taking part in my own erasure and diminishment. That part of me felt mostly invisible.

I swam along, a small gefilte fish in the Christian waters I didn't see, until something happened that made me feel like I was suddenly drowning. The notable exceptions of overt antisemitism I experienced as a child caught me completely, and devastatingly, by surprise. It was a shocking reminder that Jews were hated, and, oh yeah . . . *I'm Jewish*.

—ᗰ—

MRS. SWANSON—1967

THE YEAR I TURNED SEVEN, a certain swim team carpool family kept "forgetting" to pick up my brother Danny when it was their turn to drive. The third time it happened, it didn't seem like an accident anymore.

"Mom, they're not here yet! I'm going to be so late! The coach yelled at me in front of everybody last time!"

Danny was pacing in front of the living room window in his jacket. He had a swim bag at his feet.

"They're just ignorant goddamn people," my mom said, grabbing her purse. "Jump in the car, Danny. And be pleasant when you see them. From now on I'll take you when it's the Larsons' turn to drive."

Or a few weeks later when everybody in my class got invited to Johnny Stewart's Halloween party except for me. There were orange and black pumpkin invitations on everyone's desk but mine.

I must have looked as forlorn as I felt, because Mrs. Nelson gave me a big hug and assured me "it was a mistake," but an invitation never materialized.

"It's their loss," my mom said when I came home from school the day of the party. "And you don't like Johnny Stewart anyway. He's the butcher's kid, right? The one who brings cow eyes to school?"

"But, Mom," I said, crying hard. "Everybody came dressed up in their Halloween costume today. I was the only one in our class who wasn't dressed up!"

My mom was so angry her hands were shaking when she hung up my jacket in the closet. I'm not sure what made her madder, me not being invited or her not getting to sew one of her "creative" Halloween costumes for the party.

On these and several other occasions that fall and winter, my dad counseled patience.

"We all need to buck up and hang in there," he told us around the dinner table. "I know it's hard, but put your best foot forward, and show 'em what Jews are like. They'll eventually come around."

Show 'em what Jews are like? I wasn't sure what he meant. We're Jews, and Jews were like us . . . what else could we show them?

In the moment of silence that followed this exchange, I decided to bring up something that had been bothering me all day. Something a fourth-grader said to me on the bus that morning.

"Did we kill Christ?"

"What?"

My mom stopped spooning canned carrots on Danny's plate in mid-stroke.

"Mary Olson said that our family killed Christ. Who is Christ anyway?"

"The Romans killed Christ," my mom said.

She shook her head and gave Danny back his plate.

"They don't even know their own history."

"Just ignore her, Elisa," my dad counseled. "Don't say anything, and walk away. It's not worth fighting about."

Fighting about it hadn't even occurred to me. And how could I walk away if I was riding the bus? I started to feel worried.

"Who is Christ?" I asked again, confused.

"You're such a dweeb," Danny said. "He's Jesus. Christians think he's God. But Jews don't."

"Oh," I said, pushing carrots around on my plate as I considered this information. "So our family didn't kill him?"

"Of course not!" my mom said. "That's a ridiculous idea. Now, stop playing with your carrots and eat them."

The day we went sledding at the Millers' is one of my most potent memories.

The Millers' hill sloped down toward a narrow strip of land that separated their backyard from Mrs. Swanson's chain-link fence. None of the neighborhood kids went near Mrs. Swanson's yard. Everybody knew she wore wooden shoes and tortured kids if she caught them touching her fence.

At the top of the Millers' hill we were playing snow tag and Danny was It. There were six of us belly-down on our Flexible Flyers waiting for Danny to count us off.

"On your mark . . . get set . . . go!"

All of us bulleted down the hill and slammed hard into Mrs. Swanson's fence at the bottom. Pushing and shoving, we jumped up and took off running down the narrow strip between the yards with Danny trying to tag us out. I purposely lagged behind to tease Danny with my superior speed, when all of a sudden Mrs. Swanson threw open her back door and screamed as loud as she could.

"Get away from my yard, you dirty Jews!"

Her guttural voice stopped all of us in our tracks.

"Ya hear me, you two? Get the hell away from my fence, you Jews! You stinkin' Jews!"

There was a long moment of silence.

Without looking at any of the other kids, Danny grabbed my arm and pulled me toward home. I was worried about leaving our sleds behind, but Danny was dragging me, frantic. When we burst into the house, Danny threw himself down on the landing and started sobbing while I looked on bewildered. I couldn't figure out exactly why he was so upset.

"What is it? What's going on?"

My mom came racing out of the sewing room and up the stairs to the landing.

"What the hell happened?"

It took a minute for Danny to calm down enough to tell the story, and when he did, I couldn't remember ever seeing my mom that angry. She stomped up the stairs to the kitchen, slapped the telephone book onto the counter, and immediately got on the phone to Mrs. Swanson. Danny sat sniffling on the landing as I took off my boots, crept up the stairs in my snow pants, and peeked around the doorway while my mom screamed at Mrs. Swanson over the phone.

"You goddamn ignorant antisemite!"

My mom's face was redder than I'd ever seen it.

"If you ever . . . *ever* say another word to my children . . . one goddamn word, I will call the police and have them haul your ass into court so fast you won't know what happened. I mean that. You stay the hell away from my kids!"

She slammed the receiver down so hard the phone came off the wall and crashed to the floor with a huge CLANG.

At that moment with the phone *broken* on the floor, my mom yelling about the *police*, Danny *crying*, and Mrs. Swanson saying Jews were *dirty* . . . for the first time I understood that being Jewish was different from *not being Christian*. It was something very, very *bad*.

Something I needed to hide.

I slid my hand down the top of my red turtleneck and fingered the Star of David necklace I'd been wearing since Hanukkah. It had been a present from Grandma Goldie, and each tip of the star had a little diamond that sparkled in the light. I hadn't taken the necklace off even once yet, not even for baths.

I squeezed the star's six points between my fingertips as I listened to my mom swearing in the dining room and Danny sniffling on the landing. I reached behind my neck to unhook the necklace and headed down to my room to hide it in my underwear drawer.

CAN'T HIDE FROM THE WEATHER

Winter is not a season, it's an occupation.

—Sinclair Lewis, *The Job*

AS A MINNESOTAN, I CAN'T go any further without discussing the weather. In fact, I'm amazed I've been able to hold off this long. Poets and historians have described Minnesota's climate as "relentless" and "unforgiving." This also describes the character of many of those who settled here, including my mother. Of all the funny Minnesota jokes I've run across, not a single one is about the weather. And that's because the weather in Minnesota is no joke.

Despite the last decades of climate change, Minnesota's reputation as "the icebox of America" remains strong. In 2014 and again in 2019, Minnesota experienced temperatures colder than Mars when a polar vortex dropped temperatures as low as minus 42 degrees in International Falls, with a windchill as low as minus 74 degrees in Grand Marais. The year 2019 also saw the snowiest February in Minnesota history, with a record thirty-nine inches.

Extreme weather events in every season were a significant part of my growing up. In 1965, when I was five, civil defense sirens were used for the first time in Twin Cities history to alert residents to a severe weather threat. Six tornadoes tore across the Twin Cities that day, killing thirteen and injuring almost seven hundred. Meteorologists consider themselves lucky to be forecasting Minnesota weather patterns, because they regularly get to discuss derechos, tornadoes, flash floods, severe drought, high humidity, blistering heat, bitter cold, and whiteout blizzard conditions.

I recite these facts not only because they're impressively awful but also because I wonder how much of my mother's unhappiness and instability during my childhood was influenced by Minnesota's inexorable weather. Eighty inches of snow fell each winter between 1960 and 1970. In 1962, it was minus 32 degrees on the first day of March. In 1965, the year following the Mrs. Minnesota contest, and the same year we moved to New Hope, we had the coldest March since 1899 and the coldest September since 1868.

I'm sure my mom wasn't the only mother feeling low during those harsh winters in New Hope. According to a 2018 report from Blue Cross Blue Shield of America, Minnesota has one of the highest rates of major depression in the country and Hawaii has the lowest. The data examined medical claims from more than forty-one million commercially insured Blue Cross Blue Shield members from 2013 to 2016 and compared depression rates among states, across age groups, and by gender. Women living in Minnesota tied with women in Maine for having the highest depression diagnosis rate in the country. Is it a coincidence that both states have shitty winters? I think not.

By nature, Minnesotans aren't complainers. It's a point of pride and part of the Nordic bootstrapping quality of Minnesota Nice. Fifty years ago, before social media made griping a national pastime, Minnesotans didn't complain out loud when it was 20 degrees below. They didn't burden neighbors with their problems. They said, "Cold enough for ya?" and then helped you jump-start your car or pushed you out of a snowbank, and left you to your business. They were always ready to lend a hand, but that was the end of it.

I guess it's possible the neighborhood ladies discussed winter coping strategies each Tuesday morning at the Zealand Avenue Coffee Klatch. Maybe they confided in each other about wanting to strangle their children and about hating their husbands during the interminable months they woke up in the dark, sent their husbands to work in the dark, and made dinner in the dark. But I doubt it. Women didn't feel empowered to express these sorts of feelings back then, even to themselves.

In the winter of 1968, my mother wasn't at those coffee klatches, nor did she have many friends, even from the synagogue. I imagine she felt extremely isolated. Throw in undiagnosed "seasonal affective disorder" (which wouldn't become a term for another twenty years), a penchant toward depression (which went undiagnosed, and it wouldn't have occurred to my mother that her feelings might be something to see a doctor about), and being six weeks pregnant with my brother, David (which she probably didn't even realize yet), and you can see how she might just . . . snap.

—ᴍ—

COLD SNAP

ON A GRAY, FROSTY MORNING a few weeks into January 1968, Arlene couldn't think of a single reason to be happy the New Year had arrived. It felt just like the crappy old year to her. She lay on her back motionless under the blankets, unwilling to find a reason to get out of bed. She felt like shit. She knew she should get up and make the kids breakfast, but she was just so damn tired. She closed her eyes and felt a single tear slide down the slope of her temple into her ear. She dabbed at it with the sheet. She was pathetic.

She turned her head to the side and opened one eye. She could see a narrow slot of the room, and in that slot there was nothing but the stark mess of her life sprawled everywhere in the glaring winter light. Two loads of laundry sat unfolded on the floor next to her dresser. Sam's tennis shoes, bowling bag, and bowling shirt were heaped in front of the closet. Monopoly money and stray red and green plastic houses spilled across her makeup table. Arlene closed her eye, turned back to her pillow and exhaled heavily. She welcomed the edge of sour breath that condensed on the polyester pillowcase as she inhaled. She hadn't told anyone about the daydreams she'd been having. The ones where she left Sam and the kids.

She was tortured by these daydreams. They happened everywhere without warning. In the produce section at the grocery store. At the bus stop waiting for the kids to get home from school. She suddenly imagined herself walking away from her life in New Hope. It was like watching herself in a beautiful slow-motion movie. She followed herself from behind as she strolled confidently, *buoyantly* down Hopewood Lane on a brilliant summer day. She turned left onto Boone

Avenue and headed straight down the hill past Northwood Park, swinging her purse at her side to match the jaunty rhythm of her steps.

From the back, Arlene thought she looked like Elizabeth Montgomery from *Bewitched* (if Elizabeth Montgomery had red hair). Arlene never saw her own face during these little movies, but she knew for certain she was smiling. It was always just her walking alone on the road, her copper hair blowing in the sun, the wide-open wind of the world at her back, striding toward a future that promised nothing already known.

And then, at the reel's end, she came back to herself huddled with the other mothers at the bus stop or balancing an apple in her hand at the Red Owl. That was the torture. The punch in the stomach she felt each time her dream ended, and the movie's weightless joy gave way to the dull gray that had been creeping inside her body for months now. A thick blanket of fog had settled inside her head, and it simply would not clear. The fog was getting heavier. It was starting to seep out of her ears and wrap itself around her head and body like a shroud. She felt like she was starting to suffocate inside it.

Arlene didn't tell anyone about these feelings. Who could she tell? Her mother? Uncle Leo? They'd say, "Get over it already, Sarah Bernhardt." Sam's parents? Oy. Her friends from high school or college? She didn't have many. Moving to New Hope, working part-time, and having kids made it hard to keep friendships going. It's not like she had any friends in the neighborhood, and she certainly couldn't say anything at the synagogue. What was she supposed to do? Lean over the Oneg table after Friday night services and say, "Hey Lila, can I get the recipe for these blintzes? And by the way, ever feel like you got a black fog filling up your head, and it's inside your throat, and you're choking on it and you can't breathe?"

Yeah, right. Like she'd ever say *that* to anyone.

Arlene heaved herself onto her back. She noticed the paint starting to peel on the ceiling near the closet door. Of course, Sam was no help. She didn't even bother trying to talk to him about it. These days all he did was talk about bowling and that goddamn New Hope Athletic Association. She could barely stand to sleep in the same bed with him anymore. And the kids . . . what kind of comfort could you expect from kids?

A moment later she heard a quiet knock at the door. She turned back over onto her stomach and buried her face deep into the pillow.

THE PAIN GAME—1968

THAT FIRST MORNING MY MOM didn't come out of her room to make us breakfast was memorable because she *always* made us breakfast. It was the winter of 1968. I was eight, Danny was ten, and Lori was three. By then, my mom was acting like it was February all year long. My dad, like most dads back then, was rarely around thanks to work, bowling, and a general sense that my mom was in charge of everything on the home front. We kids were left to navigate her increasingly erratic behavior on our own and to develop our own coping strategies.

When she didn't get up, we waited in the dining room and then finally crept down the hallway and stood outside her closed bedroom door, not quite sure what to do.

Danny finally knocked, and we stood there waiting for her to answer. When she didn't, he knocked again, and we pressed our ears to the door and listened. Still nothing. Danny looked at me and I shrugged.

He knocked again, a little harder, and part of me secretly hoped she didn't answer. We'd have to get breakfast for ourselves or go without, but that might be better than getting her out of bed. Her moods were all over the place, and you never knew what was going to happen.

"Mahpppff?"

Her voice sounded muffled.

"Mom?" Danny said through the door. "When are we going to have breakfast? It's almost time for school."

"Maahppften ha door."

It sounded like she said something about the door. Danny opened it a few inches, but she didn't say anything.

"Mom?" Danny said again.

"Mahppftoo want?"

All we could see was the back of her head sticking out from the blankets. She was facing away from us with most of her mouth covered by a pillow.

"The bus is going to be here soon, Mom." I said. "What are we having for breakfast?"

She lifted her head from the pillow but didn't look at us.

"OK, OK. I'm getting up. Just go get dressed."

"We've been dressed for five hours already," Danny said.

"Shut the door both of you. Elisa, make sure Lori is dressed. I'll be out in five minutes."

"What are we having for breakfast?" I asked again.

"Hot cereal."

"I'm sick of hot cereal!" Danny said. "Why can't we have Captain Crunch like everybody else?"

My mom turned her head slowly toward us and glared murderously. I slid back into the hallway and Danny followed, pulling the door nearly closed so it was open only a crack.

"It's that or nothing, Mr. Ungrateful. You decide. Now shut the goddamn door!"

Danny did as he was told. We went to the kitchen, and I opened the refrigerator door wondering what we needed for hot cereal.

"Go sit down, Elisa. Mom's coming out!"

He punched me hard in the arm and slammed the refrigerator door.

Given our role models, is it any surprise my brother and I resorted to *Lord of the Flies* behavior? Between my father absenting himself from our family, and my mother's reliance on corporal punishment to establish some sense of "control" in her world, my older brother and I had a relationship based on pain—inflicting and avoiding it.

One of the games we played frequently during this period was called "the Pain Game." The Pain Game was Danny's invention and the rules were simple. Danny tried to hurt me as much as possible without drawing blood or making me cry. The point was to make me say "Uncle," but it was more fun for him if I didn't.

My job was to run away before Danny hurt me, or, if escape was impossible, to protect myself with psychological armor. From my perspective, I won the Pain Game by not letting Danny know that anything he did had pierced my mental shield. We were pretty evenly matched.

We usually played it in the evenings when we were supposed to be in bed. My mom put us to bed at 7:30 each night because she'd "had enough of us for one day." It took us awhile to feel tired enough to go to sleep. So, after my mom turned off our lights and padded down the hallway to her sewing room, Danny and I met in the dim downstairs hallway. Serenaded by my dad's phlegmy snoring on the upstairs couch and the muffled hum of my mom's sewing machine behind the closed rec room door, the fun and games began.

I lay on my back with my bare feet pointed toward the sliver of light that spilled from under the rec room door. Danny sat on top of my chest and used his knees to pin my elbows to the carpet. He tapped my forehead in the exact same spot over and over with the sharp knuckle of his forefinger.

He called this variation of the Pain Game "the Chinese Water Torture," although there wasn't any water involved. It was an awful game but better than "the Chinese Fart Torture," where he wrapped his legs around my head and squeezed Beanie-Weenie hotdish farts in my face.

The sharp tap of Danny's knuckle was excruciating, but I kept my eyes closed and said nothing. I knew I could spare myself a lot of pain by saying "Uncle," because Danny was usually good about letting me go. But enduring the pain and keeping silent was a matter of honor.

Not only was I stubborn, I had a vivid imagination.

I pretended I was a secret agent training for an important mission where withstanding this sort of cruelty would save my life. Tonight, I was Mrs. Peel from *The Avengers*, and my goal was to last through ten minutes of the "Chinese Water Torture" without crying.

But after five minutes it hurt so much I yelped in pain, and my mom heard me all the way in the sewing room.

"Goddamn it, you two!" she yelled from behind the closed door.

Danny stopped tapping.

"You better get to goddamn sleep right now or I'm coming out with the spoon! Do you hear me? Don't make me come down that hallway!"

My mom had a special wooden spoon that she kept in the sewing room. Originally, it was a puppet she'd made for a birthday party decoration, and it had two painted blue eyes and a red smiling mouth. During its life as a puppet, the spoon had long, curly jute hair and a little blue and white apron. But the hair and apron were long gone, and now my mom used the spoon for forcing needles through suede and leather—and for spanking us.

Danny and I both knew my mom would hit him first, but she usually gave several warning yells before she made good on her threat. So, after a few seconds of silence, he put his hand over my mouth and started tapping my forehead again.

Tap. Tap. Tap.

I tried to buck him off by rocking my hips, but he was too heavy. I brought my knees up and tried to knee him in the back of the head, but he dodged my attempts.

Tap. Tap. Tap.

I felt the tears gathering in the corners of my eyes. I rolled my head from side to side, trying to avoid the merciless point of his knuckle, but he kept landing a sharp pain in the same spot.

"Mmmphcle!" I finally said, the words muffled by his hand. I was done resisting and ready to give up. Mrs. Peel was calling it a night. But Danny clamped his hand tighter over my mouth.

Tap. Tap. Tap.

"Mmmphcle!"

I let out a loud sob.

"That's it!"

My mom flung the rec room door open.

"I'm sick to death of warning you two! When I put you to bed, I expect you to go to sleep!"

Danny jumped off me and we raced to our respective bedrooms as my mom came barreling down the hallway. From under my covers I heard the smack of the wooden spoon and Danny's screams. I pushed back the covers, crept across the hallway and peered into Danny's room. My mom had yanked his pajamas down, and she was hitting him so hard with the wooden spoon that even I felt sorry for him. Each thwack of the spoon against his bare butt echoed like a shot through the basement.

THWACK! THWACK!

I counted five strikes when suddenly there was a sharp CRACK!

For a moment it was completely quiet. And then I saw the broken handle of the spoon in my mom's hand and the rest of it lying on the bed next to Danny's shaking body.

It took all the wind out of my mom's sails. I ran into my room and leaped onto my bed seconds before she swept past my door and headed back down the hall to her sewing room. I stayed under the covers and listened over the loud pounding of my heart. She might come back with the belt for a second round with Danny or even start on me. Or my dad might wake up and tell her to "calm down" because "the veins were sticking out of her neck" which would make things worse.

When I heard the sewing machine start up, I breathed a sigh of relief. That was a very good sign.

I gave it another minute before I got out of bed and tiptoed into Danny's room. He was still sniffling, but I could tell he was relieved it was over.

"Night, Danny."

"Night, Elisa."

SEWING (IN)SANITY

Never try to sew with a sink full of dirty dishes or beds unmade. When there are urgent housekeeping chores, do those first so your mind is free to enjoy your sewing. While you sew, make yourself as attractive as possible. Put on a clean dress. Keep a little bag full of French chalk near your sewing machine to dust your fingers at intervals. Have your hair in order, powder and lipstick put on. If you are constantly fearful that a visitor will drop in or your husband will come home and you will not look neatly put together, you will not enjoy your sewing.

> —1949 *Singer Sewing Book* by Mary Brooks Picken,
> in a section called "To Sew Successfully"

BEFORE I TELL YOU HOW my family fell apart, I want to take a moment to honor the art of sewing. I believe sewing was the reason my family and my mom's sanity remained intact for several years in the mid-1960s. The final page in my mom's scrapbook has a newspaper article with the headline "Homemakers Turn Talents to Sewing." Published six weeks after the Mrs. Minnesota contest, it discusses the lifestyles of several former contestants, one of whom is my mother. The article includes interesting tidbits such as the fact that my mom liked to entertain and often served a dish called "Armenian Rice." I don't remember my mom entertaining beyond a handful of card parties and Shabbat dinners, and I cannot provide any information about the ingredients of "Armenian Rice." It's not in the *Betty Crocker Cookbook*.

The Armenian Rice struck a chord with at least one newspaper reader, because underneath the article is a letter from a woman writing to ask my mom for the recipe. The letter writer signed her name Dorothy J. Hoopes, and underneath her signature, in parentheses and quotes, she wrote "(Mrs. Lawrence L. Hoopes)."

Could there be a more perfect example of how confused women in the 1960s were about their identities? Dorothy J. Hoopes wasn't sure she could legitimately sign her own letter without using her husband's name.

The newspaper article, which was accompanied by a large black-and-white photo (see frontispiece) with the caption "Mrs. Bernick with Danny, 5, and Elisa, 3. Flowers on clothes chest match curtains," discussed my mom's formidable sewing skills:

HOMEMAKERS TURN TALENTS TO SEWING

Not only does she make her own clothes, but almost all of the draperies and bedspreads in the house. For the pink bedroom of her daughter, Elisa, 3, Mrs. Bernick made rose cafe curtains trimmed with pink and white floral print. This same fabric is in the valances at the windows and the dust ruffle for the bed. Then she quilted some of the rose fabric for the bedspread. The finishing touch to the room is an old chest, which Mrs. Bernick painted pink and then trimmed with flowers she copied from the floral print. She also made the unbleached muslin draperies for the room of son, Danny, 5. They are edged with fringe and have a row of aqua rickrack stitched just inside the border.

—Mary Hart, *Minneapolis Morning Tribune*, Monday, April 27, 1964

My mom looks happy enough in the photo. She doesn't know she'll be pregnant with Lori in six months. Despite losing the Mrs. Minnesota contest and feeling a creeping sense of malaise, at age twenty-six she was perched on the pinnacle of domestic goddesshood, and sewing was helping her keep her balance.

In *The Second Sex*, which was published in English in 1953, Simone de Beauvoir wrote about women's oppression within marriage using the concepts transcendence and immanence. Transcendent activities produced something enduring and enabled individual self-expression. Unlike cleaning, cooking, and laundry (which de Beauvoir considered immanent activities), sewing was a challenging, creative process that engaged women's artistic souls. It had a tangible impact on their self-esteem, and, by extension, the well-being of their families. Sewing was so important to my mother that she frequently gave up sleep to work in her basement sewing room long after everyone else was in bed.

Along with being a creative outlet, sewing saved money. The language of thrift figures prominently in the narratives of women who sewed through the 1950s and 1960s. Fashion articles in the *Ladies' Home Journal* included "Penny Pinching Sewing Ideas for Summer" and "The Journal's Wonder Dress to Make for Under $10.00."

My parents fought constantly about money, and the economics of sewing resonated with both of them, given their financially challenged backgrounds.

When my father complained about the cost of fabric and sewing supplies, my mother reminded him that her efforts were helping the family's bottom line. This made it easier for her to sew obsessively without feeling guilty about neglecting her children, husband, or home.

Her downstairs sewing room was her sanctuary, and her trusty Singer was her confidante and confessor. She marked the passage of seasons in yards of fabric and holiday trim. Fall was a cornucopia of High Holiday dresses and Halloween costumes. Winter was a blur of quilted snowflake vests and Hanukkah outfits. Spring's arrival was heralded not by the first poke of crocus above the snow but by Passover dresses and matzoh covers.

My mom was reliably happy when she was sewing, and this was no small thing. Although I sometimes felt like a human mannequin in the service of her obsession, I never complained when she suggested a new plaid jumper or hideous orange palazzo pants. I stood next to the cutting table with my hands at my sides, feeling her press crinkly pattern pieces against my back, and felt grateful that she was in a good mood. Often, she would hum a little nonsense tune, something that always caught me by surprise.

"Stand still. We're almost done."

I would stand silent as a statue as my mom hummed softly beside me. Inside the warm circle of her arms I relaxed a little. I felt the press of her fingertips against my shoulders, the cool slide of the yellow tape down my arm, and the brush of her hand as she gauged the distance from shoulder to wrist. The closest I ever felt to love from my mother was when she was sewing.

That said, her creativity also put me in the running for "retard of the year" (as my brother Danny so delicately put it). I rarely liked the clothes she made, and her "special outfits" were the worst. Like the sailor suit she made me wear on the first day of third grade, with a giant red bow that kept blowing into my mouth and a too-big sailor hat that kept falling over my eyes. That same year she made me go as a hobo for Halloween. I had to carry a stick over my shoulder with a fabric bag attached to collect candy, and she made me wear a Vaseline "hobo beard" covered with coffee grounds that gave me a terrible rash.

All I wanted was a costume like everyone else. Every Halloween I pleaded for a princess mask from Walgreens, and every year my mom exercised her "transcendent creativity" through spider costumes and squirrel suits.

But I see now that sewing was more than a creative outlet for my mom; it was the reason she got out of bed. It was the bargain she struck with herself each day: If you get up and get the kids breakfast, you can sew. If you get them an after-school snack, make it through dinner and homework, and get them to bed, you can sew. Sewing was the daily payoff for keeping things from spinning out of control. When she sat down at her Singer, her shoulders settled into place and her breathing slowed down. She pressed her knee against the power bar, leaned into her work, and let the high-pitched hum of the Singer lighten the dim swirl of sadness inside her brain.

Why, you might ask, was my mom so sad?

The Jewish Talmud asks, "Who is happy? She who is happy with her lot."

Being happy with her lot would never have occurred to my mother. It would have felt like accepting defeat. My mother was a competitor, someone who liked to battle. She ran at the world with a sword honed by a thirst for recognition. Every skirmish was an opportunity to win and to prove to herself and everyone else that she was worthy of love and admiration. She wanted to gain admittance into the special in-group clubs, to be desirable enough to be invited to that damn Zealand Avenue Coffee Klatch. She wanted to be wanted.

I think some of it also came down to money and the deprivations of her childhood—perhaps generations of deprived childhoods. She wanted what the in-group had: vacations, new cars, and nights in hotel rooms. She had a sense that there was something beyond mere survival; she wanted to live. Instead she got Sam Bernick and grocery lists taped to cabinet doors. She believed in the American Dream and the proverbial ladder of success. Perhaps she really did believe that money equaled happiness.

I don't know what darkness drove her, and I suspect she didn't either. There was obviously some emptiness inside her, a deep unmet need. Winning sewing and baking competitions didn't change anything, especially during the 1960s when women were starting to push for more in a world hell-bent on offering them less. It must have been exhausting to continually prove your mettle, yet never feel you've won the prize.

Being happy with her lot was untenable for my mother, and it was sewing that reliably soothed the aching, soul-sucking misery of her thwarted attempts to be, do, and have *more*.

Did the other women along Zealand Avenue feel thwarted in the same way? Some of them probably did. But for some reason, my mom reached her breaking point first. Maybe part of it was feeling like an outsider, which forced her to consider a different sort of life. Certainly, women outside of New Hope, particularly in larger cities and out on the coasts, had started envisioning different lives for themselves. I'm honestly not sure. But whatever it was, night after night, as she sat downstairs at her sewing machine trying to find meaning in the tedious life she was leading, it became clear to her there wasn't enough thread in the world to keep her life in New Hope from unraveling.

PART TWO

Departing from the Story Line

When I let go of what I am, I become what I might be.

—Lao Tzu

Life isn't about finding yourself. Life is about creating yourself.

—George Bernard Shaw

I was ready to abandon her story and tell my own.

—Elisa Bernick

—⁓—

ANOTHER JEWISH JOKE

A NEW FLOOD IS FORETOLD by the world's weather specialists. In three days, the waters will wipe out the world.

The Dalai Lama appears on television and pleads with everybody to turn to Buddhism so they will at least reach enlightenment.

The Pope goes on television and says the world must accept Christianity in order to attain salvation.

The Chief Rabbi of Israel says to the world's Jews: "We all have three days to learn how to live under water."

(RE)CONSTRUCTING THE NARRATIVE

Storytelling isn't just how we construct our identities; stories are our identities.

—John Holmes, PhD, Waterloo University

HUMANS ARE MASTER STORYTELLERS. OUR minds are designed for stories: to tell them and to be shaped by them. We are story factories spinning tales constantly, awake and asleep, casting ourselves as protagonists in the epic journey of our lives.

Psychologists believe that telling stories is the way we form our individual identities and create meaning for ourselves. We use past events and memories to unconsciously invent narratives of who we were, are, and could be.

"It is not so much our past events that shape us," says psychology professor Jonathan Adler, "but our construct[ion] and interpretation of those events and the narrative we create which, in turn, shapes who we will become."

As we shape our stories, they shape us. The telling of them becomes the truth of them. This process is like a dance with different versions of ourselves. The very nature of identity and meaning is a series of departures and arrivals from one version of ourselves to the next.

I often wonder why some people are able to "bounce back" after adversity and some are not, and I think it has to do with storytelling. The stories that travel within us, that create our memories and identities, are malleable. The way we choose to tell these stories can determine the version of ourselves we take forward into the future.

For Jews, the Bible commands us to be storytellers; to ritually remember (*zakhor*) our collective history and to pass these memories along to our children. Given recent epigenetic research that shows our genes are carriers of "molecular memories," it's likely that some of these memories are passed along through our DNA as well as through the stories, songs, and prayers we share during holidays and religious observances. Stories are the heart of collective memory.

At Passover each year we retell the story of how the Jews escaped from Pharaoh, and how this was only the first step in our liberation. We recite the words of the Jewish sages: "Not only was it necessary to take the Jews out of Egypt, it was also necessary to take Egypt out of the Jews." At my own seder table, we remind each other that we live in Egypts of our own creation. Our work is to understand the stories that enslave us today.

Jews have had centuries of opportunities to construct different storylines—many of them involving departures. Given our history of being on the run, you'd think there'd be a solid contingent of Jewish Olympians in the track and field events. But it's not speed or jumping hurdles that ensures our survival; it's the ability to adapt our stories to a new environment while retaining a separate story line. Being the "other" sets you outside the dominant culture's stories, a difficult and uncomfortable place to live. But it also means you're more likely to notice the existence of stories you're not part of and to practice authoring your own.

Growing up in New Hope, my stories existed alongside the dominant Christian stories of Jesus, Mary, Christmas, Easter—none of them mine. Each Christmas I donned my cloak of invisibility, stood on the wooden bleachers at Zachary Lane Elementary during winter choir concerts, and sang "Silent Night" and "Away in the Manger." As I silently mouthed the words "Christ the Savior" and "Little Lord Jesus" so as not to betray my faith, I was reminded that different story lines can exist simultaneously.

Stories are products of imagination, and imagination, says author and historian Yuval Noah Harari, is what separates us from other animals. Given the catastrophes that humans have survived—genocide, torture, concentration camps, abandonment, enslavement, famine, and disease—I take that to mean that we alone on Earth can invent stories of ourselves to ensure our survival—stories that are larger than the worst things that have happened to us.

In 1968, when I was eight, my mother invented a new story for herself and our family. The 1960s was one of the most turbulent and divisive decades in American history. For my mother and millions of other White suburban women, it was an opportunity to reinvent the narrative of their futures. In confluence with the civil rights movement, the Vietnam War, antiwar protests, and shifting expectations of marriage and motherhood, second wave feminism was a battle cry for independence and equality. Unfortunately, the casualty counts from the battle were enormous; families and children were blown to bits and never made whole again.

As scenes of carnage from the Vietnam War were broadcast to living rooms nationwide, the bloodless war at home—the one that eventually become known as "the Divorce Revolution"—was waged secretly behind bedroom doors and around dinner tables.

My mother's personal misery, along with her disappointment with suburban assimilation and marriage to my father, caused my family to implode in a dramatic, *traumatic* fashion. Timing-wise we were a little ahead of the national curve, far ahead of the midwestern curve, and many miles ahead of the Jewish curve in redefining "the nuclear family." The definition of *nuclear family* has its origins in the Latin *nux/nucleus*, meaning "core or kernel," but in my family's case, the atomic association of "nuclear" is a better descriptor.

We Bernicks were Jewish outsiders telling an insider's story about a mom, a dad, and four children living happily in 1960s suburban Minnesota. From my eight-year-old perspective, I thought we were mostly succeeding. But my mom's bid for reinvention changed everything. Our family's story became her departure story—until ultimately it became my own.

—⚉—

MARRIAGE GO-ROUND

IT'S EASY TO BLAME MY mom for blowing up our family (and for many years I did), but I now see that the reality is far more complicated. My dad was complicit, of course. And the institution of marriage underwent a sea change during the 1960s and 1970s. The traditional marriage arrangement based on obligation and sacrifice shifted to a "self-expressive" or "soul mate" model of marriage—one based on romance, self-fulfillment, and supporting your spouse's dreams.

Obligation and sacrifice were things my parents understood, but *romance*? Providing support for *someone else's dreams*? Those ideas were from a language my parents didn't speak. Their 1957 marriage was a union of two souls stunted by shame and selfishness. They escaped the poverty and abuse of their own families without a clue about how to navigate their relationship. With little emotional intelligence and even less experience with love, sex, or intimacy, was the outcome ever in doubt?

My mother, in particular, felt unmoored with little sense of purpose beyond her involvement with the Beth El Sisterhood; working two days a week as a dental hygienist, a job she didn't like; and tending to her home and children. She was a career woman without the option of a fulfilling career.

The women's movement during the 1960s was still too nascent to make empowerment deliveries to midwestern middle-class suburban White women. There were no consciousness-raising groups on the 3900 block of Zealand Avenue, no hunkering down around a mirror to examine vulvas in Glenda Thompson's living room.

My mom was educated enough to understand her potential worth, but she wasn't provided with the tools or a pathway to realize her potential. Nor did she have worth in a real sense. In the 1960s, a woman needed to bring a man along to cosign any credit application or to open a bank account. Women weren't allowed to have credit cards in their own names until 1974. It's stunning to think how recently women achieved financial autonomy.

Birth control pills became legal in the United States in 1960, but they weren't widely available in middle America. My mom used a diaphragm unsuccessfully and was pregnant with Danny within three months of my dad's and her marriage. Two years later she had me. She continued to use the diaphragm and continued to have more children—Lori in 1965 and David in 1968. My mother was an intelligent person motivated *not* to have children. The fact that she didn't have more effective birth control tells me there weren't other options.

I can imagine her frustration and how alone she must have felt. My dad would have been no help; he was freed from the tedious tasks of her gender-prescribed life. Any expectation of men "pitching in" on the home front was years in the future. Ladies' magazines and popular television shows were still largely preaching the White Christian 1950s gospel that housewives were living the ideal, middle-class suburban American Dream. The June Cleavers and Harriet Nelsons were all so happy—how could my mom feel differently? Why did the New Hope suburban dream feel like a nightmare she couldn't wake up from? Nothing on television reflected the roller coaster of emotions she was feeling. There was little about religious discrimination, and certainly nothing about women feeling ambivalent about raising children.

Not that everything on the airwaves was idyllic. Six o'clock newscasts brought the violent realities of real-world events directly into people's living rooms for the first time in history. It started with John F. Kennedy's assassination and continued with horrific images from Vietnam during the nation's first televised war. I was too young to remember JFK, but by the time I turned eight, the running tally of Vietnam War fatalities and my parents' bedroom battles were the reliable background music to dinner each night.

I don't remember when my parents' nightly fight moved from the rec room up to their bedroom. Or when they started fighting *during* dinner instead of afterward. It was probably around the time my dad joined an earlier bowling league and my mom started "going out."

Their fights were usually about money.

"Because, Sam, the Pontiac's falling apart, you goddamn cheapskate. It's ten years old!"

"You don't have to yell, Arlene. I'm standing right next to you."

"Well, no matter how many times I say it, you don't seem to hear me. And that's why I have to scream. MAYBE YOU'LL HEAR ME THEN!"

"Jesus H. Christ, Arlene, calm down. The veins are sticking out of your neck. You're completely out of control."

"Goddamn it, Sam, don't tell me to calm down! And no, I'm not out of control. You want to see me out of control?"

We heard a loud crash, as something heavy shattered against the bedroom wall, and then nothing but a deafening silence. In the dining room, Lori, Danny, and I stopped chewing and swallowing. Yelling was normal. Silence was not. The only sound was three-month-old David's babbling in the playpen, and the TV news anchor reading war headlines on the living room television.

"The most recent count of American soldiers dead or missing in Vietnam stands at 20,364."

A few seconds later, the reassuring thrust and parry of my parents' acid-tongued argument resumed, and we took another bite of meatloaf.

We could turn down the sound on the TV news, but my mom's volume control knob was stuck on LOUD. It's like there was a roaring waterfall inside her head, and she had to RAISE HER VOICE to be heard over the gray rush of water. I don't think she knew what she wanted to do differently, but it was obvious she didn't want to be a mother to four children and married to a man who was content with a ten-year-old car and a membership to the New Hope pool.

In her later years, when asked to recall the end of her marriage to my father, she professed to have forgotten everything that happened and would only say, "I did the best I could."

Arlene had come to the end of a story line that was clearly meant for someone else—someone dull, with little ambition. The time had come for her to reinvent herself and spin a different sort of tale.

—❦—

DISCLAIMER

I HEREBY PROCLAIM THAT SOME of the events described in the next chapter are subject to plumping.

You have been warned.

It is absolutely true that when I was eight, my mother decided to "go out" and leave me alone to babysit my four-year-old sister and baby brother with a thunderstorm rumbling in the distance. These facts are forever seared in my memory.

But I can't know her exact thoughts during these events, and I can't be totally sure about her route, destination, or timing. I am, however, one hundred percent certain about one thing, and this is very important: You are about to meet someone who entered my family's story at this time and rewrote its narrative dramatically.

ARLENE GOES AWOL—1968

(She doesn't remember, and she was doing the best she could.)

"I'm the original wandering Jew."

—Arlene Bernick

ARLENE SAT IN FRONT OF the bedroom mirror wearing only a bra and panties. Behind her on the bed, Lori and Elisa were playing the tickle game. They were shrieking, and Arlene felt like slapping them both so they'd shut up.

"Elisa, take your sister out of here! I need five minutes of peace and quiet!"

"But Mom . . ."

"Just do it! Don't argue with me!"

She watched Elisa half-drag half-carry Lori off the bed and into the hall.

"And check on David!"

She walked over and locked the door behind them.

She sat back down and stared at herself in the mirror. Middle of the afternoon already and she'd only now taken a shower. God, she looked like hell. Black circles under her eyes, hair a mess. She uncapped a stick of cover-up cream and patted some beneath each eye.

She needed to get the hell out of the house, or she was truly going to lose her mind.

She looked out the window where brooding clouds hunched low to the ground in the damp November chill. Her eyes glazed over as she envisioned the bleak winter days ahead. Months of frozen gray sky hanging above the endless prairie. Fierce snowstorms that left behind a bitter cold and a blinding whiteness that consumed everything—all movement, smells, sounds, colors . . .

"Goddamn it!"

She exhaled slowly, her breath wobbly, and drew on some eyeliner. Her hand was trembling. She had to get away from the kids for an hour. But where could she go? And how? There was no way to get a sitter on such short notice. And she couldn't ask her mother again. She'd never hear the end of it.

Arlene glowered at herself beneath the orange bangs that fell into her eyes. When was the last time she'd had her hair done? Look at this mop! Grabbing a brush, she yanked the hair back from her face with sharp, fast strokes. She pulled it tight with a twist and wrapped an elastic band around the hank to keep it in place. Then, she lifted a coppery half-fall from its Styrofoam base and jammed it down on top of her head while stuffing the ends of her hair up underneath it. Luckily, she could hide the whole mess under her fall.

She could have killed Danny the other day! Twenty-five bucks this thing cost, and there's Danny grunting and trying to bite Elisa with it! A cruel streak in that boy a mile wide.

Where the hell did he ever learn to be so mean? Mouthing off to her every chance he got. And Sam, the *putz*, does nothing. Tells him to go to his room. Sam, the medical miracle. The man without a backbone. A real man would teach his son some respect.

A spatter of leaves ricocheted against the window, and Arlene was suddenly struck by an idea that made the tiny hairs on the back of her neck tingle.

Maybe she should go by the tire place and see if Bernie was working today. He was always fun to talk to.

"Hmmmmmm."

Arlene grinned at herself in the mirror. Whenever she saw Bernie at the Beth El he always said to drop by the store anytime.

She heard a soft knock on the door.

"Mom?"

Elisa's voice was muffled.

"What? And talk louder so I can hear you."

"Can I watch TV?"

"Where's Lori?"

"Downstairs."

"Where's David?"

"In his playpen sleeping."

Arlene got up and opened the door.

"Yes, you can watch TV. I'm going to run out and do a quick errand."

She looked directly at Elisa.

"Do you think you can watch Lori and David for an hour?"

"Where are you going?"

"I'm going to do a little shopping. Your dad and Danny should be back from the game soon, but I'll be back before they get home."

Elisa sat on the bed as Arlene got dressed in a pink cowl-neck sweater, a matching skirt, dark-colored pantyhose, and pink high heels.

"Why are you getting so dressed up?"

"I'm not getting dressed up. I'm just tired of wearing *schmattas* all the time."

"Can we come?"

"No, you cannot. I really need some time to myself right now. You guys are driving me nuts."

"But what if David starts crying? And what if there's a storm? Why can't Nancy babysit?"

Arlene worked hard to keep from raising her voice. She felt her hands curl into fists and resisted the urge to hit something.

"Elisa, please. If David cries, give him his bottle. I think a third-grader can watch her little sister and brother for an hour, don't you?"

"But what if—"

"Elisa, the sooner I go, the sooner I'll be back. If there's a problem, call Grandma Goldie. You know her number. Really, you're going to be perfectly fine, and I'll be back before you know it. Now go watch TV with Lori. Go!"

Fifteen minutes later, Arlene pulled into the Silverman Tire Center parking lot and scanned it for Bernie's dark red Chrysler Le Baron. Bernie Silverman. What a great guy. He put new tires on the Pontiac a few months back and gave her a nice break on the price without her even asking.

"Come back in a few months, Red, and I'll rotate them at no extra charge," he told her with a wink.

Now Bernie, Arlene thought appreciatively, was a real go-getter. The opposite of Sam. Bernie owned his own business. He was his own man. While Sam sat around the highway department counting how many years before he could retire. Not an ounce of ambition in his body. Oy.

And Bernie had money. You could tell by the way he dressed. Not that he didn't work hard for it. Whenever she saw him at services, he was always working the angles, making the rounds, telling jokes, and slapping people on the back. She noticed the silliest things about him. How he had this nice way of chewing gum. Just a little piece of white gum that he rolled around in his mouth, snapping it softly every now and again. It wasn't at all obnoxious, and it gave his breath a nice, minty freshness.

He wore a minty aftershave too. Was it Aqua Velva? Sam smelled like soap. Cheap soap. And Bernie had a great sense of humor. He could tell a joke better than anybody, and he had a thousand of them. Sam knew two jokes. The same two rabbi jokes he'd been telling his whole goddamn life.

She shook her head. Sam was such a *putz* compared to Bernie! And Bernie's wife Sheila, now there was a little mouse. Never said a word. How they hooked up, the two of them, Arlene had no idea. People probably said the same thing about her and Sam. She checked her hair in the rearview mirror and scanned the lot again. His car wasn't here but it might be parked out back.

The last time she'd stopped by had been a month ago.

"Funny, I was just thinking about you, Red."

His deep baritone voice startled her when he came up behind her and gave her arm a squeeze with his big, warm hand.

"I was thinking it was about time for your free rotation."

He gave her a wink, and Arlene laughed. He kept his hand on her arm.

"Have ya heard this one yet? So, Rachel puts an ad in the *Jewish World* that says she's looking for a husband who won't beat her, won't run away from her, and who's good in bed. Two weeks later the doorbell rings and a guy with no arms or legs is at her house.

'I'm here about your ad,' he says. 'I don't have arms so I can't beat you. And I don't have legs so I can't run away.'

'OK,' Rachel says, 'but how do I know you're good in bed?'

The guy looks at her and says, 'How do you think I rang the doorbell?'"

Bernie gave Arlene another wink, and she started laughing. He laughed along with her, his deep baritone chuckle booming across the store.

"Actually, Arlene," he squeezed her arm slightly, "I could use a little advice from someone with your sense of interior design."

He swept an arm across the display floor.

"I'd like to make some changes to the shelving and some of these tire displays. If you're not in a hurry, would you mind if I ran a few ideas past you?"

Arlene had been flattered. He'd taken her by the hand and walked her around the store as she listened to his ideas and made some suggestions. She felt like she'd given him ideas he hadn't thought of before. She could just say she was here today to check on those displays and see how they were coming along.

Arlene parked close to the back of the lot next to a few other cars and shut off the ignition.

"Oh, damn."

A smattering of raindrops hit the windshield like an opening round of soggy bullets fired from one of the dark cloud formations above. Why hadn't she brought an umbrella? She was going to get soaked.

Should she park closer to the front door? No. Someone might see her car and start asking questions. She could just make a run for it now and get drenched on the way back out. Yes. She was here and she might as well go in. What could it hurt? She'd talked to Sheila at services a couple weeks ago about sewing Hanukkah outfits for the kids. Sheila even offered to pay her!

Since Bernie and Sheila weren't at services last night, she could just say she was driving by and thought she'd check to see if Bernie knew whether Sheila wanted her to go ahead with the outfits. They could walk around the store for a couple of minutes, he'd show her the displays, she'd ask about the outfits, and then she'd head home. Even Sam couldn't complain if she brought home some extra money sewing for Sheila.

Arlene took a deep breath, grabbed her purse, and opened the door, feeling a few raindrops pelting hard against her shoulder.

"Dammit."

She stepped out, locked and slammed the car door, and started running toward the front door.

"Whoa!"

She caught herself just in time as she skidded sideways on the wet blacktop, almost falling over in her high heels. It was slippery out here. Wouldn't that be great, Arlene thought, as she pushed through the front door. If I fell and broke my neck in Bernie Silverman's parking lot. That would set a lot of tongues wagging.

She checked her hair and patted the fall back into place as a salesman headed her way.

"Hi there, what can I do for you today? Looking for tires? We're running an early-bird special on snow tires right now. Michelins . . . the best."

"Oh, no, actually, I'm just looking for Bernie. He's a . . . I'm a . . . friend of his. Is he in today?"

"'Fraid not. He won't be back until Monday. Been gone for a week on a little family getaway with the wife and kids. Can I tell him you stopped by?"

"Oh. Uh . . . no. That's OK. I'll just come back some other time."

She glanced around the room at the tire displays. They looked the same as they had a month ago. She nodded at the salesman who returned the nod and raised an eyebrow.

"Well. Thank you."

Arlene pushed the door open and stepped out into the rain. It was coming down harder now, and she saw a flash of lightning in the distance. She ran gingerly across the parking lot, picking her way through the puddles already pooling on the shiny blacktop as a rumble of thunder boomed overhead. It was freezing. She was nearly to her car when her feet went out from under her, and she fell down hard on her left side.

"Ouch!"

She pushed herself up quickly and saw the hole in her pantyhose where she'd hit the pavement. There was an oily smear on her pink skirt that nothing would get out.

"Dammit!"

She walked the rest of the way to her car and glanced back at the tire shop where the salesman was watching her from the window. She ignored him as she opened her purse to get her keys out. They weren't in the little side pocket where she usually put them. She searched the main compartment, feeling the rain pelting her head as a drip slid down her fall and onto her nose. She wiped her nose with the back of her hand and bit her lip.

Where were her goddamn keys? Another flash of lightning. She pulled at her car door, knowing it was locked. She always locked it. A clap of thunder boomed almost directly overhead as she spotted her keys in the ignition where she'd left them. Dammit! She was drenched now. Her cashmere sweater was clinging to her wet skin, and she felt the dead, soggy weight of her fall tilting sideways on top of her head. She almost couldn't tell if it was rain or tears as she stood next to her locked car in the nearly empty parking lot knowing that in another minute she'd have to go back into the tire store and ask for help.

Arlene felt nothing in that cold, rainy moment except rage . . . rage toward everything in her life . . . rage at every goddamn reason she was freezing her ass off in this shitty suburban parking lot . . . her whiny children, her nothing husband, her ugly house, her boring life, and that goddamn Bernie Silverman away on vacation with his goddamn wife and goddamn children.

DISAPPEARING ACT

I took a hard, honest look at my ambivalence about motherhood, at my fears of not being good enough, and the loss of my identity as anything but a mother. My life was changing; my marriage was crumbling; I felt like I was being swallowed up.

—Rahna Reiko Rizzuto, *Hiroshima in the Morning*

THE NIGHT MY MOM LEFT me home alone with my younger brother and sister during a terrifying thunderstorm was a turning point for our family. Not long after she left, the power went out. By the time my dad and Dan got home from their rain-delayed football game, I was huddled in the playpen with Lori and David, all three of us sobbing in the dark.

In the tumult of those stormy hours, some essential familial glue came unstuck in my mother, and the disintegrating binding of our family narrative was revealed. At eight years old, cowering next to my siblings as lightning blazed and thunder rattled the dishes, I didn't yet understand that my mother had left us behind.

She didn't come home that night or the next. She didn't call, and even my dad didn't know where she was. I remember it all clearly because it was frightening and awful.

And then her disappearing act became a regular thing.

When you're a kid, everything your parents do seems normal, even the weird stuff. So, when my mom started disappearing every few weeks for a couple nights at a time, my siblings and I adapted pretty quickly. We got used to waking up and finding someone else in the kitchen making breakfast. It was usually Grandma Goldie, wearing a faded blue bathrobe and a scowl.

When we asked her where our mom was, her answer was always the same. "She's taking a break."

It wasn't until years later that I realized "break" was short for "breakdown." As in "nervous breakdown." Nobody discussed depression in the 1950s and 1960s. Women's "ailments" were dismissed or attributed to "nerves," "stress," or a "nervous breakdown."

I'm not sure if my mom was clinically depressed, but there's no doubt she was deeply unhappy. Nobody talked about how much she screamed, or how strange it was that she came and went so often. She would disappear for a day or two and then show up again without a word, as if she'd never been gone. Eventually we stopped asking where she was.

She was usually at Grandma Goldie's, because where else could a penniless midwestern mother of four find refuge in 1968? Even though my mom and Grandma Goldie battled, I suspect my grandmother felt some empathy for her, given that an unhappy marriage and feeling overwhelmed by raising children were finally things they had in common.

My dad wasn't around much either. He was working, bowling, coaching, or attending New Hope Athletic Association meetings. During my mom's absences, he acted like it was normal for his mother-in-law to be sleeping in the baby's bedroom and fixing meals for everyone. We children accepted this new normal as part of the Bernick family story. It was just one more way our family was different from other families.

It's possible that abandoning us every few weeks was my mom's idea of damage control. I think she sensed her ability to inflict irreparable harm, and she took steps to protect us. She had my dad install hooks on the outside of our bedroom doors so that when she got to her breaking point, she could lock us in our rooms so she didn't kill us. Being locked in our rooms was treated as a punishment, but I remember feeling a sense of relief when there was a physical barrier between us. I think she felt it too. The lock was symbolic, obviously. She could open it and smack us around whenever she wanted, but it was a visual and mental barrier. Locked in our rooms we were "safe" from her, and we couldn't get in too much trouble.

Often, she locked Lori and David in with me or Dan so we could watch them, while she barricaded herself in her sewing room. Dan and I immediately figured out how to slide a piece of cardboard up the door crack to unhook the lock if we needed to go to the bathroom or creep upstairs to get David's bottle.

Locks were an important source of protection in other ways, too. During Christmas and Easter breaks from school, and all summer long, my mom served us breakfast and then locked us out of the house. It didn't matter if it was 10 degrees below or in the sweltering 90s, we were only allowed back in for lunch and then locked out again until dinner.

Our aimless wandering was interspersed with my mom's determined efforts to "keep us out of her hair" by signing us up for summer school, camps, and memberships to the New Hope pool—all blessings of suburban White privilege. My mom pounced on any excuse to get rid of us. We used the neighbors' bathrooms more than our own. No matter how loud we complained or how many tears we shed, if there wasn't blood, my mom wouldn't let us in the house.

This meant years of serious sunburns and frostbitten toes, but her efforts may have protected us from far worse. She simply didn't have the resources to help her navigate her own unrestrained violence. I don't want to trivialize the consequences of abandonment and family violence, but it's possible my mom's serial abandonment really *was* the best she could do.

Epigenetic researchers are studying whether the propensity for abandoning your offspring can be passed along in someone's DNA. Author Melissa Cistaro raised this question in her 2015 memoir *Pieces of My Mother* after her own mother "took a break" from the responsibilities of motherhood and left Cistaro and her siblings behind.

In an interview in the *Michigan Quarterly Review*, Cistaro wondered if she, too, might have inherited the "leaving gene" that afflicted her mother and other female ancestors.

> Geneticists, after all, are studying to see whether there are genes for empathy. I kept asking myself how people are really wired, what traits from our ancestors we carry. This motif is about all the little things we don't know or aren't told, or that are kept from us, but that we carry with us—the pieces of us that feel not right, or that are confusing. I'm very much fascinated with the trauma or grief that's conceivably locked into our bodies.

Both abandonment and a lack of empathy are inherited traits that have been correlated to specific genes. In my mom's case, leaving could have been passed down through her father who continually abandoned his various (secret) wives and children. You could say that Jews, in general, have a knack for leaving—albeit mostly involuntarily.

I did not inherit the "leaving your kids" gene. Nor did my siblings. My mother was on her own here, and perhaps being left alone is what she was really after. If you look at her family of origin, almost none of her other relatives, besides her own mother and one other uncle, got married or had children. Remember the dinnertime bickering among Uncle Leo, Grandma Goldie, and Aunt Freda? This was not a group of people with the desire or ability to nurture others or forge healthy emotional connections.

Was leaving us selfish? Survival? Bravery? Protection? Abandonment pure and simple?

Whatever it was, leaving your kids and striking out on your own is never an easy undertaking, and it was especially tough back in 1968 when women had so few options. My mom had no bank account of her own, no credit card, no savings, and her only income was from working two half-days a week at Dr. Greenberg's and doing a little sewing for people at the Beth El.

What avenues of escape were open to her?

Would you be surprised if I told you there's research showing that infidelity can be passed along in people's genes? Perhaps she was biologically programmed with her milkman father's propensity for delivering cream with a side of sugar. Or maybe she thought she'd found love.

Whatever the reason, my mom's new departure story soon became loud and clear to everyone.

TURN UP THE VOLUME—1968

"MOM? ANYBODY HERE?"

On the Wednesday Mrs. Schoonover canceled Girl Scouts because Lisa Schoonover threw up on the bus, I came home to a strange car in the driveway. Normally, my mom worked at Dr. Greenberg's on Wednesday afternoons, Dan and I had Scouts, and Lori and David were at the sitter's.

I figured my mom was probably down in her sewing room with one of her "clients" from the Beth El, which would explain the unfamiliar car. I dropped my books on the landing and headed up the stairs to the kitchen. There was a note on the counter.

> *Elisa,*
> *There's a casserole in the oven. Turn the oven to 350 degrees to heat it up for a half-hour. Open a can of peaches and put out carrot sticks or open a can of peas for the vegetable. Make sure Lori and David drink some milk.*
> *Mom*

I always made dinner on her workdays, so the note wasn't a surprise. But it didn't say *when* I should turn on the oven. Now or in a little while? Was my dad coming home for dinner, or was he going straight to bowling? I wondered if I should go down and ask her.

I walked to the kitchen doorway and stood there for a moment deciding. She didn't like to be interrupted when she was with clients.

Then I heard her say something from the bedroom.

Huh?

What was my mom doing in the bedroom when clients were downstairs?

I heard her say something else from the bedroom.

"Mom?" I yelled out.

No answer.

I walked down the hallway, and halfway there I heard music playing through the closed bedroom door. That was weird. I'd never heard music playing in my parent's bedroom before. I heard my mom laugh, and right before I called out, I heard another laugh. An unfamiliar deep, booming laugh. My heartbeat thundered in my ears as I ran back down the hall, straight downstairs into the rec room and slammed the door. I turned on the TV and twisted the volume knob up as loud as it would go to drown out the hammering of my own heart.

MISSING THE STRIKE ZONE

Sam's bowling game goes to hell.
(This story comes from my dad with
some judicious plumping here and there.)

SAM ELBOWED OPEN THE DOOR to the New Hope Bowl. The low rumble of balls on varnished wood and the *crack* of bowling pins made him smile. He inhaled deeply as he strolled through the pleasant haze of salted popcorn, stale beer, floor wax, and cigarette smoke.

"Hiya, Flo!" he called to the bony permed blonde behind the snack bar.

"Hiya, Sam!" She raised her cigarette in greeting.

He caught a glimpse of himself in the mirror along the back wall. He was wearing his new bowling shirt: a short-sleeve crimson red polyester with black buttons that had "New Hope Bowl" written on the back in cursive white thread. He hadn't been sure about the red at first, but now he decided it didn't look half bad. The red set off his dark hair and eyes. He thought he looked a little like Tony Curtis in *The Defiant Ones*. Ready for action.

He stepped down into the pit area of lane seven where his crimson-shirted teammates were warming up. He set his bag on the curving blue plastic bench and started changing into his bowling shoes.

He'd just taken a pair of silver nail clippers out of his bowling bag and was trimming his nails when Norm Applebaum walked over and stood next to him for a minute. Norm stood there, hands in his pockets, jiggling his keys, before he finally said something Sam couldn't quite catch over the rumble of bowling balls and the crash of pins.

"Say again, Norm?"

"I said Lila isn't too hot for the new Sisterhood president. Says she's too pushy. How about Arlene?"

Sam shrugged.

"No idea. She hasn't said anything about it."

Norm stood there jiggling his keys.

"So, uh, Sam. Speaking of Arlene. How's she doing?"

"Fine. Keeping busy at the synagogue, sewing. Nothing new."

Norm stopped jiggling his keys and stared at the lanes. After a moment he looked at Sam.

"So, uh, I was kind of surprised to see Arlene up in Monticello last night."

Sam threw him a look.

"Whaddya talking about?"

Norm looked around and then sat down next to Sam.

"She probably didn't see me, but I saw her."

Sam kept clipping his nails. What the hell was the schmuck talking about? Arlene had a Sisterhood meeting last night. She had 'em a couple times a week.

"Ya lost me, Norm. Arlene wasn't up in Monticello last night. She was at the synagogue. What the hell would she have been doing up in Monticello?"

"That's what I was wondering."

Sam stopped clipping and stared at the man sitting next to him. Norm looked out at the lanes, barely moving his mouth.

"It was dinnertime, maybe a little later, so I stopped at Rosie's on 94 to get a nice steak before heading back to the cities. That's my regular route. 94 up to St. Cloud, St. John's, then way the hell up to Bartlett . . ."

"Yeah, so you were at Rosie's . . ."

"Like I said, I'm sitting there in Rosie's waiting for my steak, minding my own business, when who walks in the door . . . Arlene . . . with a guy."

"Are you sure it was Arlene?"

"I made sure. Like I said, I was really surprised to see her there. You know, what the hell? But with that red hair . . . anyway . . . I saw her, and I started looking around for *you* but it was just *her* and . . . a guy."

"Who the hell was she with?"

Norm stood up and looked around nervously.

"Listen, Sam. I don't wanna cause problems for you and Arlene."

"Norm, tell me who the hell it was."

Norm sighed and looked down at his shoes. His hand was back in his pocket working those keys.

"Bernie Silverman. And it looked like he and Arlene were more than just buddies, if you know what I mean."

Sam stared at Norm speechless. He shook his head and couldn't for the life of him figure out what to say.

"Sorry, Sam. Maybe there's a good reason she was up there. You know . . . some . . . reason."

Sam sat frozen on the bench. He didn't move when Norm walked over to the scoring table and sat down. He didn't move when Norm looked back at him. He just sat motionless on the bench, staring straight ahead, feeling the sharp pinch of the silver nail clippers in his palm as he squeezed them with all the strength in his body.

—ɯ—

EXILED TO THE WAR ZONE—1969

MANY OF US HAVE AN indelible memory of the moment we learned about our parents' divorce. I've already pointed out the oxymoronic nature of *indelible* and *memory*, but no matter how many times I revisit this particular memory, the indelible piece that remains is its sterility. My parents expressed so little emotion around this event, they seemed like robots. Their detachment made my own dramatic emotions and reactions seem suspect and unacceptable.

The worst part was how truly alone I felt when my parents made the decision to split up. Our family story became a different sort of outsider story. It was no longer "We're Jewish and nobody else is." It was "Our family is no longer a family, and everybody else's is." Divorce was so new back then that my brother and I didn't know a single other divorced family. We were the first.

Given the Vietnam War coverage at the time, the idea of divorce felt so dangerous and foreign to me that it conjured up six o'clock news images of jungles going up in flames and entire villages exploding in horrible fireballs. When my parents announced their divorce, it was like a bomb had been dropped on my family, and I was suddenly exiled from my real life and left to wander through a Zealand Avenue war zone with snipers hiding in the pine trees and land mines buried in the backyard.

It happened after dinner on a Sunday in early August 1969. Dan and I were in the living room reading the Sunday comics. I was almost nine and Dan was a few weeks shy of eleven. Lori, who turned four in June, was sucking her thumb on the couch and David, who was almost one, was napping in his playpen.

"Elisa and Dan, come in here, please," my mom called down the hall from my parent's bedroom.

The word *please* should have been the tip-off.

"Right now, please," my mom called again. "Both of you."

I followed Dan down the hall to our parents' bedroom.

The moment we walked through the door and I saw my parents sitting side by side on the blue bedspread, I knew something terrible was going to happen. I'd never seen them sit that close together before. I couldn't read the expression on my mom's face, and my dad was staring down at his lap. He was clasping and unclasping his hands over and over again. My heart started beating fast.

"Your dad and I have decided to get a divorce," my mom said matter-of-factly.

My mouth fell open, and I felt a prickly sensation behind my ears. I glanced over and at Dan, but he was staring at the floor.

"Your dad is not going to live here anymore," my mom continued. "But he's going to live close by, and you'll get to spend weekends with him. Lori is too young to understand what's going on, but we'll explain it to her the best we can."

My mom put her hands in her lap and stared at us.

"Do you have any questions?"

Questions? About divorce? The only thing I knew about divorce was that it was the worst thing that could happen to anybody. There must have been other divorced families in New Hope, but I didn't know any of them. There were none in our school, or in our neighborhood, or at the Beth El. We didn't see divorced families on television, or in movies, or in books.

In 1969, there wasn't a whiff of divorce on *Bewitched*, *Hogan's Heroes*, *Gilligan's Island*, *Petticoat Junction*, or *Green Acres*. The super-hip *Mod Squad* trio didn't mention divorce, the pipe-smoking dad of *My Three Sons* was a widower, and even *Julia*, Diahann Carroll's groundbreaking African American nurse, was a Vietnam War widow. *That Girl*, *The Flying Nun*. You could be single, you could be a witch, a nun, you could even (barely) be Black, but you could *not* be divorced.

I had no context. No grounding. No story line.

I looked at my dad. He was staring down at his hands, squeezing them together so hard his fingers were red. I felt my head coming unhinged from my neck and a loud whooshing sound in my ears. My temples began to ache, and tears started filling up the space behind my eyes.

"Dad?" I said, and he looked up at me. "What's Mom talking about?"

He shifted on the bed, but said nothing, and I immediately burst into tears. Dan headed out the door and, after a moment, when neither of my parents moved from the bed, I followed him.

My parents announced their divorce without a speck of emotion. They didn't offer a hug or a kind word. I don't think they were being cruel. I think my dad was overwhelmed, and my mom was "doing the best she could."

Recently, Dan told me he'd known for almost a year that our parents had been talking about a divorce, but I was blindsided. Dan went straight down to his room and shut the door. I stood in the living room with no idea how to feel or think about any of this. It's like a kind of shell shock settled over the house.

I remember walking outside and leaning against our pale yellow 1959 Pontiac Catalina, still warm from the sun. Our house had just been blown to smithereens. Everything known and normal had turned into a cloud of black ash that was drifting away higher and higher, and it was oddly comforting to stand there with my face pressed against the driver's side window, crying in the driveway, tears burning rivers down my cheeks.

—𝔪—

THE GESTALT PRAYER

(Commonly found on posters in therapists'
offices, 1969-1975)

I do my thing and you do your thing.
I am not in this world to live up to your expectations,
And you are not in this world to live up to mine.
You are you, and I am I,
and if by chance we find each other, it's beautiful.
If not, it can't be helped.

—Frederick Perls, *Gestalt Therapy Verbatim*, 1969

—∭—

REVOLUTIONARIES

The true focus of revolutionary change is never merely the oppressive situations which we seek to escape, but that piece of the oppressor which is planted deep within each of us.

—Audre Lorde, *Sister Outsider: Essays and Speeches* (2007)

DIVORCE IS SUCH A COMMON occurrence now, it's hard to remember the powerful stigma it carried back in 1969 when my parents announced their split. In 1964, Nelson Rockefeller couldn't run for president because he was divorced. In 1970, the creators of *The Mary Tyler Moore Show* were forced to change the backstory of hometown heroine Mary Richards. She went from being recently split from her husband to being jilted by her boyfriend because network executives were afraid audiences wouldn't accept a divorcée.

Sherwood Schwartz, who created *The Brady Bunch*, which ran from 1969 to 1974, originally wanted Carol Brady to be a divorcée, but network executives objected on the grounds it was too radical. Instead, her marital status, whether she was divorced or widowed, was never directly revealed. In 1969, being dead was more acceptable than being divorced.

And yet, despite the damning social stigma, the women in my family pressed forward. Not only did my Grandma Goldie divorce Grandpa Phil long before it was "acceptable," my mom pushed the envelope as well. According to the National Jewish Population Study, 80 percent of adult American Jews were married in 1970. By then, my parents had already been separated for a year. And even though no-fault divorce wasn't legalized in Minnesota until 1974, my parents were officially divorced in 1972. I guess you could say that my mom and grandmother were part of the advance guard of the Divorce Revolution.

My parents lost their minds during their divorce, my mother in particular. She was actually at war with herself, but my father was an easier target. Dismantling her marriage probably felt like a step toward freedom and reinvention, but the reality was far different. Like most women who sue for divorce, she ended up worse off financially. The Minnesota court granted her full custody of four children and very little else. No alimony, limited child support, and the challenge of raising four children alone. The daily reality of the situation intensified the precariousness of her mental state.

Once my dad moved out, wringing more child support out of him became her singular obsession. She strategized her legal gambits like a battlefield general, and she completely lost sight of how it affected us grunts on the ground. Every tasteless tuna noodle casserole was an opportunity to sling insults about my father's cheap, thoughtless character. Each Saturday morning, she lobbed verbal bombs from the top step as he tried to hustle us out the door for our weekend visits. He was a "cheapskate" and "a sorry SOB who didn't care about his own kids." The volume on her emotional rheostat was always turned up to 11.

The louder my mom got, the quieter my dad became. Soon, he was barely present. In retrospect, I think he was experiencing some form of PTSD. He was so emotionally wounded that he became a passive observer of the detritus of his marriage—detritus that included us. She painted him as a villain who didn't love us, and his increasing disengagement seemed to confirm it.

Strangely, as our family embarked on a fraught future, we four kids found ourselves both the primary source of conflict and largely ignored. My parents were consumed by the long, dramatic dissolution of their union. There ensued more than a decade's worth of court battles over child support, custody, and visitation that included high-volume driveway fights, overwhelming evidence of mental illness on the part of my mother, and imaginatively cruel acts of vengeance. My mom had my father served court papers suing for more child support *inside* the synagogue sanctuary *during* my younger brother's Bar Mitzvah.

That's not *chutzpah*, that's nuts.

While all this was going on, we kids were largely left to fend for ourselves. Dan found ways to soothe and absent himself (hello marijuana!). And since David was only a year old and Lori was four, their care fell to me, a not-quite nine-year-old.

Outliers again, we Bernick children were the first residents of a "broken home" on Zealand Avenue. By the time the term "latchkey kids" was popularized in the mid-1970s, we'd been arriving home after school to an empty house for years already. Our family may have been in the vanguard of the Divorce Revolution, but my siblings and I were just freaked-out foot soldiers doing our best to keep our heads down in the foxholes while guarding our shameful secret.

NO RESCUE IN SIGHT—1969

I DIDN'T TELL ANYBODY ABOUT the divorce. The whole thing felt so shameful I wanted to hide it in the drawer next to my Star of David necklace. I wished my parents were *dying* instead of getting a divorce. If your mom or dad died it was horrible, but at least people felt sorry for you. Getting a divorce was like admitting your family wasn't good enough to be a family anymore. Your family was so *bad* it had to *stop*. Divorce was something you did to yourself on purpose, so you couldn't ask people to feel sorry for you.

In 1969, the only acceptable story line in New Hope was about a traditional nuclear family, and I did my best to keep telling it.

But it wasn't easy.

Once my dad moved out, he immediately turned into a stranger. In reality, we probably saw each other only slightly less than before, but without daily sightings of his blue and white bowling bag on the landing, and his yellow Pontiac in the driveway, he became someone with little connection to my daily life.

He would occasionally call to say "Hi" during the week, but I had no idea what to say to him. Dan saw him at games and practices during the week, but Lori and I only saw him on the weekends. Every Saturday morning, my mom would pack our toothbrushes and clothes into a grocery bag, and my dad would pick us up for an overnight. David would stay home with my mom. I assume the general consensus was that caring for a toddler was best left to my mom.

My dad's apartment was only a few miles from our house. Before he moved out, I had never been inside an apartment. I didn't even know New Hope *had* apartment buildings. On that first Saturday morning, when we got to the turnoff to his apartment building, I briefly thought everything was going to be OK. The sign for "Shady Oak Apartments" had a giant oak tree with a hammock underneath it. I imagined us fighting over the hammock and having a picnic with my dad under the tree.

But when we pulled into the parking lot there wasn't an oak, a hammock, trees, or shade of any kind; just brown-tipped grass along a sidewalk that led from the parking lot to the front door of an ugly three-story brick apartment building.

The lobby and the hallway smelled like baked beans.

"Like I told you on the phone, it's nothing special," my dad said, closing the door behind us. "But it's OK for now."

His unfurnished one-bedroom apartment had a tiny, windowless kitchen and a dingy green shag-carpeted room that served as both a dining room and a living room. He'd bought a scratchy tweed couch to go with the carpet, and a small black-and-white TV that sat on top of a folding table. Next to the kitchen there was a brown Formica dining room table surrounded by four brown folding chairs. Lori headed for the couch, and Dan disappeared down a narrow hallway to the left.

"Like I said, it's nothing special," my dad said from the doorway, "but it'll do for now. I'm going to put this in the bedroom."

He carried our bag of clothes down the hallway.

Nothing special is right, I thought, following behind him.

I stopped and opened the hallway closet door. It was empty except for a set of barbells and a pile of weights lying on the floor. Were the barbells my dad's, or had they come with the apartment? I couldn't imagine my dad *buying* barbells, much less *lifting* them.

I closed the closet door, walked another couple of steps, and flipped on the bathroom light. No tub, just a shower with a grungy dimpled plastic sliding door. I flipped off the light and followed the green shag into the bedroom. Dan was lying on the bed reading a *MAD* magazine. The only other furniture was a wooden dresser with my dad's bowling trophies on top and a clothes hamper. I saw our bag of clothes sitting against one wall.

"Where do we sleep?" I asked.

"Well, that's your call."

He pointed to the bedroom closet.

"I've got three sleeping bags, and you can either sleep in here with me or out in the living room. It's going to be like camping until I figure out how permanent this whole thing is."

I felt a flicker of hope in my chest. Was he talking about being split up from my mom, or staying in this apartment? I didn't ask because I was afraid he only meant the apartment.

"Dan, get your shoes off the bed. You guys can watch TV for a while, and then we'll have lunch and head out."

"Where are we going?" Dan asked from behind Alfred E. Neuman's gap-toothed grin.

"I thought we could go over to Northwood Park. Toss a ball around, play on the swings, just fool around until practice, and then tomorrow, we'll go visit Grandpa Izzy and Grandma Rose."

That's the way it went for a couple of months. I crossed my fingers that nobody saw us getting into my dad's car on Saturday mornings or getting out on Sunday afternoons. I just hoped my parents would get back together before anyone found out. No matter how horribly they treated us and each other, I needed to keep telling the familiar story of our family because there was no other story to tell. I clung to the fact that my parents were separated and not divorced. This was a crucial distinction. Separation was temporary and divorce was final. I never discussed this with my parents, because I was convinced it would remind them that they'd *forgotten* to get a divorce. If I didn't say anything, maybe they'd get back together.

On the Saturday before my ninth birthday, we walked into my dad's apartment and there was a new brown La-Z-Boy rocker and a giant color TV inside a wood cabinet in the living room. It was clear he wasn't moving home anytime soon. I dropped the grocery bag of clothes in the hallway and went into the kitchen.

The only good things about my dad's apartment were the cheap cookies and diet pop he bought, neither of which my mom allowed at home. Every Saturday I'd go into the kitchen, pour myself a glass of Tab, and stand at the counter eating terrible cookies. I ate chocolate chip cookies with soapy-tasting "chips" and fake Oreos with stale chocolate outsides and vanilla frosting insides that tasted like Crisco. I dunked them into my glass of Tab and stared at the loose crumbs that floated on top of the bubbles, without a thought in my head. I'd eat a whole row of terrible cookies and start on the next row without even noticing.

It started to get harder to keep the divorce a secret, and my anxiety leaked out in strange ways. I remember walking home from school with Susan Symanski and Linda Miller, my two best friends, trying to make an important point about *The Brady Bunch*.

"I'm just saying nobody knows for sure!"

I was walking close to the curb, kicking through small piles of dried leaves.

"Nobody really knows what happened to him!"

"He's dead," Susan said. "They're both dead."

"That's the whole reason they met each other," Linda added. "His first wife died, and her first husband died. That's why they're alone. They each had three kids and . . ."

She started singing.

"That's the way they all became the Brady Bunch . . ."

Susan joined in: "The Brady Bunch . . . the Brady Bunch . . ."

"No!" I screamed and stopped walking. "We don't know that!"

Susan and Linda stopped singing and exchanged a look.

"I'm just saying . . . !"

I was shouting at them.

". . . we don't know for sure what happened to Mrs. Brady's first husband!"

This was such an important point. I had to make them see it.

"We know *Mr. Brady's* wife died," I clarified. "But they don't actually say what happened to Mrs. Brady's husband. *Anything* could have happened."

Nobody said anything, and the three of us started walking again. My tights made scratchy sounds as my thighs rubbed together. I was definitely putting on weight. Food had become my third best friend. I was starving all the time, and I was having trouble concentrating at school because all I could think about was eating.

"Like what?" Linda finally asked. "If Mrs. Brady's husband didn't die, then what happened to him?"

"Yeah," Susan said. "What else could have happened?"

"Well . . ."

I kicked a stone near the curb and watched it skitter down Zealand Avenue.

"Maybe they got divorced or something."

"No!" Susan said.

"That would be awful!" Linda said.

I kicked another stone.

"Yeah," Susan agreed. "The worst thing ever."

Linda nodded, and I didn't say anything.

"Mom?" I called, stepping inside the house. "Lori? Dan? David?"

There was a buzz of silence that meant nobody was home.

Good.

Sometimes Mr. Silverman was there with his awful laugh and that disgusting piece of gum in his mouth. I was certain the divorce was his fault. Sometimes he and my mom were in her bedroom when I got home. I tried not to think about it. The saving grace was that Mr. Silverman was already married, so he couldn't marry my mom.

I was glad Dan wasn't home. The Pain Game had mostly morphed into verbal torture. His new favorite joke was "Let's make a few bucks by selling Elisa to the circus as the new fat lady."

He said this in front of his new best friend Gary Wender, and it made me feel terrible. Sometimes when I got home, he and Gary were down in Dan's bedroom with the door shut. I figured they were smoking cigarettes because I could smell something strange seeping out under the door.

I walked up the stairs into the kitchen and hefted myself onto the counter and opened the snack cabinet. We never had a snack cabinet before Mr. Silverman. He liked to eat snacks, so I guess that was one good thing about him.

Jackpot! A new bag of Fritos and a box of potato chips! I took both and headed downstairs. I turned on the TV and sat down on the couch with the snacks next to me.

I ripped open the bag of Fritos. Over the crackle of foil, I sang along to the *Gilligan's Island* theme song.

"Just sit right back and you'll hear a tale . . . a tale of a fateful trip . . ."

I grabbed a handful of Fritos and settled into the couch cushions, crunching to the music.

"Gilligaaaaaaan . . . the Skipper tooooooo . . . the Millionaire . . . and his wiiiiiiiiife. The Movie Star . . . the Professor and . . . Mary Annnnnn . . ."

I leaned over and ripped open the Happy's Ripple Style Potato Chips. I took a handful and sat bloated and bug-eyed as the *Minnow* and its passengers washed up on the deserted island. Those poor castaways, I thought each day after school, cramming Bugles, Pizza Spins, and potato chips into my mouth.

Stuck on that island for who knew how long.

No rescue in sight.

TERRA INCOGNITA

Our children are the only people on whom we can safely take revenge for what was done to us.

—Gloria Steinem, *Revolution from Within: A Book of Self-Esteem*

FOR MY MOTHER AND MANY other women disillusioned by their straitjacketed lives during the 1960s and 1970s, reinventing themselves meant rejecting not only their marriages but also responsibility for their children's mental health.

When my mom made the decision to abandon the sinking ship of her marriage, we kids were tossed overboard without life jackets. Her new narrative meant that everyone—protagonists and minor characters alike—was set adrift without a story line. No instruction manuals, maps, or sea charts. No guidebooks or how-to videos. We were left to flail in her wake, trying to make landfall and survive through our wits, fevered dreams, and perhaps, memories hidden deep in our DNA.

It's hard to imagine a time when you couldn't turn to the internet, a bookstore, or a library to help you navigate unfamiliar terrain. Even back in 1969, you could page through *Reader's Digest* and find expert help for almost anything on the home front.

Except divorce.

When my parents announced their divorce, there was almost nothing written specifically for kids or parents to help guide them through the tortuous process of becoming a "broken home." Nowadays there are hundreds, perhaps thousands, of books and articles about divorce for every stage and age, including these:

Dinosaurs Divorce: A Guide for Changing Families
Divorce Happens to the Nicest Kids
Don't Fall Apart on Saturdays!: The Children's Divorce-Survival Book
Helping Children Understand Divorce: A Practical Resource Guide for Mom
      and Dad Break Up
On the Day His Daddy Left
When Your Parents Split Up . . . How to Keep Yourself Together

Unfortunately, back in the late 1960s the literature was pretty thin. A current voluminous list of books recommended by UCLA children's therapists includes only one book from that earlier era: *The Boys and Girls Book about Divorce* by Richard A. Gardner, MD. The UCLA group's summary of the book is not encouraging: "Audience: Ages 11–16. Long book of about 155 pages. Very outdated (1970) and oversimplified. Some good principles mixed with some outdated information. Not recommended for most kids." Nor is the publisher's description: "The author advocates helping children accept what cannot be changed. He coins 'Field's Rule' (as in W.C.) as a general principle for children whose parents continually disappoint them: 'If at first you don't succeed, try, try again. If after that you still don't succeed . . . forget it. Don't make a fool of yourself.'"

   I was eight when my parents announced their divorce. Being told to "forget" about my disappointing parents so as not to make a "fool" of myself was questionable advice. The coldness of this attitude reflects the nature of parent/child relationships back then. Unlike in the "helicopter" and "steam shovel" parenting of today, parents spent far less time attending to their children's physical and emotional needs. Studies show that in 1965, mothers spent an average of *12 hours and fathers only 4.5 hours each week* on childcare activities. Some studies show that mothers spent as little as *54 minutes a day and dads only 16 minutes a day* actively caring for or engaging with their kids.
   While the amount of time parents spend in the presence of their children hasn't changed that much, the intensive nature of their interactions has changed enormously. Time spent on "enrichment" activities like reading to children, doing crafts, taking them to lessons, attending games and recitals, and helping with homework has more than doubled. Even parents' leisure time, like exercising or socializing, is more likely to be spent with their children nowadays. This is particularly true in White, upper-middle-class American homes, but these expectations exist at all socioeconomic levels, pandemic or not, whether or not parents can achieve them.

So, if parents weren't intensively "parenting" their children back then (*parent* wasn't even a verb until the 1970s), what *were* they doing with all their time?

They were chasing the American Dream of a better life and upward mobility. They were pursuing happiness and self-fulfillment. Women, African Americans, Mexican Americans, American Indians and people in other marginalized groups were pressing for liberation, civil rights, and equality.

Mothers and fathers were busy asking for more of what they felt they deserved.

Exiting an unhappy marriage must have felt like a natural off-ramp on this road to collective reinvention. Given that between 1965 and 1975 the divorce rate went from twenty-seven percent to forty-eight percent of all marriages, this off-ramp sounds more like a six-lane freeway. And back then, children were dragged along for the ride without even seat belts to buffer the blows.

In her 1997 book *The Divorce Culture*, writer Barbara Dafoe Whitehead writes, "Nothing in the history of American childhood rivaled the scale or speed of this change in children's families." Divorce went from being a relatively rare childhood event to being "a collective childhood experience, involving a near-majority of children."

By the mid-1970s, more than a million children were newly affected by divorce each year. Up until the mid-1960s, the primary reason for avoiding divorce had been "for the sake of the children," which presumed that parents had a duty to place their children's needs above their own. But as more parents dissolved their marriages, attitudes shifted dramatically, particularly among women. Even advice columnist Ann Landers changed her story in 1972 when she said, "I no longer believe that marriage means forever no matter how lousy it is—or 'for the sake of the children.'"

As the marriage story line changed, the vocabulary describing the impact of divorce on children changed too. The term broken home was supplanted by the less catastrophic-sounding "single-parent home." Experts argued that most children of divorce bounced back after the initial trauma. The authors of the 1974 book *The Courage to Divorce* believed divorce could be a beneficial experience by "liberating children" and making them less dependent on their parents. Counting myself among this generation of kids, if we were already being neglected by our parents (literally locked out of the house, in my case), how much more "liberation" could we stand?

Opinions about the effects of divorce on kids have seesawed over the years: Kids are resilient and they'll be fine, or divorce will damage them forever. Sociologist Judith Wallerstein's renowned twenty-five-year "California Children of

Divorce project" concluded that divorce leaves children with lifelong scars that make it hard for them to establish permanent, trusting relationships.

Her conclusions remain controversial. Anecdotally, among me and my siblings, only my older brother has been divorced. My husband and I have been together for almost forty years, and he, too, is from a divorced family.

There is still little agreement about the effects of divorce on children, and recent studies continue to find conflicting results. One shows that twenty-four percent of children had their reading scores decline after divorce, while another shows that nineteen percent saw their scores increase. In one study, bullying and aggressive behavior increased in eighteen percent of kids, and another showed a fourteen percent decrease.

Despite the conflicting data, researchers universally agree on one thing: The way adults handle a divorce will affect its impact on their children. If you type "kids and divorce" into your web browser, today almost every bit of advice will include a list of things parents should NEVER do when getting a divorce. The list will include some version of the following:

> NEVER have your kids relay messages between you and your ex.
> NEVER talk bad about your ex to your kids.
> NEVER tell your kids your ex should be paying for their clothes, toys, meals, etc.
> NEVER talk about court matters with your kids.
> NEVER tell your kids it's their ex's fault you can't buy the kids anything.

Have I mentioned that no such list was available to my parents? And knowing what you know about them, do you think my father was paying a speck of attention or my mother would have cared a whit about what such a list might have recommended? My parents were walking their own paths, while my siblings and I were left wandering in the wilderness. We may not have spent forty years there like our ancestors, but sometimes it sure felt like it.

THE SWINGING TREE

"OH REALLY, SAM? YOU WANT to talk about our family?"

The four of us kids were at the dinner table listening to my mom yell at my dad on the phone in her bedroom.

"Fine. Let's talk about how you expect me to feed your kids and keep this house running on thirty-five dollars a week!"

Their dinnertime fights about money were the same as usual, except my dad lived somewhere else.

"Don't tell me to relax!"

Exactly the same.

"That's none of your business! Did you get the letter from Meshbesher?"

"Lori, drink your milk," I said, putting more Cheerios on David's tray.

"That's the only talking I'm gonna do right now! Goodbye, Sam. I'm late!"

She hung up, and we heard the clang all the way from the dinner table.

A few minutes later she came into the dining room.

"Oy, your father, he's something else," she said. "All right, I'm going now."

She was wearing a white silky shirt and a blue skirt. Her earrings and necklace had matching blue jewels that sparkled in the dining room light.

"Mommy go bye-bye?" David asked from his highchair.

"Mommy's going bye-bye, David. But I won't be gone long. Elisa, make sure Lori and David get a bath tonight. And no TV until homework is done."

"Where are you going?" I asked.

"Out."

"With Mr. 'Haaaaahh, Haaaahhhh, Haaaahhh.'"

Dan did a weird echoey laugh.

"What did you say, Mr. Smart Mouth?"

"Nothing."

"You know what, Dan?"

My mom leaned over, put her hands on the table and glared at Dan.

"That big mouth of yours is gonna get you in big trouble soon. You better watch it."

"But where *are* you going?" I asked again.

"It's nobody's business where I'm going, Elisa. Not yours and not your father's. Is that understood?"

"Yes."

My mom was so volatile during this period, it was mostly a relief when she was gone. It meant Dan and I had to babysit Lori and David almost every night, but the trade-off was worth it. With Linda Miller's Catholic family as a model, taking care of younger siblings didn't seem that unusual. Of course, leaving me and Dan in charge of a toddler and a preschooler was bound to have some drawbacks. Not only did David's diet consist solely of Cheerios and applesauce, but one evening he ended up in the emergency room with stitches over one eye because he slammed into the corner of the dining room wall during a game of indoor tag.

Dan's memory of this event is that I kept a cool head and duct-taped a (cloth) diaper around David's face to stanch the bleeding. All I remember is a lot of blood. Neither of us remember how he got to the hospital. David still has the scar and a vivid memory of doctors covering his head with a sheet of paper marked with tiny holes for the location of the stitches.

Whoever drove him, it certainly wasn't my mom.

She was preoccupied with more important things than her four children. Like having sex with Bernie Silverman and figuring out how the hell she was going to make ends meet.

"Your precious father," my mom snorted, as she adjusted an earring, "thinks I can feed all of you for a hundred and fifty bucks a month."

She snorted again.

"Well, that's all gonna change soon. A lot of things are gonna change around here."

She looked at her watch.

"For your information, Elisa, I'm going out to dinner with a friend. Now finish eating and that includes your vegetables. No more tater tots or applesauce until you eat your beans. Give David some beans too but cut them up first."

"A friend?"

I tried to think of a single friend of my mom's.

There was a honk in the driveway.

"Whoops! Gotta go. I'll be back before bedtime. Just make sure Lori and David get a bath."

She grabbed her purse from the kitchen and headed down the stairs. The screen door opened and closed. Dan looked at me across the table and shook his head in disgust.

"A friend?" he said in a high voice and tossed a tater tot at me. "Who do you think it is?"

I stared at him for a moment and then jumped out of my chair and raced to the front door. My mom was climbing into Mr. Silverman's dark red car. I heard his booming laugh before the car door slammed. I pressed my forehead against the screen door and thought about how much I hated his laugh. And everything else about him. I pushed open the screen door and took off.

"Elisa, get back in here!" Dan yelled down the stairs. "You have to watch Lori and David!"

The screen door slammed behind me.

I raced down the driveway, and as Mr. Silverman's car disappeared down Hopewood Lane, I started running in the opposite direction. The houses blurred by as I picked up speed. I wasn't sure why I was running or where I was going. There was no box I could hide in, no bus I could jump on that would keep my family from disintegrating. But running away felt like my best (and only) option.

I can't be sure, but I'd lay bets that I ran to the Swinging Tree that night. The fall my parents split up, I spent a lot of time riding that scary-as-shit rope swing. Looking back, I think it was an early attempt at self-medication.

The Swinging Tree was a century-old oak that stood on the other side of an eight-foot chain link fence that separated our subdivision from Gethsemane Cemetery. Its lowest branch was higher than the roof of our house, and there was a long, forearm-thick rope tied around it with a fat knot at the bottom. Everybody knew the rope swing was dangerous; that was part of its allure. Nowadays, there's no way parents and cemetery officials would let kids play on something so unsafe, but as I've already mentioned, adults were busy with other things.

Since this was a school night in early November, I wasn't sure anybody else would be there. Swinging season was almost over, and you needed an older kid to handle the rope. Even if someone was there, they probably wouldn't let me do it. The older kids didn't let us younger kids do it because we usually chickened out.

I'd chickened out twice already. Climbing the rickety ladder was scary enough, but being up on the swinging platform was terrifying. Not only was it twenty feet off the ground, but the tree trunk was so thick you couldn't get an arm around it, and there weren't any other branches to hang onto. You had to wedge your feet behind a block of wood and press your back against the tree while someone held onto the heavy rope for you. Then you had to maneuver the knot between your feet while the other person held onto your waist to keep you from falling forward before you were ready. And then they let you go. I hadn't even made it to the rope part yet. Both times I climbed up, I climbed right back down.

But things felt different that November night. It had been three months since my dad moved out, and even though I'd only just turned nine, I felt older.

Ancient.

I stood at the fence staring at the oak's massive dried brown leaf canopy, thinking about my mom driving away with Mr. Silverman. They were going to come back and go into my mom's bedroom, and there was nothing I could do about it. Echoes of his deep laugh boomed through my brain, and I stuck my feet through the fence rungs and started climbing.

On the other side, I walked over the rise and saw three people standing at the base of the tree: Gary Wender, his older sister Charlene, and a girl I didn't know.

It figured the Wenders would be there. Their mom worked a full-time job, so they ate dinner later than everyone else. I got closer and saw Charlene and the other girl smoking cigarettes. Were those girls old enough to smoke? How old did you have to be?

"Hi," I called out.

They didn't say anything. They just watched me walk toward them until Gary Wender, who looked sleepy as usual, sort of woke up and recognized me.

"Hey, you're Dan's little sister, right? What's your name?"

"Elisa."

"Yeah," he said, like I'd passed some sort of test. "Elisa."

He stared at me as the other two stood there smoking.

"Where's Dan?"

"Home eating dinner."

Gary nodded. He didn't ask why I wasn't home eating dinner too.

"So," he gestured to the tree. "You wanna swing?"

Gary crawled up the ladder first with the thick rope slung over his shoulder. I waited until he was lodged in the crotch of the tree. He hugged the trunk with one hand and held onto the rope with the other. When he nodded, I climbed up the ladder. I wedged my feet behind the wooden toehold and pressed back against the massive trunk.

"You've done this before, right?"

"Yeah." I lied, trying not to look down.

"Sit or stand?" he asked.

Most first-timers sat on the knot. Sitting was safer, but the rope rubbed all the skin off the inside of your legs. Standing on the knot was more dangerous. And everything felt dangerous to me at that moment.

"Stand."

Gary handed me the knot. I squatted down, keeping my feet pressed against the plank while he held onto my waist with two hands so I could maneuver the knot between my feet.

"Tell me when you're ready."

My heart was beating so hard I felt its thump in my mouth. I looked down at the two girls staring up at me, and they looked small and far away. I grabbed the thick rope with both hands and felt the rough fibers scrape my palms. I passed the rope over my right shoulder, like I'd seen the older kids do, and leaned backward as far as I could. I pushed the knot underneath my feet, trying to get both feet positioned on it without falling forward.

"Ready?" Gary yelled.

He couldn't hold onto me much longer without being pulled off the platform.

I took a quick glance around and saw the cemetery fields stretching off in all directions. The waist-high prairie grasses were rippling like a yellow and brown horse's mane in the early evening chill, and the oak's dying leaves rasped and shivered around me. Beyond the cemetery, I saw cars humming along Boone Avenue. Beyond that I saw the empty blue carcass of the New Hope swimming pool already closed for the season. And beyond that nothing but open fields.

"I gotta let go!" Gary shouted.

And he did.

The rush of wind whipped against my face as I hurtled slack-cheeked toward the ground. I hugged the rope and felt it scrape my chin and knew, with stomach-churning certainty, the rope wouldn't catch, something was wrong, I was going to slam straight into the earth and break every bone in my body . . .

And then the rope caught . . .

. . . and I was carried up and out in a long, graceful arc; the pure sensation of flying over fields and grasses as the glorious world spread out in all directions, a tan and yellow blur in the cool embrace of the oak as that long rope just kept going, far, far, beyond what I could see. And when I was feeling as full as I could, and that gnawing emptiness that never seemed to leave my belly was filled with light and air, the rope swung back toward the tree in a long, slow, glide, sailing right past the trunk and high over the fence, up and out toward the tall rooftops on the other side.

From the rope swing I could see my whole neighborhood. From Susan Symanski's house to my own nearly five blocks away. I saw the Anderson's backyard sandbox and Mrs. Thompson's sheets on their clothesline. I saw the Christmas lights on Mrs. Schoonover's house. I saw the big hill in the Westlunds' backyard where I hid from my mom's rage, and the Millers' swing set, and Mrs. Swanson's fence. My whole world was spread out in front of me . . . New Hope, Minnesota. Love it or leave it.

Leave it is exactly what I wanted to do. I wanted to ride this rope swing far enough away that I never had to see the mean look in my mom's eyes and the absent look in my dad's. Leave behind the dinner notes, and those stupid *Brady Bunch* girls, and my brother's taunts, and Lori's bath, and David's diapers, and my own fat thighs, and my mother-screaming, father-leaving, Mr. Silverman-laughing worries. Leave them all behind and fly high above the world to where all the empty places inside me were filled with calm and ease.

In a slow, majestic arc, the rope began its outward journey again, bringing the cemetery to a blur beneath my feet, back and forth, ten, eleven times, the rope marking time like a slender pendulum ticking off the moments of those long, anxious days.

STRESS FRACTURES

One of the most influential studies of the long-term effect of a stressful early home life is the ongoing Adverse Childhood Experiences Study (ACE), which was launched in the 1990s. . . . [It] identified 10 categories of childhood trauma: three categories of abuse, two of neglect, and five related to growing up in a "seriously dysfunctional household." They found that the number of these traumas a person experiences in childhood (. . . a person's ace score) correlates in adulthood with health problems ranging from heart disease to cancer. More recently, researchers . . . have found that an elevated ace score also has a negative effect on the development of a child's executive functions and on her ability to learn effectively in school.

—Paul Tough, "How Kids Learn Resilience,"
The Atlantic, June 2016

BUBBLE-SPEAK

TWO WEEKS BEFORE THANKSGIVING, MY fourth-grade math teacher asked me to stay after class.

"I don't like seeing you so frustrated, Elisa."

Mr. Webb was sitting behind his desk with his hands clasped together on top of the math book I despised.

"I know you're having a lot of trouble with fractions, and that's OK."

I didn't say anything. I just stood next to his desk and stared at his hands. He kept clasping and unclasping them. Each time he rubbed his palms together, they made a scritch-scratch sound.

"We all have things that take us awhile to understand."

Scritch-Scratch.

"So, I've decided to take the pressure off . . ."

Scritch-Scratch.

". . . by moving you into Miss Rettman's class for a while."

I looked up horrified. I might have actually gasped.

"They're just starting to learn about the metric system, and I know you'll do fine with that. Later on in the year, we can look at moving you back in here with us again."

"Miss Rettman's class?" I said, staring at him. "But, that's the low group. I can't go into the low group."

I felt tears creeping into my eyes.

"We don't think of it in those terms, Elisa," Mr. Webb said. "And you shouldn't either."

Scritch-Scratch.

I didn't tell anyone I'd been moved to the low group. On my first day in Miss Rettman's class, I was seated behind Johnny Stewart, who smelled like manure because his parents owned one of the last cattle farms in the suburbs. Halfway through the lesson on Meters, Grams, and Liters, he turned around and put a clear glass jelly jar down on my desk. Inside, there were two cow eyes floating in a viscous yellow liquid.

I stared at the milky brown orbs drifting in their cloudy sea, and I had never seen anything sadder. The sightless eyes rolled and quivered inside their murky glass prison, and I started crying and couldn't stop. I couldn't stop when Miss Rettman walked me down to the school nurse's office. And I couldn't stop when the nurse decided to call my mom.

"Mrs. Bernick, this is Mrs. Carlson, the Zachary Lane school nurse. I have Elisa in my office, and I'm not sure what's wrong, but she seems very unhappy."

I was sitting on a liver-colored plastic chair on the other side of Mrs. Carlson's desk. I looked down at my lap, and a tear fell from my chin and splattered onto my red tights.

"No, she doesn't have a temperature, but I think you need to come and take her home."

By the time my mom arrived, I was lying on a cot sniffling in the darkened back room of the nurse's office. My mom and Mrs. Carlson sat across from each other in the front office, and I could hear them clearly through the open door.

"Mrs. Bernick, can I ask you a personal question?"

"What?"

I could tell my mom was furious.

"Is there anything going on at home that might be upsetting, Elisa?"

My mom said nothing. I heard the squeak of a chair.

"Elisa's teachers tell me that she hasn't been herself lately," Mrs. Carlson continued. "And this sort of thing can often be traced to something going on with friends or family."

There was another silence.

"Actually," my mom finally said, "Elisa's father and I are getting a divorce."

A rush of blood filled the space behind my eyes. That was only the second time I'd heard the word *divorce* spoken out loud by one of my parents. The first time was in their bedroom.

"Oh my."

Mrs. Carlson didn't say anything for a moment.

"I see."

On Mrs. Carlson's recommendation, my mom brought home a book about kids and divorce. She put the book on the dining room table and made me and Dan read a chapter from it each day after school. I don't remember the name of this book. It's no longer in print, but it was one of the few available at the time. It was filled with little round bubble cartoons that were supposed to represent kids whose parents were getting a divorce. The bubbles had eyes and mouths and they talked to each other.

"I think it's my fault my parents are getting a divorce. I did something wrong, and now they don't love me or each other anymore."

"No. That's not true. It's not your fault your parents are getting a divorce. It's nothing you said or did. They still love you as much as they always did."

"Bubbles that talk to each other?" Dan said, after the first chapter. "This is so stupid."

"Yeah," I said. "Really stupid."

But actually, I wasn't sure the bubbles were stupid. I wasn't sure what to think of any of this. Was I supposed to feel everything the bubbles felt? Was there something wrong with me if I didn't?

"All I want is for my mother and my father to stay married. I think they still love each other and after a while, I know they will live in the same house again."

"That's not true. They are getting a divorce because they don't love each other any-more. They will not live together in the same house again. But that doesn't mean they don't love you."

I felt even worse when I read this particular bubble conversation. The word *love* didn't fit my family. I had no evidence that my parents had ever loved each other. And no evidence that they loved me or my siblings. My mom didn't act like she loved us, and it was hard to tell how my dad felt about anything.

Every day after school, the book talked about families "getting a divorce," but it didn't say what happened afterward. In the 1970 suburbs, a family was a mom, a dad, and kids. Once you weren't a family anymore, what were you? There was no alternative story line.

In Chapter Four, the bubbles had a conversation that made me feel physically ill.

"My Dad is going on a lot of dates with a lady I don't know. I think he's going to marry her and forget about me."

"That's not true. Even if your Dad does marry someone else, it doesn't mean he will forget about you. You will become part of a brand-new family."

Was my mom *dating* Mr. Silverman? But he was married to Mrs. Silverman. Would I have to become part of *his* family? Did that mean he was getting a divorce too? The bubbles had nothing to say about that.

Oddly enough, and in spite of the confusing bubble talks, by the end of the book, I actually felt a little better. The fact that there was a book written about families getting divorced meant mine wasn't the only one. It made everything feel slightly less dire.

"Tell your mom or dad when you are feeling sad. Ask them for a hug to make you feel better. Tell your friends and teachers too. Tell them why you are feeling sad so they can help you feel better."

Yeah, right, I thought. Like I'd ever ask my mom or dad for a hug. But I decided the bubbles were right about one thing. It was time to tell my friends about the divorce.

Late the next afternoon, I walked up the sidewalk to Susan Symanski's house clapping my mittens together in the dusky November cold. I started up their front steps and realized I had no idea what to say to Susan and Mrs. Symanski. What exact words should I use?

My parents are getting a divorce?

My parents are going to get divorced?

My parents are divorcing?

I'd never said these words out loud, and I'd never heard anybody else say them either. I looked around to see if anybody was watching. It was only 5:30, but it was already getting dark and nobody was outside.

"My parents are getting a divorce," I said out loud, my words huffing tiny smoke signals into the chilly twilight.

As soon as I said it, I knew I was going to cry. I crouched down and let the tears roll down my cheeks. I stayed there for a few minutes, sobbing quietly, hoping nobody could hear me. When I was done, I wiped my nose on my jacket sleeve and rang the doorbell. Mrs. Symanski answered on the second ring, and Susan was right behind her. I could tell they were eating dinner because Mrs. Symanski had a napkin in her hand.

"My parents are getting a divorce," I said, not even waiting until I was inside to deliver the news.

Susan burst into tears, and Mrs. Symanski pulled me into the house and gave me a big hug.

"I'm so sorry, Elisa."

Mrs. Symanski hugged me harder than I'd ever been hugged before. Even harder than Grandma Rose.

"And I'm so glad you told us."

Mrs. Symanski had been separated from Mr. Symanski for a long time. Mr. Symanski was an alcoholic who didn't live with them; he only came for holidays and to cut the grass and shovel. Susan never talked about her dad and never visited him. It occurred to me that being separated and being divorced weren't that different—they were just two different kinds of awful.

"Do you want to stay and eat dinner with us?" Mrs. Symanski asked.

"Ummmm. . . . no thank you."

As I turned to leave, Mrs. Symanski pulled Susan into a hug, and I felt a little bad that I interrupted their dinner and made them cry. But overall, I felt better. Walking down their driveway, blowing warm clouds into the chill, I somehow felt lighter and more solid at the exact same moment.

I cut through the Earles' backyard, went up the Westlunds' hill, and knocked on the Millers' back door. Mrs. Miller opened it, and behind her I saw Linda clearing a mess of congealing spaghetti plates off the dining room table. I heard the other five Miller kids screaming from the basement playroom.

"You can go downstairs if you want," Mrs. Miller told me. "But Linda can't play until she finishes her chores."

Mrs. Miller was wearing a stained pink-and-white polka dot apron that she had sewed herself. I knew this because the shoulder ruffles stood up at different heights. She had just given herself a new Toni home permanent, and the tight brown curls all over her head didn't move.

"I didn't come over to play. I just wanted to tell you that my parents are getting a divorce, and my dad doesn't live here anymore."

"Oh, Elisa!"

Linda dropped some silverware on the table.

"That's terrible!"

"Oh heavens, that *is* terrible!" Mrs. Miller said.

She shook her head so hard that her tight helmet of curls actually wobbled a little.

"That's just awful, Elisa. Come inside, you poor thing."

I stepped inside, and Mrs. Miller patted my shoulder awkwardly. I could tell she and Linda were genuinely horrified by my news. Not only was divorce generally unacceptable, but the Catholic Church considered it a mortal sin, and the Millers were good Catholics. A decade down the road, the Miller family's state of grace would evaporate when they got their own divorce, but at that moment, Mrs. Miller saw my "terrible" news as an opportunity for some neighborly proselytizing.

"Oh, you poor thing," she said again, switching to a strange, teacherlike voice.

"It will be good for you to play over here in the weeks ahead. In a house where there's a healthy family with two parents."

She put her arm around my shoulders and turned to Linda.

"Leave the dishes for now. Let's all go sit in the living room."

The living room?

I raised my eyebrows in amazement at Linda. I'd been in the Millers' house a thousand times, but I'd never once set foot in their living room. Not because kids weren't allowed, but because the Millers' living room always looked like a clothes bomb had gone off in it. There were huge piles of half-folded laundry covering the couch, the chairs, and the beige carpeted floor. Mountains of it. The ironing board was permanently set up near the front windows, and it was heaped with blue and white plaid Catholic school uniforms and short-sleeved white shirts.

I followed Mrs. Miller and Linda into the dark living room. She turned on a lamp near the couch and another between two fat red chairs that were also covered with laundry.

"Linda, let's clear off the couch so we can all sit down."

Linda gave me an irritated look and started picking up laundry. While I waited, I looked around the room and saw a small silver cross hanging above the front door. On the wall over the couch, there was a larger wooden cross hanging next to six framed pictures of the Miller kids when they were babies. Each baby was wearing a long, ruffled white nightgown, and each photo had a fancy framed award next to it that said "Baptism Certificate" in silver script. On the wall behind the red chairs, there was a large gold-framed oil painting.

What the . . . ?

It was Jesus's crucifixion. I'd seen it in a book, but never this close-up. I stared at the blood dripping down Jesus's sad, pale face and the glowing halo of thorns on his head. His eyes were closed, and his head was hanging down at an uncomfortable angle. He was naked except for a skimpy loin cloth. I got the same feeling in my stomach as when I watched the Holocaust films at the Beth El.

"OK, Elisa," Mrs. Miller said. "You can sit down now."

She patted a spot on the couch between her and Linda.

"I know you're feeling sad about your family's terrible situation."

Mrs. Miller wrinkled her brow sympathetically when I sat down.

"Being without your father at home must really be hard."

I thought about Mr. Miller never being home because he had to work three jobs to support Linda's family. My mom called Mr. Miller "the only living Catholic saint."

"You know, Elisa," Mrs. Miller put her arm around my shoulders. "When we're feeling sad, going to church always makes us feel better. Right, Linda?"

Linda nodded, but I knew she was lying. She was always complaining about how much she hated going to church.

"If you ever want to come to church with us, you're more than welcome. In fact, you could spend the night with Linda tomorrow and come with us on Sunday morning. Right, Linda?"

"Sure," Linda said without any emotion. "That would be fun."

"And Elisa," Mrs. Miller looked deeply into my eyes. "We don't need to tell your mother if you'd rather not. It could be our special secret."

I considered Mrs. Miller's offer. I looked across the room at Jesus with his caved-in chest and the blood dripping from the nails pounded into his hands and feet. If he was part of this secret, I didn't want anything to do with it. I'd already learned that "special secrets" didn't make me feel any better.

"No thank you," I said, jumping up from the couch. "I sleep at my dad's apartment on the weekends. I have to go."

I could feel their eyes drilling into my back as I threaded my way through laundry and headed for the back door.

—〰—

GRIT

Resilience
1: capable of withstanding shock without permanent deformation or rupture
2: tending to recover from or adjust easily to misfortune or change
—*Merriam-Webster Dictionary*

IT'S ONLY IN HINDSIGHT THAT I realize what was so important about this moment. It wasn't the Jesus painting or the talking bubbles, or even Mrs. Symanski's wonderful hug. It was my conscious decision to tell people about the divorce. There on Susan Symanski's steps in the gloaming chill of that November evening, I intentionally chose the words to describe my situation, and it was the beginning of my own departure story. It was my fledgling realization of the power of words and of seeing my narrative as something separate from my mother's. I wasn't just a character in her story, I was the author of my own. It was the moment I felt the tiniest kernel of *me* inside *my* story; and instead of running away or hiding my fear and shame in a drawer, I sensed the possibility of saying something different.

Resilience is often defined as the ability to maintain coherence or continuity in one's life story. It's the capacity to adapt to stress and create meaning from chaos—something researchers believe accounts for the endurance of Holocaust survivors and those of other traumatic events.

"We are constantly rewiring our brains based on past experience and the expectation of how we need to use them in the future," says neuroscientist Huda Akil.

Given that epigenetic memories are written into our very cells, with the potential to recall generations of adversity, is it possible that Jews and other victims of long-term trauma have a predisposition for resilience? We certainly hear a lot about the negative consequences of historical trauma, but there are likely to be positive consequences, or at least possibilities, right? As a recent *Discover* magazine article put it, "The mechanisms of behavioral epigenetics underlie not only deficits and weaknesses but strengths and resiliencies, too."

Studies show that resilient children have certain things in common: a strong bond with a supportive caregiver, teacher, or mentor; a psychological makeup that allows them to meet the world on their own terms; and an internal locus of control.

Locus of control is a personality trait that exists on a continuum. People with an *internal* locus of control believe *they* can influence events and outcomes. They tend to take more responsibility for their actions, good or bad. People with an *external* locus of control blame outside forces for the trajectory of their lives: things like bad luck or authority figures. Most people exist somewhere between the two extremes.

I think the link between locus of control and resilience is storytelling. Resilient children adapt to stressful situations by intentionally spinning stories of their own survival. They cast themselves as action heroes inside their own tragedies.

When I consider the trajectory of my mom's life, I see a resilient person with a confused locus of control that led to a muddled story line. She certainly had a strong desire to influence events and outcomes. But like most women of her generation, she didn't feel her own *agency* in the world. She was a victim of bad timing. She was fighting to tell a different story, to find a better version of herself, but where were her examples? When she looked at the stories available to her, what did she see? Women who didn't get first names. Or bank accounts. Or broad career options. Or invitations to the Zealand Avenue Coffee Klatch. She was Jewish and female in a world that diminished both. She was at the whim of outside forces, with little ability to achieve success on her own terms.

She was also raised in a verbally abusive family, continually subjected to criticism, hostility, and "emotional over-involvement toward family members"—factors all correlated with an external locus of control and depression. Resilience relies on the ability to establish at least one emotional connection, and she, unfortunately, felt very much alone. Like generations of Jews and other traumatized populations, she also had serious attachment issues. If much of your history is spent losing people around you to cattle cars, slavery auctions, and death marches (and a twin sister's brain aneurysm), you're going to be wary of creating emotional bonds.

For my mother, with no sympathetic role models or mentors, no financial independence, and limited career opportunities, resilience must have felt a lot like desperation. For many years, her claim that she was "doing the best she could" during our childhood felt to me like she was ducking responsibility for her actions. But now I think she was telling the truth.

You could argue I grew up in a similarly abusive and traumatic household. My mom and I are both Jewish and female; we share a history and many of the same epigenetic memories of marginalization and trauma. So why did I fare so much better? What accounts for *my* resilience?

Aside from having a more pronounced internal locus of control, I think the central difference is that *I grew up in an environment where telling a different story was possible.* My shifting circumstances enabled me to reinvent myself and adapt to a changed environment.

Unlike my mom, I had the significant advantages of middle-class money and suburban White privilege from the get-go. I had Girl Scouts, an innovative school district, a women's movement that had picked up steam, and strong female role models in books, in movies, and luckily, in several of my teachers. Mrs. Symanski worked a seemingly glamorous job in downtown Minneapolis (I think she was an executive secretary). Even my *mom* worked part-time.

Everywhere I looked I saw stories of smart girls and interesting women with lives that stretched beyond their homes and children. Nellie Bly, Pippi Longstocking, Anne of Green Gables, Mary Richards, Lucy Ricardo, Marlo Thomas, Harriet the Spy, and Mary Poppins were just a few of the willful, independent females whose stories presented a rich stew of synonyms that included *plucky, driven, courageous, accomplished, intrepid,* and *intelligent.*

As a Jew with insider/outsider status like my mother, I was already sensitized to the possibility of there being alternative stories. But I sensed my own agency in a way she never did. My story had the potential to be larger than hers because I had different material to work with and more confidence that the world would let me tell it.

Unfortunately for my mom, even with the advantages of White assimilation, the potential story lines for a desperately unhappy 33-year-old part-time dental hygienist with four kids ages two, five, ten, and twelve were pretty limited in 1970 midwestern America. She was drowning, and Bernie Silverman must have felt like a lifeline, so she grabbed on. She chose an ambitious, aggressive man whose rough manner was similar to her mother's (and the opposite of my dad's, whose frugal timidity must have felt oppressive). It would have been easy for her to mistake Bernie's volatile attentions for love.

My mom's road to reinvention was filled with potholes and roadblocks. Bernie was a married man with several children of his own. She continued to struggle financially, and her escalating war with my father over child support seemed to be a losing battle. My mom was the epitome of a "loose cannon" during this period. I did my best to stay out of her line of fire, but she had my brother Dan trapped in her crosshairs.

—⚒—

OUT IN THE COLD

AS THE WINDS WHIPPED ICE and snow across the prairies in December of 1972, I avoided going home whenever I didn't have to babysit Lori and David. Nearly every day after school I headed to Northwood Pond to skate until it got dark and the warming house closed.

Sometimes I kept skating after they locked the doors and everyone else drifted home to dinner. I'd set my boots on top of a snowbank and glide over the ice with the first stars barely visible in the wide, cobalt sky. Nothing but frozen breath, silent snowbanks, and the juicy crunch of my skate blades as I propelled myself faster and faster through the dark until my fingers and toes were long past numb.

When I finally headed home, I took the long way up Hopewood Lane so I could watch families eating dinner in their brightly lit dining rooms. I liked being an invisible presence in the dark, moving just outside the pools of amber light spilling from those cheerful scenes. As I watched mothers and fathers laughing with their children, I imagined they were telling knock-knock jokes or talking about something silly that happened at school.

I huffed warm breath into the frigid twilight and listened to my boots squeak in the snow as I walked up the long, curving hill. Christmas lights careened along roof edges, snowflakes melted against my cheeks, and the world felt like my own silent snow globe filled with gentle possibilities.

At the top, I turned left onto Zealand Avenue, and my own house came into view. Across the street, the Millers' nativity scene blinked on and off beneath their red and green Christmas lights. Our house didn't have any Christmas lights, of course, but the outside garage light was on, and the flakes of snow falling through its glow looked cozy. There were lights on in our living room, the kitchen, and the sewing room downstairs. It looked like any other house where the people inside were laughing and telling jokes.

I stood at the foot of our driveway and contemplated that for a moment. Clearly, it was impossible to tell anything about what was going on inside a house from the outside.

I walked up the driveway, kicking through the snow that had already fallen, and pushed open the front door.

"Elisa Rae Bernick, what time is it?"

My mom was standing at the top of the steps with a spoon in one hand and a hot pad in the other.

"What time were you supposed to be home, young lady?"

"5:00."

"And what time is it now?"

"I don't know. I don't have a watch."

I kicked my boots onto the doormat.

"It's almost six, for your information. You're an hour late."

"Sorry. There's no clock in the warming house."

I unzipped my jacket and hung it on the banister.

"Well, then maybe you won't be skating after school anymore if you can't figure out how to get home on time. Hang up your jacket in the closet, and get up here and set the table. Just set it for three. Dan's not eating."

"Why not?"

"Because his big mouth got him in trouble again, and he has to stay in his room during dinner."

"What'd he say?"

"None of your business unless you want to skip dinner too."

I set the table as my mom banged pots around in the kitchen. I put a fork and napkin on Dan's placemat before I remembered he wasn't eating. My mom had really been on the warpath lately, and Dan was almost always her target. At first, I considered myself lucky. Now I was worried about Dan. My mom blew up at the littlest things, and Dan just didn't seem to get it. Why didn't he shut up?

When I ask Dan about his memories of this period in our lives, he has a hard time dredging anything up. He says he's blocked a lot of things, which isn't surprising. This was a particularly awful time for him. He was a stand-in for my dad, and my mom used him constantly as a punching bag for her anger and frustration. Nothing he did was right, and she continually punished him for minor infractions and threatened to "send him to live with his father." With nothing to lose, Dan embraced his role as a smirking thirteen-year-old on the precipice of a lifelong relationship with marijuana.

He says he doesn't remember the specifics of this particular night, but the events are seared into my memory. Even then I think I realized my mom had a new exit plan, and Dan wasn't part of it.

She started yelling at him from the top of the stairs.

"Dan, it's snowing. I want you out there in fifteen minutes to shovel the driveway! Lori, turn off the TV and come up! Bring David with you!"

"Mom, it's going to snow all night," I called from the dining room. "He might as well wait until morning to shovel."

She walked into the dining room with a murderous look on her face.

"Mind your own goddamn business or you'll be the one out there shoveling. Get the milk out, and sit down and shut up. No one asked for your opinion."

She went back into the kitchen as Lori came racing into the dining room and scrambled up into her chair. She was singing a little nonsense tune to herself.

"Hi, Lori."

"Hi."

"Where's David?"

"Sleeping on the couch."

My mom came back into the dining room and set a bowl of tuna noodle casserole and a bowl of canned green beans down on the table. She picked up my plate and started dishing out the food. It looked disgusting. I knew better than to say anything, but I couldn't help curling my lip. Lori imitated me and scrunched up her mouth.

"What? You two don't like it?"

My mom paused in midspoonful and glared at us.

"No, it's not that," I said. "It's just . . . we had the same thing last night."

"That's right," she said, spooning it out again. "And thanks to your precious father you'll probably have it again tomorrow night, too."

Oh boy, I inwardly groaned. *Here we go.* I automatically looked across the table to roll my eyes at Dan and felt a jolt at his empty chair.

"Your precious father tells the judge he can't afford to pay more for you guys, which is a load of crap, and so you end up eating this for dinner."

She slammed the plate down in front of me.

"You have a complaint about the food? Call your father. And if you don't like it, you can go to your room and have nothing for dinner."

She spooned tuna noodle hotdish onto Lori's plate and left the dining room without a word. She padded heavily down the hallway to her bedroom and slammed the door.

A few minutes later she came out and walked to the top of the stairs.

"Dan! Get out there and shovel. Now!"

There was no response from downstairs.

"Did you hear me? If you aren't out there in two minutes, you're gonna be very sorry!"

No response.

"Two minutes, Dan!"

She went back down the hallway and slammed the door again.

Ten minutes later, as I was clearing the table, she went downstairs. A few minutes later she dragged Dan up to the landing.

"You keep asking for it, Dan. Night after night. You just never know when to keep your mouth shut, do ya?"

"Yeah, guess who I learned that from?"

I went to the top of the stairs and saw Dan putting his winter coat on over his pajamas. My mom smacked him hard on the side of his head.

"You got a big mouth, you know that? Get your boots on, Bigmouth. You better hope your dad gets here soon or your mouth's gonna freeze shut and you won't be able to open it again to talk so smart to me. Take your bag and get out there."

Dan walked out the front door holding a torn paper grocery bag filled with clothes. He wasn't wearing a hat or mittens, and he didn't look back. My mom slammed the door and locked it behind him. She saw me at the top of the steps.

"What are you looking at? Clean the kitchen if you're done eating."

My mom stomped back downstairs, and I ran to the window to watch Dan kick his way to the curb. It was snowing heavier now, and he dragged his feet down the driveway, making long tracks in the snow. When he got to the curb, he stood there, head down, with his hands shoved into his pockets and the bag of clothes at his feet. After a minute he turned around and looked up at the house. I waved at him, but he didn't wave back.

The torn grocery bag of clothes in the snow sticks out clearly in my mind. I remember my mom locking the door behind him. The harsh finality of her actions. I recall the frantic intensity of her anger and my own anxiety about Dan not having a hat or mittens. I have written about this moment in poems and in other stories over the years, but strangely, *neither my dad nor my brother remembers it.*

Am I making this whole memory up? It's possible. I remember this night being the last time Dan lived with us. Dan says he remembers a grocery bag of clothes, but he thinks his final exit happened a few months later.

He says he didn't get any special warning. He came home from school, and my mom told him to get in the car. She had packed his things in a couple of boxes in the trunk, and there was a grocery bag of his clothes in the back seat.

"I'm done putting up with your crap, Dan. I've had enough."

He had no idea where they were going.

"Your father can deal with you now full-time, because I'm done with you. And I mean it this time."

"Where are we going?" Dan asked dully from the backseat.

"Oh, you'll see soon enough."

Dan smirked at her.

"You think it's funny?"

My mom raised her eyebrows at him in the rearview mirror.

"You and your saintly father won't be laughing in a few minutes."

Dan says she just kept talking about how cheap my dad was, and that she couldn't afford to feed all of us. I know she was having a hard time making ends meet during this period. She started buying powdered milk, and we ate from huge blocks of government cheese. Could we have been on food stamps? I have no idea. Years later my mom told me Bernie paid for our groceries and kept our family afloat for almost a year. My dad says he paid her what the court told him to pay. I suspect they were both telling the truth.

"Your goddamn father," my mom said to Dan in the rearview mirror. "What's he think? I can use air to pay the bills? I can use pixie dust to buy food for you guys? Well, starting today he'll see how much it costs to feed a teenager."

She pulled into the highway department parking lot.

"Grab the bag," she told him.

She steered Dan by the back of the neck to the reception desk.

"Can I help you?"

"Please let Sam Bernick know he has visitors. Go sit down, Dan."

"Certainly," the receptionist said. "Can I tell him who . . . ?"

"Just get him out here right now."

"Well . . . ummm . . . just a minute, please."

By this point, my dad was a manager at the highway department. It was the middle of a workday, and he says he got a call back in engineering that someone was here to see him. He was surprised to see my mom waiting for him at the reception desk.

"Arlene, what is it? I'm in the middle of a meeting."

My mom pointed to Dan, who was hunched silently in one of the orange plastic molded chairs against the wall. His paper bag of clothes was sitting on the chair next to him.

"Dan, what are you doing here?"

"He's yours now, Sam. I can't deal with him anymore."

"Arlene, it's the middle of a workday. I'm in a meeting. I can't talk about this right now."

"That's your problem. I've had it with him. You deal with him now."

The receptionist was staring at them.

"Have you lost your mind? I can't deal with him right now. I'm working! Take him home and I'll call you later."

"No, Sam. I'm not taking him anywhere. He's your son. He's your responsibility as much as mine. I don't want him anymore. That's it. I'm done with him!"

My dad looked at the receptionist and stepped closer to my mom, lowering his voice.

"Arlene, he cannot just sit here in my office. I'm in the middle of a very important meeting right now. Please take him home, and I'll come and get him when the meeting is over. OK?"

"No, Sam. That's not OK. Maybe now you'll know how I feel taking care of your children all day long without any help."

"Arlene! Please!"

"Good luck, Sam. Have fun with your son. You son of a bitch."

"Goddamn you, Arlene."

My mom left without even looking back. If she had, she would have seen my dad throw up his hands and stalk back to his meeting while Dan sat frozen like a statue in the orange plastic chair next to his clothes. He didn't move a muscle. Not even a twitch. Even his mouth stayed frozen in a smirk. The only sign that he was alive were the hot, white tears beginning to slip down his cheeks.

—ɯ—

ABANDON (VERB)

CEASE TO SUPPORT OR LOOK after (someone); desert.

Synonyms: leave, leave high and dry, turn one's back on, cast aside, break with, give up, indulge, surrender, yield, renounce, relinquish, dispense with, disclaim, forgo, disown, disavow, discard, wash one's hands of, forsake, maroon, quit, strand, ditch, dump, fling, jettison, junk, scrap, shed, shuck, throw away, throw out; hand over, surrender, escape, take off, vacate, withdraw; abjure, cut off, reject, renounce, repudiate, separate (from); sacrifice; distance; disregard, forget, ignore, neglect, cancel, abort, call, call off, cry off, drop, recall, repeal, rescind, revoke, scrap, scrub, abrogate, annul, invalidate, nullify, void, write off; recant, retract, take back, withdraw; countermand, reverse, roll back; break off, discontinue, end, halt, stop, terminate; hold back, interrupt, suspend; give up, stop doing, knock off, lay off (of), pack (up or in), cease, close, conclude, end, expire, finish, halt, leave off, shut off; pause, taper off; throw up; round (off or out), terminate, wind up, wrap up, abjure, abnegate, bag it, bail out, cede, remit, drop, forgo, leave, leave high and dry, leave holding the bag, leave in the lurch, opt out, quit, quit claim, resign, retire, sell out, step down, vacate, waive withdraw, yield, accede, admit, back off, back down, back off, back out, back pedal, backtrack, balk, beg off, bow out, cave in, chicken out, concede, cop out, demur, give ground, give in, go back on, have no fight left, hold back, pull back, pull out, recent, recoil, renege, resign, retreat, submit, take back, wimp out, withdraw, betray, be unfaithful, bite the hand that feeds you, break faith, break promise, break trust, break with, commit treason, cross, deceive, deliver up, delude, desert, double-cross, fine, forsake, go back on, inform against, jilt, knife, let down, mislead, play Judas, play false, seduce, sell down the river, sell out, stab in the back, trick, walk out on, cut, discontinue, interrupt, pause, rest, suspend, cancel, desist, drop, kill, postpone, scrub, withdraw, can, cast, eighty-six, eject, fire, fling, flip, forsake, give the heave ho, heave, hurl, launch, pitch, quit, reject, renounce, scrap, shed, shy, divorce oneself from, disavow, discard, sling, slough, toss, belittle, negate, minimize, disclaim, contradict, disaffirm, disallow, disown, disparage, forswear, gainsay, minimize, negate, recant, refuse, reject, renounce, repudiate, retract, revoke, spurn, traverse, turn back on, wash hands of, drop, throw overboard, bring down, topple, slump, cease, give notice, jettison

ABANDON (NOUN)

COMPLETE LACK OF INHIBITION OR restraint.

Synonyms: uninhibitedness, recklessness, lack of restraint, lack of inhibition, wildness, impulsiveness, impetuosity, immoderation, wantonness, carefree, freedom from constraint, added spices to the stew, with complete abandon, abandonment, ease, lightheartedness, naturalness, unconstraint, unrestraint, ardor, enthusiasm, exuberance, fervor, spirit, warmth, zeal, zealotry, zealousness; carelessness, heedlessness, impulsivity, indiscretion, insouciance, recklessness, thoughtlessness; unselfconsciousness, casualness, offhandedness; excess, excessiveness, immoderacy, incontinence, indulgence, intemperance, licentiousness, permissiveness, wantonness, wildness; blank check, carte blanche, free hand, energy, animation, bounce, buoyancy, cheerfulness, eagerness, ebullience, effervescence, exhilaration, fervor, friskiness, gayness, get up and go, high spirits, juice, life, liveliness, pep, pepper, spirit, sprightliness, vigor, vitality, sap, zest, zip, flexibility, full play, free rein, full swing, laissez faire, latitude, laxity, leeway, liberty, opportunity, own accord, play, plenty of rope, power, prerogative, privilege, profligacy, boldness, brazenness, candor, directness, ease, impertinence, license, spontaneity

—𝔪—

MUTATION AND ADAPTATION

AN ADAPTATION IS A MUTATION, or genetic change, that helps an organism, such as a plant or animal, survive in its environment. Due to the helpful nature of the mutation, it is passed down from one generation to the next. As more and more organisms inherit the mutation, the mutation becomes a typical part of the species. The mutation has become an adaptation. An adaptation can be structural, meaning it is a physical part of the organism. An adaptation can also be behavioral, affecting the way an organism acts. Adaptations usually develop in response to a change in the organism's habitat.

—https://newsela.com/read/natgeo-elem-adaptation/id/44438/

LOOKING FOR THE EXITS

IN THE *MEDIUM* ARTICLE "Jewish Trauma May Be Passed Down Through the Generations," writer Gila Lyons discusses the possibility that Jews have a genetic predisposition toward sensing danger and are always looking for the exits. Like me, Lyons wonders, "Is there some inherited resilience, or compulsion to keep surviving and thriving?"

Thriving didn't seem to be my mom's strong suit, but she certainly had a compulsion to survive. And she was always looking for the exits. Literally and figuratively. Whenever we entered an auditorium or an unfamiliar room, she immediately looked around for the escape routes.

"You never know when you're going to have to get out in a hurry," she'd say, gesturing to the exit signs.

Although I found most of my mom's advice irritating, stupid, or dead wrong, she nailed this one. Everyone needs an exit strategy, and my mom had a zillion of them. Exiting was her superpower. When things became untenable, she ran away. Sometimes she brought us along, but many times she didn't. She was a serial abandoner. I think she believed her unhappiness and unrealized dreams were a function of location. It was part of her confused locus of control. She was convinced that starting over in a new place would magically make everything better.

In the spring of 1973, about a year after my parent's divorce became final, my mom decided to move us to California. At the time, I had no idea why. It's not like she discussed it with us. We were minor characters in her new story line. She announced we were moving and petitioned the court for permission to move us out of state. I was twelve, Lori was about to turn eight, and David was almost five.

Since Dan was almost fifteen and living with my dad, the court decided he was old enough to choose whether to stay with my dad or leave with my mom. It was no surprise which parent he chose. I didn't get a choice, legal or otherwise. During the court hearing, my dad asked the court to reduce his child support payments so he could afford to fly us back to Minnesota "several times a year" (which didn't happen). The court agreed to his terms, and my mom was free to go. Free to run away with even less money and three kids to support. I suppose she considered that a victory, of sorts.

She moved us to La Habra, California, a town thirty miles southeast of Los Angeles. It had forty thousand residents and the nickname "Guadalahabra" for its growing Mexican American population. It was part of suburban Orange County and undergoing the same migration patterns as the rest of the country: upper- and middle-class Whites moving out of the urban core and into the suburbs. Orange County was also experiencing a large influx of mostly White Christian newcomers from the southern and midwestern United States, many of them from Minnesota. These new Golden State residents were attracted by Orange County's unique gospel of righteous self-empowerment and prosperity.

Unlike Los Angeles, which had one of the country's largest Jewish populations outside of New York City, Orange County had relatively few Jews at the time. It was a hotbed of conservatism, with one of the country's most active member- ships in the ultra-right-wing John Birch Society and a national reputation for racism and antisemitism.

I'm not sure how much my mom knew about Orange County before she moved there. My Aunt Berta, my mom's younger sister, had been living in Cali- fornia since 1966. She says my mom didn't discuss her move to La Habra with her, my Grandma Goldie, Aunt Freda, or any of the other relatives who had moved to Los Angeles several years before. The move was kept under wraps until it actually happened.

According to my aunt, there was a Jewish dentist in Orange County with a Twin Cities connection who needed a dental hygienist. It makes sense that my mom would have lined up work before she moved; she was living on fumes at this point. And given her prickly family relationships, she wouldn't have wanted to live too close to her California relations. The move to La Habra probably came down to the job location and what she could afford.

We ended up in a generic housing development, a ubiquitous feature of Or- ange County then and now. As a Minnesotan, my mom was undoubtedly wowed by the development's kidney-shaped swimming pool and the shiny avocado tree in our concrete backyard, perks that came with our monthly Association dues. I don't remember much about the move or our first couple of weeks in California. Maybe I felt a certain sense of excitement and adventure. I'm sure I was happy that Bernie wasn't around; he was the slimiest of slime balls, and it wasn't just because of his slicked-back hair. Maybe we had two weeks of paradise in our new California home. Maybe it felt like a new beginning. Maybe my mom was happy. Maybe I was too.

I don't remember any of that.

What I do remember is Bernie showing up at our door with four large suit-cases two weeks after we moved to California (he left his wife and kids behind). I suppose this was the plan all along: send my mom ahead to get us settled, and then have him join us. But once he showed up at our door, settling in California was not an option for me. I soon discovered that Bernie was an even bigger creep than I imagined, and it wasn't long before I, too, started looking for the exits.

—ɯ—

SNOW BUNNY GETS LOST IN LA LA LAND

Lost really has two disparate meanings. Losing things is about the familiar falling away, getting lost is about the unfamiliar appearing.

—Rebecca Solnit, *A Field Guide to Getting Lost*

WHERE THE HELL WAS I?

I was looking for the band room, but I was completely lost in a maze of hallways filled with lockers, and I really had to pee.

Shit!

I set my clarinet down and pulled out my ninth-grade winter schedule. Why did I let my mom talk me into taking band this quarter?

Crap! Dammit! Shit!

Now I knew why my mom swore so much . . . it felt good.

I spotted a group of eleventh-graders coming toward me down the hall, and I pretended to be opening my locker until they passed. Dan was an eleventh-grader, but here in California they looked different. Especially the girls. Eleventh-grade California girls looked very . . . *mature.*

I focused on my schedule. Band was in C4 R16. I picked up my clarinet and walked along the hallway until I found a room number. C3 R23. I was such a spazz! Where the hell was I?

I spotted a Boys bathroom sign at the end of the hallway. The faceless figure on the door was wearing pants, and someone had drawn a long black snake coming out of the front of them. I looked around for the Girls bathroom. At least I could pee before I had to be a total doofus and ask someone where the band room was.

I turned the corner and saw the *Girls* bathroom sign. This faceless figure was wearing a dress that someone painted red, white, and green. Christmas colors, I thought, as I pushed open the door . . . and immediately wished I hadn't. Four tough-looking brown-skinned girls standing at the sinks swung around and glared at me. They were obviously not expecting company.

"Hey! What the hell?"

A girl with slashes of bright blue eye shadow and thick eyeliner took a step toward me.

"What the fuck are *you* doin' in here?"

"Uh . . . nothing," I said, backing up. "Sorry."

I turned to go.

"Wait!"

A girl who was shorter than the others waved me over. She had giant silver hoop earrings and was wearing a brown beret with a bright orange eagle patch on the front of it. The eagle had some kind of animal dangling from its beak.

"Come here."

Eagle Girl gestured to one of the stalls with her thumb.

"Go ahead and use it."

She looked at me with sleepy, dangerous eyes, and I knew I should run like hell right now.

"Uh . . . that's OK."

"*I said use it.*"

Eagle Girl held out her hand.

"We'll hold your stuff."

The other girls laughed and exchanged knowing glances as I swallowed hard. I felt just like that dangling animal on her patch.

"Thank you," I said, feeling even more like a scared dork, as I walked over with my books and clarinet.

"Give 'em to 'Pita."

Eagle Girl pointed to a girl wearing a tight pink tube top that barely covered her enormous breasts. I handed her my books and held out the clarinet. The girl grunted when she took it.

"What the hell is in here?"

"A clarinet."

I'm such a dork, I thought, as I turned and walked to the nearest stall with my head down. I locked the door behind me and immediately saw there was no toilet paper. *Dammit!* There was no way I was going back out there to find toilet paper. I pulled down my shorts, and there was complete silence in the bathroom except for the sound of me peeing.

I thought about the girls waiting out there. I'd seen them fighting in the lunch room. They hitchhiked after school with their thumbs out and called out to the cars in Spanish. They elbowed people in the hallway and dumped your lunch tray on the floor if you accidentally sat at a table you didn't know was theirs. I stared at the graffiti on the back of the stall door. There was a skull smoking a cigarette and a red, white, and green fist with chains wrapped around it.

I was in deep shit.

When I finished peeing, I did my best to drip dry. On top of everything else, I was going to have to walk around with wet pee underwear for the rest of the day.

Dammit!

I was about to stand up when a stubby hand with peeling red fingernail polish poked under the door holding a wad of toilet paper.

"Take it."

I reached out and took the toilet paper.

"Thank you."

I flushed the toilet and stood there for a moment behind the locked stall door. The whoosh of the flush ended, and there was silence.

This could be very bad.

I took a deep breath, unlocked the door, and walked out. All four girls were staring at me. It was like they'd paid their admission, and they were waiting for the show to begin.

"So . . . ," Eagle Girl said. "Do you know who we are?"

She gestured to herself and tipped her head back to indicate the rest of them.

"Yes," I said.

Eagle Girl nodded with the tip of her tongue showing.

My mouth was dry, and I cleared my throat.

"You're eleventh-graders."

The four girls stared at me for a moment, and then all of them cracked up, with Eagle Girl laughing the loudest.

"Oh, *chiquitita! ¡Que bueno!*"

She laughed again and shook her head. When she stopped laughing, the others stopped too.

"We are *Chicanas. Chee-CAH-nas!*"

She strolled over to me and stood very close. We were about the same height, so I was looking straight into her eyes.

"*Chicanas.* Say it."

"*Chicanas.*"

I said it with exactly the same accent she did.

Eagle Girl raised an eyebrow.

"Good."

She sauntered back to her friends.

"Where are you from?"

"Minnesota."

"Where?"

They all looked puzzled. I felt like such a dweeb.

"Minne*soda*. It's near Canada. It's . . . really cold. With lots of snow."

"Ohhhhhhhh," Eagle Girl said and nodded. "You are very far from home. Like a little . . . bunny. A little white snow bunny."

She chuckled, and all the other girls laughed.

"Well, Snow Bunny, you came to a very bad place. We eat bunnies here."

I swallowed. They had my stuff. If I ran, I'd have to leave my clarinet behind. I looked at the girl who was holding my books. She grinned and drummed her peeling red fingernails on top of my math book and nudged the instrument case with her toe. Standing next to her was another girl with a big silver cross hanging around her neck that glinted in the fluorescent lights. She pulled a cigarette out of her purse.

"This is *our* bathroom," Eagle Girl said, coming close to me again. "*We* own it. *Nobody* uses it but us."

I nodded.

"I promise I won't *ever* use it again."

"I know you won't," Eagle Girl said, and smiled. "But you used it today."

She raised an eyebrow.

"So now you must pay us."

She held her upturned hand directly in front of my nose and wiggled her fingers.

My heart started racing.

"Uh . . . I don't have any money with me today," I stammered. "But I can bring some tomorrow . . ."

"No!" Eagle Girl snapped her fingers. "Now!"

My heart was leaping in my chest, and I knew that something very bad was going to happen.

"No money, no stuff."

Eagle Girl shook her head.

"Or . . ."—she looked around at the other girls—"maybe we'll find a different way for you to pay."

All the girls laughed.

My cheeks were burning. Out of the corner of my eye, I saw the flash of a flame as the girl with the silver cross lit the cigarette. Eagle Girl stepped closer, and I smelled sweat. I couldn't tell if it was mine or hers. What were they going to do to me?

A second later I smelled something else. The sweet burnt smell of marijuana. I'd never smoked it, but I knew what it was. It reminded me of Dan. And home.

"Hmmmm . . . ," I said and inhaled deeply without even knowing it.

I did the same thing every time I smelled that smell. And I smelled it a lot in California. Down near the gym lockers. Outside in the courtyard on the way to English. After school walking home near the fence. Every time I smelled it, I inhaled and made the same wish. *Oh God, I wish I was back in New Hope with Dan, and my friends, and my dad. Anywhere but here . . .*

"You smoke?" Eagle Girl said, surprised.

I saw an opportunity.

"Yeah," I lied.

Eagle Girl raised her eyebrows and exchanged a look with the other girls.

"Maybe this snow bunny isn't so White as she looks."

"Here," Eagle Girl held out her hand to the girl with the cigarette. "*Andale*, Tonietta."

She snapped her fingers, and Tonietta handed her the cigarette. I now saw it was actually a different kind of cigarette.

"Dis shit's from *Oaxaca*," Eagle Girl said. "*Muy bueno*."

She held the cigarette to her lips, sucked on it and breathed in deeply.

"*Muy fuerte*," she said in a strangled voice, and then held it out to me.

I took it from her and brought it to my lips exactly as she did. I thought of Dan and the burnt smell. He smoked this. I sucked deeply on the cigarette, just like Eagle Girl, and I immediately felt a powerful, searing bullet of smoke reach down my throat and explode in my lungs. I doubled over and started coughing as all the girls stood around laughing.

"I warned you, Snow Bunny," Eagle Girl said, laughing and exhaling smoke into the bathroom. "Good strong shit from *Mexico*!"

They all kept laughing as I coughed and coughed. When I finally regained my composure, the other girls were passing around the cigarette. After a moment, Eagle Girl nodded at the girl holding my stuff. She handed me the books and slid the clarinet case forward. I bent down and picked it up.

"Snow Bunny," Eagle Girl said, with that sleepy, dangerous look in her eyes, "you are very smart or very stupid."

She pushed me back a step.

"But now you should hop away, and don't ever come in here again."

She shoved me hard toward the door, and I pulled it open and ran.

After school, my throat raw and still feeling a little light-headed from that hit of pot, I walked down the sidewalk past a group of brown girls huddled near the fence. They were speaking Spanish, and I felt an urge to run, but I kept my head down and gripped my clarinet tighter. They didn't even look at me. Out of the corner of my eye, I saw they all had skulls and Mexican flag stickers on their backpacks.

I couldn't tell if they were the same girls from the bathroom. There were a lot of Mexican girls at school . . . no . . . I mentally corrected myself. *Chee-CAH-nas*.

At the end of the fence, I turned left on the sidewalk that bordered the busy four-lane highway leading to my subdivision. Across the street, there was a girl hitchhiking in the opposite direction. She had long blonde hair, jean shorts, and tall red cowboy boots. Cool boots, I thought, admiring their shiny black heels and the way they came to a sharp point in front.

As I pulled even with her, a blue pickup truck honked and pulled over. She ran to it, climbed in, and the pickup pulled out into traffic and the girl was gone. Like she'd never been there at all.

I watched the truck until it was out of sight. That looked so easy. Just jump in and whooooosssssh . . . you magically disappeared. If only I could hop into somebody's truck and magically disappear all the way back to Minnesota.

Minnesota.

All I wanted was to go back to my friends, teachers, and, yes, even my neglectful dad and stoned brother. My dad had remarried during the previous winter, and he and his new wife had bought out my mom and moved into our old house in New Hope. I wanted to be back in my old room, in my old neighborhood. Mostly I wanted to be away from Bernie.

I calculated the two-hour time difference. Dan was probably playing hockey on Northwood Pond this very minute.

Oh . . . to be skating on Northwood Pond.

There was an ache in the back of my throat as I imagined myself gliding over the ice under the early stars. Orion still low and barely visible. Nothing but cold silence and the crunch of my skate blades moving faster and faster through the dark.

I walked down Palm Drive until I reached Rushton Lane. Even after all this time, I still had to look at the street sign to make sure it was the right turnoff. All the houses looked the same here. Brown shingles on top of brown and tan houses. Every house was painted the same two colors, and each had a shiny lemon tree or avocado tree in the front yard with white rocks and aloe plants underneath. It all looked fake. Especially in December with Christmas decorations. Why would anyone put snowmen, icicles, and reindeer in their yard when it was 80 degrees out?

The house across the street from ours had a life-sized nativity scene out front. It reminded me of the Millers', except the Millers' camel and sheep were kneeling in snow, and here they were kneeling in white rocks. The underground sprinklers were on, and the three wise men were getting soaked. I wondered if The Association had okayed that nativity scene. My mom had already had some run-ins with The Association. She'd put a *mezuzah* on the front door frame, and The Association said it was an "exterior modification" and threatened to charge her $500 if she didn't take it down.

I walked up our driveway and kicked a stone at Bernie's car. It hit one of his tires and left a white mark. Score!

Bernie was bad news with a capital BS. For "bullshit" and "Bernie Silverman." I thought about the girl hitchhiking in those cool, pointy red cowboy boots. Nobody would mess with you if you had boots like that. You could walk into any bathroom you goddamn wanted. And you could protect yourself from a creep like Bernie Silverman.

BAD WITH A CAPITAL BS

I'M GUESSING MY MOM IMAGINED a different story line for herself in California—one that included some approximation of happiness. But every day after school, I opened the door and heard her same old fury spilling down the stairs from the bedroom. She and Bernie fought constantly, mostly about when he was going to marry her.

"Hang in there just a little bit longer, Dollface. Don't slow down before the finish line."

"Goddamn it, Bernie! Stop saying that! Why do we have to wait if the divorce is final?"

"I told you. We can't get married until I get her name off everything!"

The thought of my mom marrying Bernie made me want to vomit. There was no way I was sticking around if she married him. I walked into the kitchen and slammed my math book onto the counter.

"No goddamn way!"

David gave me a disapproving look.

"No saying bad words, Elisa."

Lori and David were at the dining room table with crayons spread out between them as *Love American Style* blared in the background. They both had blonde hair and tans. Perfect California children. Lori had a sheet of homework in front of her: a cat wearing a spacesuit surrounded by a whole page of floating clocks.

"I'm supposed to change the hands to fifteen minutes later, and color the clocks that are noon and midnight." Lori said. "And guess what?"

"What?"

"Melissa Hardeen invited me to swim at her pool tomorrow."

Oh great. My third-grade sister has more friends than I do.

"And Bernie says it's OK."

"Who cares what Bernie says. He's not our dad."

"Bernie is my California Dad, and Dad is my Minnesota Dad."

"We only have one dad, Lori!"

I glared at her, but she just shrugged and went back to her clocks.

A few minutes later my mom stomped into the kitchen.

"Set the table, Elisa. We're eating early tonight."

"Why?"

"Because I said so, that's why. And Lori, you and David pick up all those crayons."

"I'm doing homework."

"You can finish after dinner. Don't argue with me! Why is everybody always arguing with me? What are you watching? Turn off that TV right now!"

"Jeez, Mom," I walked into the kitchen for silverware. "Don't take it out on Lori. It's not her fault you and Bernie were fighting again like two-year-olds."

My mom turned from the stove and held up her finger.

"You better watch your mouth, Elisa. I mean it."

When my mom turned away, I caught Lori's eye, held up my finger and mouthed, "I mean it."

Lori laughed.

A minute later Bernie stalked into the room. He went over to the TV and changed the channel.

"The drawdown of US military personnel in Vietnam continues . . ."

"Goddamn Nixon should be hitting those damn Gooks . . ."

"Bernie," my mom said. "Turn that off."

"Mom?" I asked. "Can I get some cowboy boots?"

I saw that girl with the red cowboy boots in the lunchroom today. Not even the *Chicanas* messed with her.

My mom was reading the back of the Hamburger Helper package.

"Cowboy boots? Don't be ridiculous."

"The only people who wear cowboy boots are dirty Mexican beaners and ignorant shit kickers," Bernie said. "Hey, I got a new one. What do you call a Mexican with a broken lawnmower?"

I ignored him.

"Unemployed."

Bernie's laugh boomed through the dining room, and my mom rolled her eyes.

"Mom, please? There's this girl at school who has red cowboy boots, and I really want some! Please!"

"You want cowboy boots?" my mom smirked at Bernie. "Ask your father for the money."

"That's right," Bernie said. "Tell him it's an early Hanukkah present. I'm sure he'll run right out and buy you some."

He snorted, and they shared a derisive chuckle. My mom and Bernie constantly harped on how cheap my dad was. It seemed to be the only thing they agreed on.

"Fine," I said, and dropped the silverware on the table in a clatter.

"I'll call him right now and ask him."

My mom rolled her eyes.

"Ask him on Sunday when he calls."

"No, I'm going to call him right now!"

"Stop being ridiculous, and set the table."

"Goddamn it, Mom! I want to call Dad!"

"Hey!" Bernie walked over to me and shook his finger in my face. "What did I tell you about swearing?"

I stood at the table with my heart hammering in my chest.

"Huh?"

He moved his finger, so it was barely an inch away from my face. I wished I had the guts to bite it.

"If I hear one more swear word come out of your mouth, I will personally take you over to the sink and wash it out with soap. Do you understand me?"

I didn't say anything.

"I said . . ."

Bernie slammed his fist down on the table. Lori jumped, and David covered his head as the silverware rattled, and some of the crayons rolled off onto the floor.

"Do you understand me?"

I kept my head down. Bernie was standing so close I could smell the gum in his mouth.

"Yes."

"Good."

He bent down to pick up the crayons on the floor.

"Here you go, Lori," he put them back on the table. "I like your clocks. What color are you going to make this one?"

He pointed to her paper.

I left the silverware on the table and walked out of the room. My mom followed.

"Where are you going?"

"I'm calling Dad."

I started climbing the stairs.

"And I don't give a shit what you think."

"Elisa! Enough with the swearing already."

She lowered her voice and raised an eyebrow.

"You heard what Bernie said."

"I don't give a shit what Bernie said!"

I glared down at her. Neither of us moved for a moment.

"Fine." She started walking back to the kitchen. "Do whatever the hell you want. Call your father."

I started up the stairs.

"But make sure you call collect!"

I don't remember if I called my dad that afternoon. I'm sure I wanted to, but calling collect was a big deal back then because long-distance phone calls were so expensive. Adjusted for inflation, a ten-minute direct-dialed Sunday phone call from New Hope to California cost twenty-five dollars. Operator-assisted collect calls and nonweekend calls were even more expensive, so my dad and I talked only once a week on Sundays when he called, and they always ended with me pleading with him to bring me home.

"Elisa, if it were up to me, you could stay with me. But the court says you have to be with your mother."

"But what does the court know?" I asked. "And why does Dan get to stay there?"

"We've been over this a lot already. He was old enough to decide, but you weren't. The court thought you'd be better off with Mom."

"The court doesn't know Mom!" I yelled into the phone. "The court doesn't know me!"

My dad sighed his familiar sigh.

"Elisa . . . you have to tough this out and make the best of a bad situation. Just for the rest of the school year, and then I'll bring all of you home for the whole summer."

"But why can't we visit before then?"

"Airplane tickets are really expensive."

"I don't want to stay here. Bernie's a creep!"

Usually, my mom picked up the downstairs extension to end the call.

"Elisa, get off the phone. Bernie needs to use it."

Silence.

"Say goodbye to your dad and hang up."

My dad and I waited until she clicked off.

"Elisa, it's gonna be OK. Let's talk about this next week."

"Dad . . ."

"And California! Wow! Palm trees! We've already got a foot of snow here, and you get to wear your swimsuit!"

He brought up the weather every time we talked.

"And you have to help with Lori and David, remember? You're their big sister. They need you."

"I know."

"Listen, I gotta go. This is getting expensive. I'll call you next weekend, OK?"

"OK," my voice wavered.

"Bye, Elisa."

"Bye, Dad."

A REAL NIGHTMARE

THAT NIGHT, I COULDN'T SLEEP. Everything felt one hundred percent wrong. Everything. And how would any of it ever be right?

I thrashed around and woke up panting and hot from a terrible dream. I was being chased through an icy landscape, and I couldn't get my footing. I kept slipping and falling, looking for something to hang onto, and something behind me was getting closer . . .

"No!"

I looked at the clock. It was 11:30.

I threw off the covers and pulled up my nightgown to get some air. I lay there in the dim wedge of light coming through the doorway, feeling hot and disoriented. I could hear my heart pounding over the quiet whoosh of cool air pushing through the floor vents. I tried to calm myself by imagining that I was flying high above the clouds. That's what I did on nights I couldn't sleep. I conjured up a constellation-filled sky and pretended that I was winging my way through the darkness . . .

And then I heard a noise outside my door. My eyes flew open and I lay motionless, my heartbeat galloping in my temples. I'd heard this sound before, late at night. Nights with other terrible nightmares. It was a small, quiet noise that scared me to death. I heard it again. The quiet snap of Bernie's gum as he stood outside my door, looking in.

REMEMBERING AND FORGETTING

THERE'S AN INTERESTING LINK BETWEEN the way humans think about the past and the way they think about the future: The same region of the brain is activated when we're asked to *remember* something as when we're asked to *imagine* an event that hasn't happened yet.

"The future is never a direct replica of the past," says psychology professor Jonathan Adler. "So, we need to be able to take pieces of things that have happened to us and reconfigure them into possible futures."

Our memories become the stories we tell ourselves about the future.

What if I told you I don't know if Bernie sexually abused me? I remember him at the door, in my room, and near my bed. And that's it. Until I started writing this book, I had rarely thought about him or even considered this possibility. When I asked Lori if Bernie ever sexually abused her, all she remembered is never wanting to be left alone in the house with him. On nights our mom was gone, she had friends sleep over or she climbed out her window. Like me, she didn't remember if any abuse took place, and like me, she hadn't given it much thought.

Neither of us felt we were hiding or repressing these memories. Maybe nothing happened. Maybe something did, and we both "forgot" it. Either way, we seem to have largely written Bernie out of our story.

Does this seem shocking? Unbelievable?

Maybe. Maybe not.

"For better or worse, stories are a very powerful source of self-persuasion," says psychology professor John Holmes. "Storytelling isn't just how we construct our identities, stories *are* our identities. Evidence that doesn't fit the story is going to be left behind."

The idea that we "disappear" evidence that doesn't fit a particular story is an empowering thought. Not only do we unconsciously edit, revise, and invent plot points in our personal narratives, we can *intentionally* do this by remembering things differently or not at all.

In a 2014 TED Talk, author Judith Claybourne describes the negative self-image she'd constructed based on what she thought were "factual" childhood memories that turned out not to be true. As an adult, she decided to intentionally change the stories of her upbringing to create more positive memories and forge a different identity for herself in the present day.

"Every time we remember something, we alter it, so why not go in and change memories yourself?" asks Claybourne. "The unconscious mind accepts what we do and what we think now as real. The stories we tell ourselves about ourselves create who we are."

This is a powerful notion with enormous potential for freeing us from prisons constructed by stories of traumatic events. Not only does the human brain unconsciously remember what never happened, it can be intentionally trained to forget what really did. Forgetting is a protective device, a survival mechanism. Although we may not be aware of it, we are continually burying or reinventing stories of our worst moments. Our identities are created by the stories we tell ourselves—what we include and what we leave out. The provocative idea here is deciding to reinvent specific memories by remembering them differently, *by telling different stories of the past, and by telling stories of the past differently.*

It has taken me years to decide which stories to tell and which to forget—and to understand that I have a choice. For a long time, I only told stories bounded by my own fury and helplessness. The telling of them was a chance to tongue the wounds of my childhood over and over, to constantly reprise my sense of victimhood and powerlessness.

The stories I've included here are carefully curated and set within a specific context. They are not simply a recitation of painful events, but rather tales that serve a larger purpose. Although it may not yet be obvious, inside these stories I am the hero of my own traumatic memories. What you are reading is the conscious reinterpretation of my past and future—and of my mother's as well.

Each of us inhabits a life filled with traumas large and small; some of them we know about and some we don't. Some of them we experience personally, and some of them are passed along through our genes and collective histories. But we can decide which of these stories we are going to tell and how to tell them.

We can adapt our stories to an environment that continuously presents us with opportunities for reinvention as our self-knowledge, culture, vocabulary, and expectations change.

I'm not suggesting we all start whistling a happy tune and forget the catastrophes of our lives. Individual and collective traumas and tragedies are the binding force that defines our historical memory and individual identities. Rather, I'm suggesting we examine the role that memory plays in our lives and how we put memories to use.

So many of our individual and collective pasts are stories of abandonment, abuse, enslavement, victimization, and suffering. The question is, What benefit do these stories have for our own lives and the futures of our children and our communities? Does honoring our pain require us to eternally tell only the worst parts of our stories? Does the continual retelling of them continue to enslave us? Does reliving and defining ourselves solely through past trauma "honor" a tragic experience, or does it limit our power and agency to shape and be shaped by a different, larger story?

By now you have a pretty good sense of my mother. Do you think I've included all the "worst" stories in this book? Hardly. And what of Bernie? Did I bury memories of his abuse? If so, I'm grateful. Writing this book has helped me understand how selective our memories are—neither memory nor meaning depends on history. In every culture and life, some catastrophes are remembered, and others are forgotten. Before COVID-19, how many tragic stories of previous pandemics did your family tell? The flu pandemic of 1918 killed twenty million to fifty million people; there were more than ten thousand deaths in Minnesota. Why aren't memories of this catastrophe a bigger part of our collective trauma?

History is nothing but a record of selective remembering and forgetting.

So, what if we curate our memories to select for a different future? What if we intentionally "remember" stories that emphasize resilience rather than victimization? What if we tell our stories using words like *determination* rather than *despair*? *Reinvention* rather than *resignation*? *Transformation* rather than *capitulation*? Why run away when we can free ourselves? Liberation tells a different story than lying low.

The words we use matter, and the vocabulary of possible futures is enormous.

There is debate in the field of trauma recovery about whether revisiting traumatic memories is necessary for healing, or whether it may in fact be harmful.

Mental health professional Nkem Ndefo, whose father was a Nigerian immigrant and mother an Ashkenazi Jew, believes there's a difference between healthy and unhealthy storytelling.

She doesn't advocate the wholesale jettisoning of historical memory and experience, but she does see the potential of creating a personal narrative where the story of your identity is larger than only your past oppression and suffering.

"There are places we need to fight," says Ndefo. "There's struggle, there's work, and there's fight. But if we're always in that state, the ideas that we generate will be fight ideas. They'll be struggle ideas. I don't want to live in a world with the DNA of fight and struggle. I want some of the visioning to happen from a settled, connected, and peaceful place."

This idea of choosing to tell stories from a "peaceful place" feels revolutionary in a world where rage and hate are go-to choices on the slim menu of appropriate responses to past wrongs. It suggests that there are alternative ways to respond to both individual and historical trauma, a menu with a broader range of options that can help you tell your story differently. The stories in this book are told from a peaceful place. If that surprises you, you haven't yet finished reading my tale.

The way we remember and tell trauma stories varies widely across people and cultures, as do the ways that communities and individuals interpret and respond to these narratives over time.

Jews, for example, have a highly ritualized method of remembering trauma. We memorialize it in stories and holidays where we feast, fast, atone, admonish, and collectively mourn. For psychiatry and neuroscience professor Rachel Yehuda, what's interesting about this is that "these days occur on a specified time on the calendar. They start at a certain time. They end at a certain time, and then so too the effects end."

Having a ritualized way to control the long-term effects of trauma makes practical sense for a population that has endured so much of it. It makes it possible to remember and honor trauma without continually reliving it. (You may have heard the old Jewish joke that the theme of most Jewish holidays is "They tried to kill us, G-d helped, we survived; let's eat!")

Trauma stories can be a source of both distress and resilience. You can intentionally tell the story of being wounded as a tale of survival. For traumatized individuals, and perhaps even for traumatized cultures, intentionally reinventing the narratives of the past might be a way to reclaim memories that can help in healing from historical trauma. This is not a magic cure for overcoming the effects of genocide, but it *is* an opportunity to recognize the power that stories have to shape our identities.

"I cannot shake the belief that the ways in which we tell the story of our reality shapes that reality: the manner of telling makes the world," says David Treuer in his book *The Heartbeat of Wounded Knee*. "And I worry that if we tell the story of the past as a tragedy, we consign ourselves to a tragic future."

Treuer grew up on the Leech Lake Reservation in northern Minnesota with an Ojibwa mother and a Jewish father. He questions the power of historical trauma and what he calls "blood memory" to determine the life and legacy of an individual or a culture. He wonders why some catastrophic events create lasting trauma that determine our trajectories while others seemingly don't. He points to his father, who was a Holocaust survivor.

"He experienced so much more trauma than I can even imagine, losing his entire family, losing his homeland, his language and culture, fleeing for his life.... He was marked by trauma, but it did not determine the shape of his life."

Before I wrote this book, it was almost impossible for me to consider telling a story of my mother that was larger than her abuse and abandonment. It felt too much like letting her off the hook.

You may be thinking, "Wait a minute. Almost all of these stories are about abuse and abandonment!" I'll concede that—up to a point.

But haven't I also presented my mother's actions in a larger context? Haven't I given possible reasons for her behavior? Described how being Jewish, being raised by neglectful and abusive parents, and being female during a specific time and place in history restricted her options and irrevocably influenced her behavior? Can you see, as I do, that she alone does not bear sole responsibility for the way our family unraveled?

She may not be Glinda the Good Witch, but neither is she the Wicked Witch of the West. By releasing her from a false omnipotence, I have freed myself from her eternally damaging power and acknowledged her humanity.

Telling a different story doesn't necessarily mean erasing trauma from your life or pretending it didn't happen. You don't have to "give up" the precious pain that defines you, but you can reinterpret it as something that has contributed to your resilience, rather than your victimhood. You can set that past pain apart from the story you are telling about yourself today. You can choose to live somewhere other than trapped inside a story of anger and powerlessness.

Leaving stories behind and creating new ones in order to tell a different story of the future may sound trite, disrespectful, and impossible, especially when you're talking about centuries of deep wounds and intergenerational trauma. But it comes down to each of us making choices as individuals, and choices as communities, about how to tell the stories of our lives. The environment we live in is constantly shifting, and our stories can too.

"A story can be a gift like Ariadne's thread, or the labyrinth, or the labyrinth's ravening Minotaur," says Rebecca Solnit in her book *A Field Guide to Getting Lost*. "We navigate by stories, but sometimes we only escape by abandoning them." Back in 1973, when I was thirteen and lost in the labyrinth of La Habra, California, doing my best to avoid a Minotaur named Bernie, my mother's story line was leading nowhere I wanted to go. She was trapped in her own bad choices, but those choices didn't have to be mine. I was ready to abandon her story and tell my own.

TRUTH AND LIES

THE NEXT DAY AFTER SCHOOL, I walked into the house and heard my mom and Bernie screaming at each other upstairs with an intensity I'd never heard before.

"You're a goddamn liar, you asshole!"

My mom was bellowing like an enraged animal.

"You told me you were divorced months ago!"

"Arlene, shut up for minute and listen!"

Uh oh, Bernie, I thought, heading for the kitchen. *Now you're in trouble.*

"Lori . . . ," I called, before remembering she was swimming at a friend's house. I poked my head into the kitchen, but David wasn't around either.

"Why should I listen to you?"

My mom's voice was a fusillade of fury.

"Everything you say is a lie! I bet you've lied about everything, right? Right? Mr. Full-of-Shit Bigmouth Liar!"

"Goddamn it, Arlene! Don't call me that!"

"Liar? You don't want to be called a liar?"

There was a moment of silence, and then my mom's voice abruptly changed.

"Let go of me right now!"

"You shut up and listen."

"Ow . . . stop it!"

When I heard my mom start crying, I took the stairs two at a time. They were in the middle of the upstairs hallway, locked together and struggling. Bernie was twisting one of my mom's arms behind her back, and she was trying to get away. Her face was blotched with scarlet spots, and she was crying hard.

"Mom!"

"Elisa!" she sobbed. "Call the police! Call them right now!"

Bernie's face was red, and he was sweating and breathing hard.

"Do it, Elisa! Tell them to come and get this goddamn liar out of my house!"

Call the police?

"Don't you do a goddamn thing, Elisa!" Bernie glared at me. "Your mother and I are just having a little . . ."

"He's a liar, Elisa!" My mom was crying harder now. "They're all goddamn liars. Let go of my arm!"

Bernie let her go.

"Arlene. Calm down."

There was a purple mark on her arm where he'd grabbed it.

He flicked his eyes down the stairs.

"Get the hell out of here, Elisa. This is between me and your mother!"

"Mom! Should I call the police?"

She didn't say anything. She just rubbed her arm.

"Should I have them take Bernie away?"

Bernie laughed, like the whole thing was a big joke.

"Listen, kid," he took a step toward me.

"You don't get it yet, do ya? Your mom doesn't give the orders around here anymore. *I* do."

He pointed to his chest.

"*I'm* the new Captain. Not you! Not your dad! And not your mother, who . . ."— Bernie wrapped his arm around my mom's shoulders—"God knows, hates me at the moment. But deep down she knows we're meant to be together. Right, Red?"

He kissed my mom's cheek.

"Mom?"

She didn't say anything.

"*I'm* the Captain," Bernie said again. "And when I say jump . . ."

He let go of my mom and walked toward me.

"You're gonna jump."

He stopped a few inches from me and stood there rolling that little piece of white gum around in his mouth.

"Got it, sport?"

He leaned in and poked my chest hard with his finger.

I stared at his finger for a moment. And then I raised my hand to my forehead and saluted.

"Aye aye, Captain Kangaroo."

"You little bitch."

Bernie slapped me hard across the face, and I staggered backward.

"Bernie!" my mom yelled.

She took a step in my direction and then stopped.

"I'm the boss here, Arlene, and she's gonna have to learn that! If she doesn't like it, she can leave!"

Bernie stormed past me down the steps. The front door opened and slammed shut. I put my hand on my burning cheek and started crying.

"You can't marry him, Mom! You can't!"

I was sobbing now.

"Oh, Elisa."

My mom walked over shaking her head.

"When are you gonna learn to keep your mouth shut?"

She tried to pull my hand away from my face.

"Let me see your cheek."

I shrugged her off.

"He lied about being divorced! He's a liar! You said it!"

"Elisa . . . ," she just kept shaking her head. "You don't understand what's going on here, OK?"

"I hate Bernie!"

I was crying harder now.

"And he hates *me*. I can't live with him. I can't!"

The tears were pouring down my face.

"Please don't marry him!"

"Oh, Elisa."

She let out a deep sigh as I stood in front of her sobbing. She rubbed her arm and looked in the direction of the stairway.

"This might be hard for you to understand, but I love Bernie, and I will not let you or anyone else come between us. That's just the way things are, so you're going to have to accept that and find a way to live with him. Now go hold a cold washcloth on your cheek. I have to get Lori and David."

I stood in the hallway holding my cheek as my mom headed down the stairs and out the front door. The house was silent except for the sound of my sobs.

"I HAVE A COLLECT CALL for Sam Bernick from Elisa Bernick," the operator said. "Will you accept the charges?"

"What?" my dad said.

I knew he would be confused. I'd never called collect before. And he was at work. Even back in Minnesota, I rarely called him at work.

"Elisa?"

"Sir, will you accept the charges?" the operator repeated.

"What?"

"I have a collect call for Sam Bernick from Elisa Bernick. Will you accept the charges?"

"Uh . . . yeah! Elisa, what's going on? What's wrong?"

I touched my throbbing cheek and felt a jolt of fury.

"Bernie slapped me really hard on the cheek! I can't stay here anymore!"

"What? He *slapped* you?"

"Yeah! Really hard! I can't live with him. I need to come home."

"Put your mother on the phone."

"She's not here. She went to get Lori and David."

"You're there alone with Bernie?"

"No. He's gone too."

A huge sigh.

"Elisa, I'm very upset that Bernie slapped you. That's not OK with me."

I heard someone else's voice in the background.

"What?"

He was talking to someone.

"No! Tell 'em I'll be right there!"

"Dad?"

"Oh boy. It's nuts here today. There's a Christmas party going on, and the guys are waiting for me."

"Dad, please! Just say I can come home!"

"Elisa, listen. Stay away from Bernie until I talk with your mother. OK? I'll call her this weekend, and we'll figure something out. Just stay away from him. Got it?"

"But, Dad . . . !"

"Honey, I gotta go. And you can't call collect unless it's an emergency. These calls are really expensive!"

"Dad . . ."

After my dad hung up, I sat with the phone to my ear and listened to the dial tone. Didn't he understand this *was* an emergency? I couldn't stay here anymore! My eyes filled with tears, and I wished I was a tiny bird who could fly through the phone line all the way back to Minnesota.

THE NEAREST EXIT

I DROPPED MY THUMB WHEN I saw the green taxi coming down the ramp. It slowed as it passed me, but I ignored it.

Sorry, buddy. Wish I had money for a ride.

I kicked at the gravel and set my backpack down. This was harder than I thought. Where was all the traffic? The girl with the cowboy boots had made it look so easy. I shielded my eyes from the long rays of the setting sun and thought about how late it was getting. It was at least 8:30. Maybe later. I squinted into the sun at the horizon line. I didn't have much light left.

Out of the corner of my eye, I noticed the taxi had pulled over to the shoulder of the ramp and was just sitting there. A minute later a blue car headed toward me down the ramp. I stuck out my thumb and pasted on a smile, but it didn't slow down.

Dammit!

I kicked the gravel again. My mom must be home with Lori and David by now, and Bernie was probably back too. They could be driving around looking for me right this minute.

I considered that possibility and rolled my eyes.

Not likely. Poor Lori and David. Stuck with Bernie.

How could I leave them alone with Bernie? I touched my bruised cheek. Shouldn't I protect them? *Could* I protect them?

I heard the grind of gears and saw the taxi driver slowly backing up the ramp in reverse. He stopped about ten feet from me and honked. I shook my head, but he rolled down his window and signaled me forward with his hand.

I hoisted my pack, walked over, and looked at him through the open window. He was wearing a Dodgers baseball cap, and he looked Mexican. Or *Chicana*. Or whatever they were called. There were blinking Christmas lights strung around his windshield, and a picture of a praying lady wrapped in a hooded blue cape was hanging from his rearview mirror.

"I don't have any money."

"Where you going?" he asked, with a strong accent.

Definitely Chee-CAH-na.

"The airport."

"LAX?"

The taxi driver stared at me for a moment.

"How old you are? 'leven? Twelve?"

"Sixteen," I lied, as a red car sped past down the ramp.

"I gotta go. Bye."

I started walking back to my spot.

"Hey! ¡*Chiquita!*"

I ignored him.

"The hitchhike is no good," he called out. "The cops they will arrest you."

I turned around and stared at him.

"Why you are doing this? Your mama is worried, I bet."

I snorted.

"You don't know my mom."

As I turned away, the taxi door opened behind me.

"OK, *chiquita*, come here," the driver called out. "I take you to LAX."

"I already told you I don't have any money."

"I go to LAX anyway," the driver called back. "I have two daughters. The hitch-hike no is good. Many bad people 'round here."

I turned around.

"Really? You'd take me to the airport? For free?"

The taxi driver took off his baseball cap and scratched the top of his head. He had a little bald spot on top, just like my dad. He had a round belly like my dad too. He made the sign of the cross in front of his chest with his baseball cap.

"*Dios Madre*," he said, still scratching the top of his head. "Come on, *chiquita*."

He put the baseball cap back on, opened the passenger door, and waved me over.

"Les go."

In the taxi's backseat, I rode with one hand on my backpack. The colorful blanket under my bare thighs was a little scratchy, and a spicy flower scent rushed in through the open windows. It mingled with the spicy smell of Mexican food inside the taxi. My stomach rumbled. I had no idea how far away the airport was.

The taxi driver hadn't said anything since I got in, but I'd seen him look at me a few times in the rearview mirror. In the glow of the blinking Christmas lights I saw a big silver cross swinging from the mirror behind the praying lady. The radio was turned to a Spanish music station. I couldn't understand the words, but I bobbed my head to the beat.

"Ah," the taxi driver said into the rearview mirror. "You like *norteño* music?"

I nodded as we sailed along the freeway. It was almost night now. I was glad I wasn't still standing on the side of the road with my thumb out.

"Thanks again for the ride," I said over the music. "I really appreciate it."

"What time your flight is?"

The taxi driver watched me in the mirror.

"Um . . . ," I looked out the window. "About 9:30."

"You miss it. We have still fifteen minutes to LAX."

"That's OK. I'll just take the next one."

The taxi driver turned down the radio. He stared at me in the mirror.

"You no have ticket?"

I didn't say anything.

"You no have ticket. All alone you hitchhike. You are running away, *sí*?"

He kept looking at me.

"Running away from home no is good, *chiquita*. Tell me where you live, and I take you. No charge. You *Mama* and *Papi* worry."

"No, they don't." I shook my head. "At least my mom doesn't."

I met the taxi driver's eyes in the mirror.

"And I'm not running away *from* home. I'm running *to* home. To my dad in Minnesota."

He raised his eyebrows, and I nodded.

"My dad is waiting for me to call him from the airport. He's bringing me home."

The driver looked at me a few more times in the mirror as we drove.

Speeding through the darkness with the *norteño* music and my own heart throbbing loud in my ears, I wondered what I was going to say to my dad. And what I was going to do if he said no.

"OK, *chiquita*, I wait for you here."

We pulled up in front of the passenger terminal at LAX, and the lights were suddenly bright in my eyes.

"Telephones, they are inside the doors. You *Papi* know you are calling, *sí*?"

"Oh yeah."

I opened the door.

"He's waiting for me to call."

I grabbed my backpack and started to get out, but the taxi driver reached back and put his hand on my backpack.

"This stay here."

"What?"

"Then I know you come back. If you *Papi* no buy you a ticket, I take you back to your *Mama*. *¿Entiendes?*"

I let go of my pack and heaved a sigh.

"Oh-*kay*."

"And I know if you no tell the truth."

He lifted a finger in warning, and then he kissed his fingertip and touched the picture of the praying lady.

"I have daughters. *Andale, chiquita*."

He pointed to the doors.

"I wait here."

I stood at a bank of pay phones and pressed the telephone receiver to my ear as the operator and I waited for my dad to pick up. The phone rang three times, four times, five times. . . .

"Miss, do you want me to keep trying?" the operator asked.

"Just a couple more times, please," I said and squeezed the receiver even tighter. *Come on, Dad. Pick up the phone!*

"I'm sorry, Miss," the operator said. "Nobody is answering."

I willed myself not to cry.

"Thank you."

I hung up and pressed my forehead against the telephone, wondering what I was going to do now. I let out a quivery sigh and whispered sternly to myself.

"No crying!"

The woman at the next telephone turned to look, but I ignored her and picked up the receiver again like I had somebody else to call.

Why didn't my dad answer? Where was he?

I closed my eyes, suddenly exhausted. After a moment, something occurred to me.

It's two hours later in Minnesota. Of course he isn't at work. He's at home!

With my heart racing, I started over. On the fourth ring, my dad picked up.

"H'lo?"

He sounded weird, and I realized I'd woken him up.

"I have a collect call from Elisa Bernick for Sam Bernick, will you . . ."

"Uh . . . wha? . . . from . . . Elisa?"

Please accept the charges! Please.

"Oy."

I heard him sigh deeply.

Please! It's an emergency!

"OK. I'll accept the charges."

The operator clicked off.

"Elisa. What's going on? What the hell time is it?"

"Dad"—I felt the tears threatening again—"I need to come home."

"Elisa, it's late."

He stifled a yawn.

"Can we talk about this . . ."

"I'm not going back there. No matter what. I'm *not.*"

"Go back?"

I could tell he was waking up now.

"Elisa, where are you?"

"I'm at the airport."

"Where?"

"The airport. LAX. Can I come home?"

"Oh my god, how the hell did you get to the airport? Does your mother know where you are?"

"No," I started crying. "Dad, please, I miss you. I miss Dan. I don't want to live with Bernie and Mom."

"You ran away to the airport?"

"You said if I hated it here, I could come home. Well, I hate it here!"

"Elisa, what the hell's going on? Do you have any money?"

"No. I don't have anything with me. I just want to come home.

"It's winter here. You don't have a coat or boots . . ."

"Dad, please!" I wiped my nose on my sleeve. "We can buy those things!"

"Elisa . . . your mother has custody . . ."

"I'm *not* going back there. No matter what. Please . . . just let me come home."

"Oh boy, oh boy."

I heard my dad breathing heavily into the phone. And then silence.

I closed my eyes and pressed the receiver as hard as I could against my ear as the tears slipped down my cheeks.

Please, Dad. Don't say wait or be patient or it's too expensive or the courts won't let you . . .

"Elisa, honey . . ."

Or we'll figure something out or we'll talk about it on Sunday . . .

"Listen carefully."

I knew he was going to say no. I just knew it. And then what was I going to do? I wasn't going back to my mom and Bernie. No way. But the taxi driver would know . . . so I'll have to leave my stuff . . .

"Elisa, are you listening?"

"Yes."

The tears were falling harder now.

"I want you to go to the Northwest Airlines counter and give them your name. I'll get you on the next flight to Minneapolis."

My heart was beating so hard in my ears, I wasn't sure I really heard him.

"What? Really, Dad?" I couldn't stop crying now. "Really?"

I heard my dad sigh, but this time it sounded different.

"Yes, Elisa. You're coming home on the next flight. You just get yourself to the Northwest Airlines counter, and tell them who you are. I'll handle everything from this end. Do you understand?"

"Thank you, Dad." I wiped my nose with the back of my arm. "Thank you so much. Thank you . . ."

"It's OK now. Stop crying, OK?"

My dad's voice was quivery.

"OK."

"I'll see you soon."

I ran outside to the taxi. There were tears streaming down my cheeks and I was smiling wide.

"He said yes! He really said yes! I'm going home!"

The taxi driver smiled. He got out of the taxi and handed over my backpack. He patted me awkwardly on the back.

"I so happy for you. *¡Feliz Navidad, chiquita!*"

"*¡Feliz Navidad!* And thank you so much!"

I hoisted my backpack and headed inside. When I got to the doors, I turned back and waved at him.

"Happy Hanukkah!"

Nose to the window, I watch the wing lights race down the runway as the airplane picks up speed. The powerful thrust of the engines forces me back against the seat, and a rush of air fills my ears. There is a bump, and then suddenly . . .

I'm flying.

I stare out the window as the city lights fall away, and there is only darkness and the small glowing wing lights tracking our route through space. Looking at my reflection in the small oval of night, I feel my chest crack open and something warm, like happiness, spills out. It's like I told the taxi driver—I'm not running away *from*, I'm running away *to*. They're completely different. Running away *from* is running for cover. It's hiding and making myself smaller. But running away *to* is like skating on a frozen pond beneath a star-filled sky—it's propelling myself through space, fast and strong.

"Here I go," I whisper softly to the grinning girl looking back at me in the window.

I press my cheek against the cool glass as I hurtle through space, a powerful arrow of blue light streaking toward my future, constructing a story line that is all my own.

EPILOGUE
Evolving Story Lines

If I focus on the story of the history and not the story of what came out of it, which is a story of survival, triumph, and love, then I could miss out on the healing.

—Vanessa Jackson, president of Healing Circles

I WROTE THIS BOOK ALMOST fifty years after these events took place, and to be honest, I have no memory of hitchhiking to LAX. I remember calling my dad and going to the Northwest Airlines counter, but the whole taxi driver thing . . . I made that up . . . at least I thought I had until Lori convinced me it was true. She says I told her about the taxi ride years ago, right after it happened, but I have no memory of it. Or . . . I guess I did remember it, but I didn't remember that it was true. My confusion over this event was, in part, the genesis for this book. The fact that I was so sure this "true" story was fiction made me wonder about the nature of truth and memory—and why we often can't tell the difference.

What I do know for a fact is that I abandoned my abusive mother when I was barely thirteen—a survival lesson I obviously learned from her. And perhaps she learned it from her parents. And so on and so on. What stories of reinvention do we all carry in our bodies?

Initially, I thought that writing this book was about forgiveness—being able to see my mother in a more generous light so I could forgive her for being a fallible, difficult human. But when I researched this idea, I discovered that in Judaism, forgiveness is not designed to be easily given. The sinner is required to *ask* for forgiveness—something I suspect my mother would have little interest in doing. More importantly, she is no longer around to even consider it.

Although my connection to the spiritual aspects of Judaism has always felt tenuous, one of the most enduring rituals in my life has been our Passover seder. For the past thirty-five years, we've hosted a seder guided by a *Haggadah* my husband and I cobbled together and continue to reinvent through the additions of poetry and philosophical musings. This dovetails with a powerful theme underlying many Jewish rituals: Words make the world. Retelling the story of Exodus is just one example.

At its heart, Passover tells the story of the Jews' departure from slavery and exile to freedom and redemption. The traditional *Haggadah* phrase "He took us out from slavery to freedom . . . and from servitude to redemption" has been interpreted and reinterpreted over the centuries. Certainly, part of it refers to the Jews' departure from a slave mentality: the idea that we remain victims for as long as we believe we will be.

The Jewish sages posit that because Pharaoh had never given anyone permission to leave the country, the Jews couldn't fathom trying to leave of their own accord. In order to leave Egypt, they had to break out of the victim mentality to become free to achieve their full spiritual potential. Freedom in this sense is not just the absence of oppression but the presence of a meaningful route to self-fulfillment. The Jewish tradition differentiates between fate (*yi'ud*), and destiny (*goral*). Fate is the hand of cards we are dealt. Destiny is how we choose to play them. I interpret this as choosing which story to tell.

Part of telling the Passover story is to remember past hardships, but it is also to remember our purpose and identity in this world. Rather than living in a state of forgetfulness, we are commanded to live in a state of memory and consciousness that induces us to make ourselves and the world a better place.

For Jews, adapting our collective memory to the present has allowed us to last through thousands of years of history—something that itself is a continual subject of reinvention and reinterpretation. The Jewish historian Yosef Hayim Yerushalmi says the entire history of Judaism is a history of interpretation. "But it is not only the interpretation of a text, or a set of texts, it is also an ongoing interpretation of experience."

For Yerushalmi, "history" is the story not only of what happened *but of how what happened was interpreted*. "So long as there is a sense between the generations of continuity, then it doesn't really matter that the interpretations of one age and the interpretations of another age will be very different. Jewish memory is at its heart an ongoing contest of interpretation, dialogue, and debate by Jews trying to define the law, the experience, the faith, which becomes the tradition."

I like the idea of memory and its reinterpretation as the path to redemption. Whether you're Jewish or not, memory's selectivity and its continual evolution are the keys to adaptation and survival. Recognizing that trauma stories can be a source of both distress and resilience, reinterpreting my own memories, and telling the stories in this book in the context of my resilience is the path I have taken to freedom and redemption.

I wish I could tell you that my mother and father walked that same path, but I cannot. Despite many opportunities to establish emotionally rich relationships with his children and grandchildren, my father has been unable to see the value of things that don't carry a price tag. I believe his emotional potential was stunted when he was a child, and his life has been dictated by the sense of unworthiness that he learned from an antisemitic culture, Grandpa Izzy, and also from my mother. I'm not sure he ever recovered from what he perceived as her betrayal.

When my dad found out about my mom's affair from a guy on his bowling team, he fell apart and never quite came back together again. For forty-five years, he seethed with the shame and humiliation of her rejection—something that confirmed his low self-esteem. Maybe some part of him still loved her, if what they felt for each other could be described as love. Or perhaps he felt like he'd held up his end of the bargain, and she'd reneged on it.

Whatever it was, many years after their divorce, he demanded an apology from her. I suppose he thought it would allow him to put her betrayal behind him. But of course my mom refused. Not because she wanted my dad to suffer, but because what he wanted didn't matter to her. Not even a little. He was like an irritating fly she'd swatted away and forgotten about. For her, the past was the past. Done. Finished. But my dad kept her infidelity alive and tasted a little bile every day as he held out for an apology that never came. For him, the most galling thing of all was her lack of contrition.

I have never felt particularly close to my father, but despite our emotional distance, I have never forgotten how he saved my life when I was thirteen by departing from the safe path and doing something profoundly out of character. He accepted my collect phone calls, bucked the court's custody order, and bought me an expensive airline ticket home on a moment's notice. I like to think there was some epigenetic force at work that helped him see I was drowning, and he was my lifeline.

As for my mom, things remained rocky between us. She and Bernie eventually married, and then divorced a decade later. I didn't speak to her much during my teens and twenties. Lori remained in California, but moved as far away from my mom as possible. David moved back to Minnesota when he was in his twenties.

I spent my thirties trying (and failing) to develop empathy toward my mom, myself, and others. Becoming a mother myself in 1994, and again in 1999, gave me a trajectory toward tenderness that provided a fragile bridge to my mom. Being able to see her as "Grammy" rather than "Mom" made things a little easier.

We spoke weekly by telephone, and she visited Minnesota periodically. As far as I could tell, she couldn't see much beyond her own little bubble. Most of our conversations were her complaints about my siblings and predictable stories about how someone mistook her for someone *much* younger. This, of course, became a running joke among me and my siblings.

After my mom divorced Bernie, she was content to live alone with few friends or personal connections. For thirty years, she moved from apartment to apartment, still believing that her departures and arrivals would magically make her happier. Her relationship to Judaism remained the most consistent thread of her identity. She joined a Reform Jewish temple wherever she lived, she sang in the choir, and when she turned sixty, we all flew out to California when she became a Bat Mitzvah.

She always enjoyed being the expert in the room and wanted to share her Jewish knowledge, so after twenty-five years in dental hygiene, and another decade as a moderately successful interior decorator, my mom became a Hebrew tutor for kids studying for their Bar and Bat Mitzvahs. They called her "Miss Arlene," and she developed a reputation as a strict but effective teacher.

She continued to sew, knit, and do embroidery. She gave small handmade gifts to her students and clients, and she sent scarves, sweaters, and hats to family in Minnesota as Hanukkah gifts. She was a fierce Scrabble and Mahjong competitor, with little patience for chitchat and an irritating tendency to gloat. Winning was always her goal. She enjoyed her grandchildren in limited doses and remained geographically and emotionally distant. She was a critical, narcissistic presence at any gathering. My siblings and I found her difficult, and both she and my dad were consistent sources of disappointment and frustration—but aren't we all?

In August of 2016, my then seventy-eight-year-old mother arrived in Minnesota for a two-week visit. By this point, my brother Dan was divorced and had moved to California, not far from Lori. When my mom came for her infrequent visits, she stayed with David's family (he is married with two kids) because I couldn't tolerate having her in my house. By then, I had created specific boundaries, and she understood they were the price of admittance to my life. I was in the early stages of writing this book, and my mom and I had a date to go out to dinner the evening after she arrived so I could "interview" her about her childhood.

But the next morning something happened that instantly changed all of our story lines yet again: My mom had a stroke that ended her independence. Although she remained mostly fine physically, the stroke affected her ability to speak, understand, and remember things. For the first time in her adult life, she became dependent on others for her care, and her story became something radically different.

Now this is where the plot takes another strange turn. It may be hard to believe, but after my mom had spent her life finding fault and seeking out the worst in every situation, the stroke transformed her into a more pleasant, joyful version of herself. I know this sounds improbable, but I have heard stories of this happening to others after a brain injury. My mom became, against all odds, a delightful person to be around! It was as if, as my Aunt Sharon so aptly put it, "she forgot what she was so angry about."

Hers was such a dramatic transformation that I found myself reexamining everything I felt about her. I realize it may be hard to understand how I could somehow abruptly soften toward my mom after a lifetime of her abuse, but it might be easier once you read an example of our conversations.

A week or so after her stroke, I was in her hospital room. The nurse and I had given her a shower, washed her hair, changed her bedding, and put a new gown on her. She told us she felt great. Clean. Then she got into bed and looked around.

"Where's my left hand?" she asked. "I had two of them."

I laughed and picked up her left hand and said, "It's right here, Mom."

She gave me a half grin and then, a little exasperated, said, "Ha ha. No really. Where's my left hand? I'm cold."

I was trying to figure out what she was talking about. I was thinking, "OK, left hand, she had two of them, she's cold . . ." and I spied the two red booties she had had on before the shower.

"Oh, Mom, are you talking about these?"

I walked over and held up the booties.

"Of course," she said matter-of-factly. "My left hand."

Do you see what I mean? The old Arlene would have snapped at me and told me to "stop goddamn monkeying around." But in this new story line, my mom had hilariously forgotten many parts of herself, including her worst parts.

It became an opportunity for me to do the same.

With ongoing occupational therapy and consistent care from me and my brother David, my mom was able to live alone in a studio apartment at a nearby assisted living facility. She was content with the few belongings that made their way to her from California. We played a lot of cards; she loved Kings in the Corner, but Gin Rummy was too hard. Sewing, knitting, reading, and cooking were out of the question, but she could eat food that was prepared for her, wash her dishes, and do her own laundry.

My mom spent her days busy with paint-by-number kits and finely detailed "adult" coloring books. She laughed a lot and enjoyed daily visits with others at the care facility. She wasn't mentally feeble, but receiving and retaining information was difficult. Her humor and intelligence were intact, but sometimes she made sense and sometimes she didn't. Even though she was aware of these new limitations and felt frustrated by them, she accepted them and largely remained content in her own company. I was impressed by how adroitly she adapted to her profoundly changed circumstances.

Her biggest complaint was the Minnesota cold (again, with the weather). She had never weighed much, and after her stroke she was down to one hundred pounds. By the end of September, even with the thermostat turned up to 80 degrees, she was wearing her winter coat, gloves, and a hat *inside* her apartment. We spent hours trying to figure out how to keep her warm. It was harder than you might think, given that we didn't trust her with a space heater.

At the end of February 2017, not long after my sister Lori was diagnosed with melanoma and about a month after my mom's seventy-ninth birthday, I was standing in my mom's apartment hallway knocking on her door.

"Hi, Mom, it's me. Open the door. I've got some groceries."

It had been six months since her stroke. They were forecasting a snowstorm, so I wanted to make sure she was stocked up.

"C'mon, Mom, open up."

I waited a few moments, and then I heard an eerie noise inside her apartment. A garbled, guttural sentence without words.

My heart sped up, and I put the groceries down.

"Mom? Are you OK?"

Oh shit. Oh shit.

I tried the door, knowing it was locked. She always locked it. Locks were still so important to her. I dug in my purse for the extra key to her apartment that I'd never used because she insisted on locking and unlocking the door herself. That little bit of control she wouldn't give up.

Where the hell was the key?

When I finally got inside, she was lying on her back on the bed. One side of her face was drooping, and her left arm was hanging uselessly. Her eyes were wide, and she was making low, guttural sounds, trying to talk with a tongue that wouldn't work.

"Mom, it's Elisa. You're having another stroke. I'm going to call an ambulance."

I frantically made the call and sat next to her while we waited. I stroked her forehead and her cheek, trying to calm her down, but she kept trying to speak, panicked.

"Calm down, Mom. Try to calm down. You're having a stroke. The ambulance is coming."

I wished she would stop trying to talk. I worried that she was in pain. How long had she been alone and panicked?

The unit nurse and the activities director arrived with the paramedics, and they got her on a stretcher. As I followed behind them, I looked around at the coffeemaker she insisted on buying but never remembered how to use. Ditto with the microwave. I pulled the cord on the humidifier.

"Can you turn the thermostat down and lock up?" I asked the nurse.

"Of course."

"But wait," the activities director said, and I could tell she was confused. She loved my mom. Just that morning my mom had given her a beautiful color-by-number picture from one of her adult coloring books.

"It will be cold when she gets back," she said, knowing how much my mom hated the cold.

I shook my head as the paramedics headed to the elevator with my mom.

"I don't think she's coming back."

I walked beside the stretcher holding my mom's hand as we headed outside and down the icy sidewalk to the ambulance. My mom said one last thing before they loaded her into the ambulance, and even through her garbled speech I understood her perfectly.

"Ith thold," she said.

My mom's last words were about the Minnesota weather.

The stroke and my mother's transformation at the end of her life transformed me as well. They allowed me to become her caregiver—to literally care *for* and *about* her. I had no way of knowing she would live only six months after the initial stroke. I thought I would spend years caring for her, and I consciously chose to stop running away from her and to run toward her instead.

Although ultimately short-lived, this profound shift altered both of our stories. I was able to admire her great resilience in the face of trauma, and she was able to acknowledge her vulnerability and ask for help. She was able to thank me for stepping up—something that made us both cry.

The final months of my mom's life allowed me to reinvent the story I'd been telling about her. It freed me from the prison of anger where I'd been trapped for so many years. This was no accident. I *intentionally* transformed the narrative

I constructed about my mother. Yes, I have told you stories of her abuse, and my goal is not to excuse or forget her behavior. But through my research and writing I am now able to more clearly see the depth and complexity of the challenges she experienced—and to see her resilience in the face of them. And most importantly, I have been able to tell these stories in the context of *my own* resilience.

Each of our individual memories alters the trajectory of our family's past and future. The stories we tell are always a departure from someone's truth and always an opportunity for reinvention. Yes, the narratives we invent feel immutable, but they are not. They are an opportunity to consciously acknowledge the inevitable reinvention of our own truths—including the traumatic and painful events of the past, in order to create more positive opportunities in the future.

When I think of my mother now, she is a gentler version of herself. Someone I can actually be fond of. This reinterpretation feels like a remarkable gift. You may feel I've still cast her as a villain. But for me, she is no longer the Wicked Witch of the West. If nothing else, this book is an opportunity for my remaining siblings, children, nieces and nephews, and those who follow behind them to remember my mom as someone who really *was* doing the best she could.

After all, our memories are the stories we tell ourselves about the future.

Defren, Arlene, Age 79, of Sacramento, CA, died peacefully in St. Paul, MN, on March 3, 2017. Arlene was a runner-up and Jewish trailblazer in the 1964 Mrs. Minnesota contest. She enjoyed sewing, singing in the temple choir, and competing fiercely at Mahjong and other games. She is survived by two siblings, four children, and eight grandchildren. She will be missed by friends and family in both Minnesota and California, where she was a long-time resident.

—*StarTribune*, March 7, 2017

ACKNOWLEDGMENTS

Thanks to the Association of Writers and Writing Programs (AWP) Writer to Writer mentorship program, and in particular Leslie Schwartz, who counseled me to raise the stakes and write this as something other than a novel.

Thanks to Ann Regan at the Minnesota Historical Society Press for your early encouragement, and to Gary Dunham at Indiana University Press for your willingness to take this project on.

Thanks to Lorna Landvik, Nora Murphy, and Kate Hopper. Your willingness to share your experiences and resources made this journey easier.

Thanks to the patient readers of the earliest drafts of this book: Bridget Murphy, Laura Zelle, Rachel Breen, Suzanne Stenson O'Brien, and Larry Lavercombe. Your support and suggestions made this a better book.

Thanks to John Wareham, the media librarian at the *Minneapolis Star Tribune*, for your generous help in tracking down articles and photos related to the 1964 Mrs. Minnesota contest. And also to Amy Barickman, whose deep knowledge of Mary Brooks Picken supplied some necessary answers.

Thanks to Kathryn Bernick for her thorough documentation of the Minnesota Bernick family. It planted the earliest seeds of my interest in how my family arrived on these shores.

Thanks to David Bernick, Dan Bernick, Ruby Bernick-Langworthy, Harvey Defren, Sharon Defren, Berta Steele, Sam Bernick, and Joan Bernick. I appreciate your willingness to share your memories, idea, and stories with me so that I could write this one.

My eternal thanks to my husband, Michael Roehr, and my children, Cleome Bernick-Roehr and Asher Bernick-Roehr. The food, songs, jokes, travels, stories, and love we share continually create the most important and wonderful memories of my life.

And finally, my thanks to Lu Lippold, who read every draft with great heart and keen insight. Your humor, patience, encouragement, and confidence in my ability to tell this story made all the difference.

APPENDIX

1840s–1850s: German Jews arrive and organize Mount Zion Synagogue in St. Paul.

1869: Eastern European Jews organize Sons of Jacob Synagogue in St. Paul.

1878: German Jews found Shaarai Tov Synagogue in Minneapolis (later renamed Temple Israel).

1880: Minnesota's population is 780,773. There are 500 Jews, mostly German, living in Minneapolis.

1882: Yiddish-speaking Eastern European Jews begin to arrive in Minnesota as a result of Russian pogroms, rampant antisemitism, and poor economic conditions in other countries. They are primarily small merchants, peddlers, and factory workers in the nascent garment trade. Tailoring and peddling are Eastern European specialties. The banking and lumber industries are closed to Jews and anyone not part of the Anglo-Saxon elite.

There is early friction between the Eastern European Jews (my ancestors) and the earlier-settled and wealthy, mostly German, Jews. The newcomers are poor and uneducated; they are refugees rather than immigrants. They continue to speak Yiddish and practice traditional customs.

1900: Minnesota's population is 1,300,000. Fewer than 5,000 Minnesotans are Jews, and most live in the Twin Cities with a small outpost in Duluth.

1903: **Haim Berniker** (my great-uncle) arrives in St. Paul from a small shtetl called Deretchin in "the old country" on the border of Russia, Poland, Lithuania, and Bielorussia (now Belarus). His wife's brother pays his passage, and his wife and children join him five years later. He changes his name to "Hyman Bernick" soon after his arrival, in an effort to be more "American."

1905: Highland Park becomes St. Paul's primary Jewish neighborhood and is home to most of the city's synagogues. My grandfather will eventually settle here, and my father will grow up here.

1910: The Twin Cities' Jewish population has doubled to thirteen thousand people. Of the Minnesota population, 99 percent is White, 0.3 percent is Black, and 0.5 percent is "Other." It isn't clear whether Jews are considered White or Other. Probably Other.

1910: Minneapolis racial covenants stipulate that the "premises shall not at any time be conveyed, mortgaged or leased to any person or persons of Chinese, Japanese, Moorish, Turkish, Negro, Mongolian or African blood or descent" (https://minnesotareformer.com/2020/11/13/9445/).

1911: The nation's quota system dramatically limits the number of Jews and African Americans who can attend private colleges and many professional schools, including the University of Minnesota.

1914: **Shmuel Berniker** (my great-grandfather) joins his brother **Hyman Berniker** in St. Paul after working as a tanner in Derechin. He leaves behind a pregnant wife and five children ranging in age from five to fourteen. My grandfather **Isadore Berniker** (Itze, Izzy) is the oldest. Shmuel changes his name to "Samuel Bernick" soon after he arrives in Minnesota. He works as a mattress maker to earn enough money to bring the rest of his family over.

1915: Of Minnesota's population, 70 percent is foreign-born or has at least one parent who is foreign-born. Germans and either Catholics or Lutherans account for 25 percent. The remainder are Nordic immigrants: Norwegians, Swedes, Icelanders, and Danes, who far outnumber Germans and are mostly Lutheran.

1919: An advertisement in the *Minneapolis Tribune* offers "restricted" housing sites overlooking Lake of the Isles that could not "be conveyed, mortgaged or leased to any person or persons of Chinese, Japanese, Moorish, Turkish, Negro, Mongolian, Semitic or African blood or descent." That same year, the Minnesota legislature bans real estate restrictions based on religious faith or creed.

1920s: The "tribal twenties" are marked by racism, antisemitism, and anti-Catholicism. Marine City, Minnesota, has three thousand members of the Ku Klux Klan.

1920–1965: Jewish businesses make up half of all businesses operating along Plymouth Avenue on Minneapolis's North Side.

1921: *Isadore Bernick* (my grandfather), then twenty-one, shepherds his remaining four siblings (*Soreh, Michal, Hohem*, and *Avram*) and his mother, *Chana*, on the long journey to the United States. They enter the US via Canada (Quebec is the port of entry). They are not religious, but they are somewhat educated. My grandfather speaks fluent Yiddish, Polish, and Russian. The youngest sibling, *Rochel*, who was still in utero when Samuel left for the US six years earlier, does not make the journey. She died of malnutrition the previous year.

1922: My grandfather works as a tailor at Gordon and Ferguson on Wacouta Street in downtown St. Paul.

1922: The Beth El Synagogue is the last synagogue to be formed on the North Side of Minneapolis. It is the only one to affiliate with Judaism's Conservative movement. It will eventually become my mother's synagogue, and mine as well.

1923: Two Jewish students are denied rooms in dormitories on the University of Minnesota campus because the idea of living with Jewish students makes other students "uncomfortable."

1924: Xenophobic feelings after World War I are directed at recent immigrants and their families, Jews in particular. The clamor to restrict immigration results in a national quota system.

1925: In light of the antisemitism that Jews face in the Twin Cities, my grandfather considers changing his last name from "Bernick" to "Berns." He decides against it when he learns it will cost twenty-five dollars.

1926: My grandfather *Isadore Bernick* marries *Rose Golda Short*. He is twenty-six and she is eighteen. There are rumors that her parents have paid him to marry her because she has a low IQ (possibly as low as 70, according to my father). Isadore is a poor foreigner, while Rose is the American-born daughter of a respected Jewish St. Paul property owner (three apartment buildings in the Selby/Dale neighborhood). It is probably considered a good match.

1930: *Norman Bernick*, my dad's older brother, is born. The story behind his significant developmental delays is clouded in secrecy. Either he was born with hydrocephaly and his brain was damaged by a botched forceps delivery, or my grandmother Rose dropped him on his head when he was a newborn.

1931: My mother's father, **Phillip Defren**, the eleventh of twelve children who arrived in the United States with his family in 1902, moves to Minneapolis from Brooklyn, New York. He is a bigamist who leaves behind two wives and an unknown number of children. Originally heading to California to escape the authorities, he runs out of money in Minnesota and finds work as a milkman. Details of his past remain mysterious. There are rumors of his having up to six wives in at least two states, and an unknown number of children.

1930s: Virulent antisemitism is advanced by the Silver Shirts, a popular fascist organization with a strong following in Minnesota. Jews, particularly in Minneapolis, are shut out of civic life and social organizations. Discrimination in employment and housing is legal and accepted. Jews in the Twin Cities are restricted from buying homes and property in many parts of the cities, and few Northern Minnesota resorts welcome them. Jewish professionals—doctors and lawyers—are excluded from practicing at hospitals and law firms.

1935: **Phillip Defren**, age forty-two, marries **Goldie Gelb**, thirty-five, my maternal grandmother. She is a harsh disciplinarian who comes from a family of nine children, most of them smart and argumentative. Her people, who are originally from Eastern Europe, landed in Philadelphia, then Chicago, and moved to Minneapolis. She is a customer along Phillip's milk route. Goldie doesn't know about his other wives and kids. She is not considered a beauty, and she feels fortunate to find someone to marry at her age. Phillip and Goldie live in North Minneapolis with Goldie's parents, Anna and Julius (a tailor), and Goldie's siblings Esther, Freda, and Leo. Goldie's new husband Phillip is a charming, artistic, handsome, secretive rake who contributes little financial support to the family.

1935: **Samuel Bernick** (my father) is born in St. Paul.

1936: My mom's brother, **Harvey Defren**, is born in Minneapolis.

1937: My mom, **Arlene Defren**, and her fraternal twin sister **Elaine Defren** are born in Minneapolis. The siblings are not close.

1937: There are 43,700 Jews in Minnesota: 31,560 of them are in Minneapolis, 11,000 are in St. Paul, and 1,000 are in Duluth. They represent 0.9 percent of the state's population and 1.7 percent of the total population of the Twin Cities.

1938: Help wanted ads in Minnesota newspapers state "Gentile" or "Gentile preferred."

1938: The Jewish Community Relations Council is formed to combat antisemitism in Minnesota.

1939: The Twin Cities' Jewish population peaks at forty-four thousand people. There are 16,260 Jews in Minneapolis, 3.5 percent of the city's total population. Almost 70 percent (11,018), including my mom's family, live on Minneapolis's North Side.

1939: Iona Jackson, head of the Dental Hygiene Program in the University of Minnesota's Dental School, invites Renee Rappaport, Rose Olesky, and Rosa Lee Feinberg to withdraw from the program after a month in classes, based on the judgment that no dentist would hire a Jewish hygienist. She says she is trying to be "helpful." (My mother entered the University of Minnesota's dental hygiene program in 1955, not long after the "cap" on Jewish students was lifted.)

1940: My mother's younger sister **Berta Defren** is born in Minneapolis. My mother considers her a competitor for the scant attention of their parents. The family attends the Beth El Synagogue on Minneapolis's North Side. The family is extremely poor. Phillip financially and emotionally neglects **Goldie** and the children. Goldie depends on her argumentative, unmarried siblings (**Leo**, **Freda**, and **Esther**) to support her and her children. Leo is the only one with a college education, and none of the siblings marry except for Goldie. Arguing is the primary method of communication.

1940: Charles Lindbergh, the famous aviator and antisemite from Little Falls, Minnesota, and son of Swedish immigrants, becomes the spokesperson of the noninterventionist America First Committee. He charges Jews with trying to pressure the United States to enter into World War II.

1941: G. R. Higgins, director of the newly built University of Minnesota Student Union, writes a letter to Cornell's student union director Foster Coffin complaining about the "Jewish use of the building." He cannot find them "committing a specific sin," but he feels "burdened" by their presence.

1944: My great-aunts **Freda** and **Esther** join the armed services in the Women's Army Corp (WAC) in World War II, while **Leo** joins the US Army.

1945: Hubert H. Humphrey is elected mayor of Minneapolis and forms the Mayor's Committee on Human Relations. The committee actively seeks to combat racial and religious discrimination within the city. The mayor's committee surveys Whites about housing and race in Minneapolis. Of the Whites surveyed, 43 percent object to Jews living in their neighborhood and 85 percent object to Blacks living there.

1946: In *Common Ground* magazine, journalist Carey McWilliams describes
   Minneapolis as "the capital of anti-Semitism in the United States." He
   notes the lack of antisemitism in St. Paul.

1947: Almost half of all Minneapolis Jews are working blue-collar jobs.

1948–1951: The Jewish community raises $1.75 million and builds Mount Sinai
   Hospital in South Minneapolis. It is the first nonsectarian hospital in the
   state where Jewish doctors and other minorities can practice. It is the most
   modern hospital of the time, and it attracts prestigious doctors and garners
   respect in the community. Eventually it offers graduate-level teaching and
   educates the University of Minnesota's medical students.

1948: The US Supreme Court declares restrictive residential covenants to
   be illegal, invigorating the efforts of such organizations as the American
   Jewish Congress to eliminate antisemitic discrimination in housing.

1950: The University of Minnesota still allows people who run boardinghouses
   approved for student residences to restrict student renters by race, religion,
   and foreign birth.

1950–1965: Minneapolis's Black population grows from 1 percent to 4 percent
   of the city's total population, and most newcomers settle on the North
   Side.

1950: My mother's family moves from Minneapolis's North Side to
   Robbinsdale, a Minneapolis suburb. They find a cheap house large enough
   for my mom's family and Goldie's three siblings to move in together to
   make ends meet. My mom and her siblings are the only Jewish kids at
   their schools. Goldie hates not having Jews around and takes the kids back
   to the old neighborhood in North Minneapolis after school each day to
   attend Hebrew school.

1955: *Arlene Defren* and *Sam Bernick* (my parents) meet at a dance sponsored
   by Sigma Alpha Mu, the Jewish fraternity at the University of Minnesota.

1956: Sam graduates with a degree in engineering, and my mother graduates
   with a dental hygienist's license.

1957: My parents get married and move into an apartment in St. Paul.

1958: My mom's twin, *Elaine,* who is married and pregnant, suffers a serious
   stroke. She loses the baby and lives partially paralyzed for three months
   before dying. The family does not discuss her death, and she largely
   disappears from family lore. My mother will name me after her by
   putting an *E* in front of "Lisa." It's a name my father will never be able to
   pronounce correctly.

1962: Grandma *Goldie* divorces *Phillip,* citing "irreconcilable differences" after
   he walks out on her immediately following *Berta's* high school graduation.

Goldie does not know that Phillip is married to other women or that he has been having an affair with the secretary of the creamery (who will become his next wife). She only knows that she is done with marriage.

SELECTIVE TIMELINE OF THE JEWS (AND MY FAMILY) IN THE MINNEAPOLIS SUBURBS OF ROBBINSDALE, CRYSTAL, ST. LOUIS PARK, AND NEW HOPE, 1950–1970

1950: My mother's family moves from the North Side of Minneapolis to Robbinsdale, Minneapolis's oldest suburb. Robbinsdale has a downtown, a grade school, Whiz Bang Days (an annual Fourth of July celebration), and a high school. My mom and her siblings are the only Jewish students attending Robbinsdale schools. The nearest synagogue is on Minneapolis's North Side, six miles away.

1950–1970: The Minneapolis suburb of St. Louis Park (aka "St. Jewish Park") becomes a center of Twin Cities Jewish life. Jewish families arrive from the inner city, drawn by cheap housing and by the lack of housing restrictions that keep Jews out of other nearby suburbs. By the time filmmakers Joel and Ethan Coen and former senator (and comedian) Al Franken are growing up in the area, it is roughly a quarter Jewish and home to many of Minneapolis's major Jewish institutions.

1950–1960: Almost half of all housing in the suburbs offer Federal Housing Administration (FHA) or Veterans Affairs (VA) financing, which includes zoning requirements that ensure economic and age homogeneity and that preserve residential class separation and housing values (racist covenants).

1953: Over the objections of resident farmers, the suburb of New Hope incorporates as a city with six hundred residents. It comprises six square miles and is located twelve miles northwest of downtown Minneapolis. It has no discernible downtown and few sidewalks.

1954 The US Supreme Court's *Brown v. Board of Education* decision desegregates schools.

1954: The St. Louis Park High School student newspaper, the *Park High Echo*, has a front-page article entitled "Choir Honors Easter with Spiritual Works" that is accompanied by a large picture of an open Bible with the caption "My Redeemer Lives." Inside is a sketch of a cross, captioned "Christ the Lord Is Risen."

1954: The Anti-Defamation League, a branch of B'nai B'rith, presents a booklet to the St. Louis Park superintendent of schools that includes a schedule of the Jewish holidays and suggestions for teachers.

1956: The Interstate Highway Act (also known as the Federal Aid Highway Act) becomes law. Congress funds 90 percent of the cost of a forty-one-thousand-mile highway system.

1956: A new Robbinsdale High School is built to serve the rapidly developing suburbs of Robbinsdale, Crystal, and Golden Valley.

1957–1962: A "segregation index" created by the University of Wisconsin shows that financial and spatial segregation in Minneapolis is more severe than almost any other major metropolitan area in the country. (It remains so today.)

1957: **Sam Bernick** and **Arlene Bernick** (née Defren) get married at the Beth El Synagogue in North Minneapolis.

1958: My dad is hired as a civil engineer by the Hennepin County Highway Department.

1958: The *Park High Echo* includes an editorial about Hanukkah.

1958: My brother **Danny Bernick** is born at Mount Sinai Hospital, the only Twin Cities hospital to allow Jewish doctors to practice.

1959: The Rondo neighborhood, a center of St. Paul's Black community in close proximity to the State Capitol, is razed for the construction of Interstate Highway 94.

1960: **Elisa Bernick** (me) is born at Mount Sinai Hospital. My mother spells my name with an *E* in memory of her deceased twin sister *Elaine*.

1960: My parents move with me and my brother Danny into a three-bedroom house in a new development in the Minneapolis suburb of Crystal (next door to Robbinsdale). They put a $3,600 down payment on the house and buy it for $25,000 using my mom's savings from her job teaching dental health in the St. Paul schools. My mother keeps a kosher house: separate sets of dishes for milk and meat; kosher meats only.

1960s: TV shows shift to a suburban backdrop with *My Three Sons, Father Knows Best, The Brady Bunch,* and *I Love Lucy* (this last show starts in an apartment and then shifts to the suburbs).

1960: Suburban school district 281 includes parts of seven municipalities, among them Robbinsdale, Golden Valley, Crystal, New Hope, and Plymouth, encompassing more than thirty-two total square miles.

1960: The population of New Hope is 3,552. The minority population (Jews) is 0.25 percent. The Black population equals 0.

1960: The Beth El, a Conservative Jewish synagogue on the North Side of Minneapolis with nine hundred families, builds a youth center in St. Louis Park to serve members of the congregation who have already relocated. This is my family's synagogue.

1960: Rival athletic teams toss bagels at St. Louis Park High School's Jewish players.

1963: Rev. Martin Luther King Jr. speaks to an audience of three thousand at Northrop Auditorium at the University of Minnesota.

1963: Black players on the Minnesota Twins baseball team are forced to live in segregated quarters during spring training in Orlando, Florida. Outrage ensues.

1964: Dayton's department store introduces four mannequins "representing the Negro race" in its window displays.

1965: My sister **Lori Bernick** is born at Mount Sinai Hospital.

1965: My family moves into a brand-new four-bedroom house in New Hope, where there are few other Jews. It is much cheaper to build a house there than in St. Louis Park, where most of the other Jews have moved. We no longer keep kosher because it is too expensive, my mom is fed up with it, and there are no kosher meat markets nearby. Still, we do not eat pork or shellfish.

1965: Enrollment in school district 281 increases from 9,410 in 1955 to 23,537 in 1965. The district's building boom results in nineteen new elementary schools by 1970.

1966–1969: My parents drive my brother and me to the Talmud Torah in St. Louis Park after school three days a week to attend Hebrew school, because the Talmud Torah bus won't come to New Hope to pick us up. My favorite part of Hebrew school is the chocolate milk and chocolate chip cookies.

1966–1972: The Minneapolis Talmud Torah religious school experiences a 35 percent decline in enrollment.

1968: My brother, **David Bernick**, is born at Methodist Hospital.

1968: The Beth El Synagogue moves permanently to St. Louis Park. It is the last synagogue to leave Minneapolis's North Side, and nearly the entire Jewish community has moved away by the time it leaves.

1968: The Jewish Community Relations Council of Minnesota provides superintendents of Minnesota schools and the president of the University of Minnesota with a calendar of Jewish holidays for 1968 through 1973, with a note that reads, "We are hopeful that having a schedule of these holidays so far in advance will avoid scheduling conventions, examinations, etc., on days when Jewish youngsters and adults observe their Holy Days."

1969: The *Park High Echo* includes a two-page spread with the headline "Today's Youth Envision Religion Through Confused, Questioning

Eyes." A survey of three hundred students finds that Jews are more
likely to socialize with other Jewish students because "Jews at Park are
uncomfortable in a society that is largely Christian," and that Christmas
carols in school cause alienation among Jewish students. It also reports
that more Jewish students than Christian students feel discriminated
against by teachers.

1969: Zachary Lane Elementary opens, and I am in its first fourth-grade
class of students. It is a nontraditional, open, team-oriented school that
emphasizes individual learning and fewer textbooks.

1970: After a request from a local church, the St. Louis Park school board
votes to change "Christmas Vacation" to "Winter Vacation" and "Easter
Vacation" to "Spring Vacation."

1970: St. Louis Park High School begins teaching a course on minorities.
Mrs. Paula Beugen, the police records clerk, gives a training session at
the school called "What City Employees Should Know about the Jewish
People." She describes situations in which a city employee might be
confronted with Jewish people in an official capacity, cultural and religious
differences that might create those situations, and how to deal with them.

1970: Armstrong Senior High School is built to serve New Hope, Golden
Valley, and Plymouth students.

SELECTIVE TIMELINE OF "THE DIVORCE REVOLUTION," 1960–1975

1960: I am born.

1960: The Food and Drug Administration approves birth control pills.

1960: 25 percent of marriages end in divorce.

1961: JFK establishes the President's Commission on the Status of Women.

1963: Betty Friedan publishes *The Feminine Mystique*, which describes the
dissatisfaction felt by middle-class American housewives with the narrow
role imposed on them by society. The book becomes a bestseller and
galvanizes the modern women's rights movement.

1963: Congress passes the Equal Pay Act.

1964: Congress passes the Civil Rights Act, which outlaws discrimination
based on race, color, religion, gender, or national origin.

1965: The US Supreme Court establishes the right of married couples to use
contraception.

1965: My sister Lori is born.

1965: Governor Art Rolvaag creates the Minnesota Commission on the Status
of Women. A study by the group finds widespread discrimination against

women in employment, maternity benefits, and admission to professional schools at the University of Minnesota.

1966: The National Organization for Women (NOW) is founded by a group of feminists, including Betty Friedan. It is the largest women's rights group in the US and seeks to end sexual discrimination, especially in the workplace, by means of legislative lobbying, litigation, and public demonstrations.

1969: California becomes the first state to adopt a no-fault divorce law, which allows couples to divorce by mutual consent. By 1985, every state has adopted a similar law. Laws are also passed regarding the equal division of common property.

1969: My parents separate.

1970: 33 percent of marriages end in divorce.

1971: *Ms.* magazine is first published as a sample insert in *New York* magazine; three hundred thousand copies are sold out in eight days. The first regular issue is published in July 1972. The magazine becomes the major forum for feminist voices, and cofounder and editor Gloria Steinem is launched as an icon of the modern feminist movement.

1972: My mom and dad officially divorce.

1972: Sociologist Judith Wallerstein begins a study of 131 children and their families who are going through the divorce process over a period of twenty-five years. She will publish her findings in 2000 and conclude that children really aren't "resilient" and that divorce leaves children to struggle for a lifetime with the residue of a decision their parents made.

1972: The Equal Rights Amendment (ERA) is passed by Congress and sent to the states for ratification. The amendment reads, "Equality of rights under the law shall not be denied or abridged by the United States or by any State on account of sex." It has yet to be ratified.

1973: The landmark US Supreme Court ruling *Roe v. Wade* makes abortion legal.

1974: Minnesota passes a no-fault divorce bill.

1975: 48 percent of all marriages end in divorce. The divorce rate stays consistently near 50 percent for the next thirty years.

SELECTIVE TIMELINE OF THE JEWS (AND MY
FAMILY) IN CALIFORNIA, 1945–1973

1945–1965: Thousands of war veterans and others, along with their families, move west. This includes Jews in one of the greatest migrations in US Jewish history. In 1948, the Jewish population in Los Angeles is 250,000. By 1951, there are 330,000 Jews living in LA, and by 1965, the Jewish community numbers half a million, and LA is one of the largest Jewish population centers in the country. Among its residents are my mom's uncle **Abe Gelb**, who makes a living playing piano in bars all over Hollywood, and uncle **Red Gelb**, a sign maker, who ended up on the West Coast after stints in the Merchant Marine during World War I and World War II.

1955: Disneyland opens in Anaheim (Orange County) with eighteen attractions, at a cost of $17.5 million. Opening day ceremonies are overseen by Ronald Reagan, Art Linkletter, and Robert Cummings. The park charges admission for attractions and a general admission at the front gate to keep out certain "undesirables." The park is strategically located near a major freeway and far from public transportation and the center of Los Angeles, so access is limited to those who can afford automobiles.

1960s: Unlike Los Angeles, suburban Orange County has few Jews or racial minorities. It has a national reputation for hardcore conservatism with a crackpot edge. *Fortune* magazine calls it "nut country." According to the *Los Angeles Times*, "Orange County held a tension between midwestern traditionalism and California's drive for reinvention." The fast-growing, mostly White gated communities allow politicians to exploit fears of the "outsider."

1960: John F. Kennedy is elected president; however, Richard Nixon beats him in California by 35,623 votes, propelled by a 62,884-vote margin in Orange County, Nixon's birthplace.

1963: James B. Utt, the US representative from Orange County, claims the United Nations is training "a large contingent of barefooted Africans" in Georgia to take over the country.

1964: Lyndon Johnson is elected president—but in Orange County he loses to Barry Goldwater, who takes almost 56 percent of the vote.

1965: Orange Country is home to thirty-eight chapters of the conspiracy-minded, ultra-right-wing John Birch Society.

1965: The University of California at Irvine is founded and attracts a significant number of Jewish faculty members.

1965: The Orange County Board of Rabbis is founded.

1965: In Delano, California, Cesar Chavez and Dolores Huerta found the United Farm Workers (UFW) association, which becomes the largest and most important farm worker union in the nation. Huerta becomes the first woman to lead such a union. Under Chavez and Huerta's leadership, the UFW joins a strike started by Filipino grape-pickers in Delano. The Delano Grape Strike and Boycott becomes one of the most significant social justice movements for farm workers in the United States.

1966: My mother's sister **Berta** moves to California, accompanied by Grandma Goldie. Berta stays and gets married. **Grandma Goldie, Aunt Freda,** and **Aunt Esther** bounce back and forth between Minnesota and California for several years before relocating to Los Angeles for good in 1968.

1967: Ronald Reagan, who makes his home in Orange County, becomes governor of California.

1967: The Brown Berets, a Chicano paramilitary organization that stresses "direct action," is created in Los Angeles. Wearing brown khaki uniforms and a distinctive Brown beret, the organization, led by its founder David Sanchez, soon forms chapters throughout the Southwest.

1967: The first Chicano Studies program in the United States is created at California State University at Los Angeles.

1967: Disneyland debuts "Pirates of the Caribbean," which immediately becomes its most popular attraction.

1968: Several years after its passage, the Immigration and Nationality Act of 1965 goes into effect and opens the door to non-European immigrants, primarily from Latin America, Africa, and Asia.

1968: The Mexican American Legal Defense and Educational Fund opens its doors, becoming the first legal fund to pursue protection of Mexican American civil rights.

1968: Mexican American high school students in East Los Angeles stage walkouts to protest the inferior education they receive in the Los Angeles school system. The "blowouts" at Wilson, Lincoln, Roosevelt, and Garfield high schools last for a week. Eventually, as many as fifteen thousand students in schools throughout the city walk out in sympathy strikes. The students eventually win a series of concessions from the board of education.

1968: Popular televangelist Robert Schuller, who moved from the Midwest to Orange County in 1955, adds a thirteen-story "Tower of Hope" building on the north side of his drive-in church. It is the tallest structure in Orange County and is topped by a ninety-foot illuminated cross.

1969: The Jewish Harbor Reform Temple in Newport Beach is refused entry into the Harbor Council of Churches.

1969: Fifteen hundred young people attend the Chicano Youth Liberation Conference in Denver, where Mexican Americans are encouraged to think beyond assimilationist politics to embrace goals of self-determination. The conference includes discussions of feminism and sexism within the movement.

1969: Chicana activists in Long Beach take the name Las Hijas de Cuauhtémoc and work to distinguish themselves from other feminist movements.

They critique their exclusion from both the mainstream male-dominated
Chicano nationalist movement and the second wave feminist movement.

1970s: At the start of this decade, 80 percent of California's residents are non-
Hispanic Whites. Migration to the Sunbelt boosts Orange County's Jewish
population. Over the next few years, the Latino population in Orange
Country more than doubles from forty thousand to ninety thousand,
lured by construction jobs, service positions, and better schools.

1970: La Habra, California, has a total area of 7.4 square miles and a population
of 41,350 primarily White Christian residents.

1970: Heading one of the nation's first megachurches, televangelist Robert
Schuller begins national broadcasts of his weekly "Hour of Power"
television program.

1970: Four Kent State University students are killed and ten are wounded when
members of the Ohio National Guard fire on demonstrators protesting the
US bombing of Cambodia. Eleven days later, two students are killed and
twelve are injured at Jackson State College in Jackson, Mississippi, during
an antiwar protest.

1970: Disneyland closes five hours early when three hundred "Yippies" enter
the park as part of "National Yippie Day." In a strange twist, my brother
Dan and I are there with Uncle Leo! We are visiting California, and
Disneyland is the highlight of our trip. Police from several nearby cities are
called in, and six Yippies are arrested after scuffles with police (who are
dressed in riot gear). The Yippies hold a smoke-in on Tom Sawyer's Island,
raise the Viet Cong flag on Castle Rock, and march down Main Street
harassing the Disneyland Marching Band by singing "We are marching to
Cambodia." Dan and I are sad that we have to leave "the Happiest Place on
Earth" earlier than planned.

1970: Chicano antiwar activists from local colleges and members of the Brown
Berets lead a march in East Los Angeles that draws thirty thousand
demonstrators.

1970: Women of the Brown Beret movement, Las Adelitas de Aztlán, separate
themselves from the men to tear down stereotypes about the role of
Chicanas.

1971: The First National Chicana Conference takes place in Houston, and six
hundred Chicanas establish a platform and formally declare themselves
an integral part of the Chicano movement. The discussion includes equal
access to education, reproductive justice, and formation of childcare
centers. The conference is fraught with discord as Chicanas from
geographically and ideologically divergent positions spar over the role of

feminism within the Chicano movement. These conflicts lead to a walkout on the final day of the conference.

1972: "I Am Woman" reaches the top of the popular music charts and earns Helen Reddy a Grammy Award. The song, with its words "Hear me roar," becomes an anthem of the second wave women's movement.

1972: The Equal Rights Amendment (ERA) is passed by the US Senate and is sent to the states for ratification.

1972: Conservative leader Phyllis Schlafly's "Stop Taking Our Privileges" campaign turns political opinion against the ERA and contributes to its defeat.

1973: *My mom* moves *me, Lori,* and **David** to La Habra. Just shy of thirteen, I attend Sonora High School as a ninth-grader. Past demographic statistics are unavailable, but current statistics show that 77 percent of Sonora's student body is "of color," 64 percent is Latino, and 49 percent of the student body comes from economically disadvantaged households.

1973: Adjusted for inflation, a ten-minute direct-dialed Sunday phone call from New Hope to California is twenty-five dollars. Operator-assisted collect calls and nonweekend calls are significantly more expensive.

1973: The airline industry is still regulated by the US government. It is illegal for an airline to charge less than $1,442 in inflation-adjusted dollars for a flight between New York City and Los Angeles.

NOTES

Listed below are the sources from which I have quoted without full attribution.

MEMORY IS A SLIPPERY FISH

After writer Elizabeth McCracken reread Beverly Cleary's Ramona Quimby books as an adult, she tweeted, "87% of my kindergarten memories are in fact plagiarized from *Ramona the Pest*." The tweet is available here:
https://twitter.com/elizmccracken/status/496846505500622852

"Even memories which are detailed and vivid and held with 100 percent conviction can be completely false," says University of London professor Chris French.
Daily Briefing, "How Reliable Is Your Memory? (Not Very.)," *Advisory Board*, August 15, 2016, https://www.advisory.com/daily-briefing/2016/08/15/memory.

Something writers Brenda Miller and Suzanne Paola describe as "plumping the skeletal facts with the flesh of the imagination."
Brenda Miller and Suzanne Paola, *Tell It Slant* (New York: McGraw Hill, 2012), 154.

"History is never a 'given'; it is always a 'creation.'"
Annette Atkins, *Creating Minnesota: A History from the Inside Out* (St. Paul: Minnesota Historical Society Press, 2007), xv.

Additional Sources

Melissa Dahl, "Your Fondest Childhood Memory May Not Have Really Happened," *The Cut*, September 4, 2014, http://nymag.com/scienceofus/2014/09/your-fondest-childhood-memory-may-not-be-real.html.

Erika Hayasaki, "How Many of Your Memories Are Fake?," *The Atlantic*, November 18, 2013, https://www.theatlantic.com/health/archive/2013/11/how-many-of-your -memories-are-fake/281558/.

"How Real Are False Memories?," *CNRS News*, January 16, 2017, https://news.cnrs .fr/articles/how-real-are-false-memories.

Julia Shaw, "The Memory Illusion," *Scientific American*, June 13, 2016, https://blogs .scientificamerican.com/mind-guest-blog/the-memory-illusion/.

Julia Shaw, "What Experts Wish You Knew about False Memories," *Scientific American*, August 8, 2016, https://blogs.scientificamerican.com/mind-guest-blog/what-experts -wish-you-knew-about-false-memories/.

Kelly Tatera, "Are All of Your Memories Real?," *The Science Explorer*, September 2, 2015, http://thescienceexplorer.com/are-your-memories-real.

"THE GREAT JEWISH INVASION"

When Russia swallowed large chunks of Poland, one population was found to be indigestible—the Jews.
> Linda Mack Schloff, *And Prairie Dogs Weren't Kosher* (St. Paul: Minnesota Historical Society Press), 1996.

McClure's, a popular US magazine, ran an article with the headline "The Great Jewish Invasion."
> Burton J. Hendrick, "The Great Jewish Invasion." *McClure's* magazine, February 1, 1907.

A DEPARTURE FROM MINNESOTA NICE

Statistics about religion and population:
> "U.S. Religious Landscape Survey: Religious Beliefs and Practices: Diverse and Politically Relevant," June 2008, https://www.pewresearch.org/wp -content/uploads/sites/7/2008/06/report2-religious-landscape-study-full .pdf.
> "World Population Review," 2021, https://worldpopulationreview.com /states/minnesota-population.

DECAMPING TO THE SUBURBS

"Though still not as assimilated into mainstream Minnesota culture . . ."
> Jacob Cohn, Maggie Goldberger, and Maya Margolis, "Religious Diversity in

Minnesota Initiative," Carlton College, https://religionsmn.carleton.edu
/exhibits/show/st-louis-park-eruv-jewish/history/1800s/movement
-of-jews-out-of-the-no

EMIGRATION TO ASSIMILATION

Something linguist Deborah Tannen says is common among Eastern European
Jewish transplants. Tannen describes this way of speaking as "high-involvement"
and "cooperative overlapping."

"Interrupters: Linguist Says It's the Jewish Way," *The Jewish News of Northern
California*, May 12, 2000, https://www.jweekly.com/2000/05/12
/interrupters-linguist-says-it-s-jewish-way/.

According to one study, by the end of World War I, only 20 percent of US Jews kept
kosher. By 1967, it was down to 5 percent. We were just part of the larger trend.

Linda Mack Schloff, *And Prairie Dogs Weren't Kosher* (St. Paul: Minnesota
Historical Society Press, 1996), 86.

Both the Holocaust and Israel gave Jews a degree of critical distance from the
mainstream American whiteness, a sense of otherness even in the midst of being
ardently embraced by the mainstream.

Karen Brodkin, *How Jews Became White Folks* (New Brunswick, NJ: Rutgers
University Press, 1998), 141.

MAKING A BETTY CROCKER BREAK FOR IT

Even in 1971, only 1 percent of Jewish mothers in the United States held jobs outside
the home, while nationally, more than half of all mothers did.

Linda Mack Schloff, *And Prairie Dogs Weren't Kosher* (St. Paul: Minnesota
Historical Society Press, 1996), 132.

MRS. SAMUEL BERNICK REACHES FOR THE CROWN

In 1953, Billboard magazine called it "a cheesecake parade." But in 1954, the whole
thing was reincarnated as something less of a beauty pageant and more of a domestic
goddess talent show.

Manisha Aggarwal-Schifellite, "The Long, Strange Life of the Mrs. America
Pageant," *Jezebel*, January 5, 2016, http://pictorial.jezebel.com/the-long
-strange-life-of-the-mrs-america-pageant-1750888725.

JEWISHNOTCHRISTIAN

My mom was nine and my dad was eleven in 1946 when journalist Carey McWilliams described Minneapolis as "the capital of anti-Semitism in the United States" in *Common Ground* magazine.

> Laura Weber, "From Exclusion to Integration: The Story of Jews in Minnesota," *MNOPEDIA*, https://www.mnopedia.org/exclusion-integration-story-jews-minnesota.

CAN'T HIDE FROM THE WEATHER

Extreme weather events in every season were a significant part of my growing up. In 1965, when I was five, civil defense sirens were used for the first time in Twin Cities history to alert residents to a severe weather threat.

> Paul Huttner, "50 Years since 1965 Twin Cites Tornado Outbreak," *Updraft Blog, Minnesota Public Radio,* May 4, 2015, https://www.mprnews.org/story/2015/05/04/50-years-since-1965-twin-cites-tornado-outbreak.

I recite these facts not only because they're impressively awful, but because I wonder how much of my mother's unhappiness and instability during my childhood was influenced by Minnesota's inexorable weather.

> Charles Fisk, "Graphical Climatology of Minneapolis-St. Paul Area Temperatures, Precipitation, and Snowfall (1820–Present)," *ClimateStations. com,* https://www.climatestations.com/minneapolis-2/.

According to a 2018 report from Blue Cross Blue Shield of America, Minnesota has one of the highest rates of major depression in the country and Hawaii has the lowest.

> "Major Depression: The Impact on Overall Health," May 10, 2018, *Blue Cross Blue Shield Association,* https://www.bcbs.com/the-health-of-america/reports/major-depression-the-impact-overall-health

SEWING (IN)SANITY

Fashion articles in the *Ladies' Home Journal* included "Penny Pinching Sewing Ideas for Summer" and "The Journal's Wonder Dress to Make for Under $10.00."

> Marcia McLean, "Constructing Garments, Constructing Identities: Home Sewers and Homemade Clothing in 1950s/60s Alberta," 2006, *Textile Society of America Symposium Proceedings,* 328.

(RE)CONSTRUCTING THE NARRATIVE

"Storytelling isn't just how we construct our identities, stories are our identities," —
John Holmes, PhD, Waterloo University

Sadie F. Dingfelder, "Our Stories, Ourselves," *Monitor on Psychology* 42, no. 1
(January 2011): 42, https://www.apa.org/monitor/2011/01/stories.

"It is not so much our past events that shape us," says psychology professor Jonathan
Adler, "but our construct and interpretation of those events and the narrative we
create which, in turn, shapes who we will become."

Julie Beck, "Life Stories," *The Atlantic*, August 10, 2015, https://www
.theatlantic.com/health/archive/2015/08/life-stories-narrative-psychology
-redemption-mental-health/400796/.

Recent epigenetic research shows that our genes are carriers of "molecular
memories."

June Javelosa, "Scientists Have Discovered How Memories Are Inherited,"
World Economic Forum, December 4, 2018, https://www.weforum.org
/agenda/2018/12/memories-can-be-inherited-and-scientists-may
-have-just-figured-out-how/.
Helen Thomas, "Study of Holocaust Survivors Finds Trauma Passed On to
Children's Genes, *The Guardian*, August 12, 2015, http://www.theguardian
.com/science/2015/aug/21/study-of-holocaust-survivors-finds-trauma-passed
-on-to-childrens-genes.
Siddhartha Mukherjee, "Same but Different," *The New Yorker*, April 25, 2016,
http://www.newyorker.com/magazine/2016/05/02/breakthroughs
-in-epigenetics.

Stories are products of imagination, and imagination, says author and historian Yuval
Noah Harari, is what separates us from other animals.

Yuval Noah Harari, "What Explains the Rise of Humans?," filmed at
TEDGlobalLondon, video, 06:27, https://www.ted.com/talks/yuval
_noah_harari_what_explains_the_rise_of_humans/transcript?language=en.

MARRIAGE GO-ROUND

The institution of marriage underwent a sea change during the 1960s and 70s. The
traditional marriage arrangement based on obligation and sacrifice shifted to a "self-
expressive" or "soulmate" model of marriage; one based on romance, self-fulfillment,
and supporting your spouse's dreams.

Eli J. Finkel, "The All or Nothing Marriage," *New York Times*, February 14, 2014, https://www.nytimes.com/2014/02/15/opinion/sunday/the-all-or -nothing-marriage.html.

Not that everything on the airwaves was idyllic. Six o'clock newscasts brought the violent realities of real-world events directly into people's living rooms for the first time in history.

Ronald Steinman, "The First Televised War," *New York Times*, April 7, 2017, https://www.nytimes.com/2017/04/07/opinion/the-first-televised-war.html? action=click&pgtype=Homepage&version=Moth-Visible&moduleDetail= inside-nyt-region-1&module=inside-nyt-region&region=inside-nyt -region&WT.nav=inside-nyt-region.

DISAPPEARING ACT

In an interview in the *Michigan Quarterly Review*, Cistaro wondered if she, too, might have inherited the "leaving gene" that afflicted her mother and other female ancestors.

Melissa Cistaro, "On Pieces of My Mother: An Interview with Melissa Cistaro," interviewed by Katie O'Reilly, *Michigan Quarterly Review*, September 28, 2015, http://www.michiganquarterlyreview.com/2015/09/on-pieces -of-my-mother-an-interview-with-melissa-cistaro/.

Would you be surprised if I told you there's research showing that infidelity can be passed along in people's genes?

Susan Scutti, "The Roots of Infidelity: Surprising Genetic and Financial Factors Link to Cheating," *Medical Daily*, May 27, 2015, https://www .medicaldaily.com/roots-infidelity-surprising-genetic-and-financial -factors-link-cheating-335236.

Even without a genetic component, there's plenty of sociological research showing infidelity runs in families.

Laura Dang, "Science Has Bad News for People Whose Parents Have Cheated," *NextShark*, September 3, 2015, https://nextshark.com/cheating -runs-in-family-study/.

THE GESTALT PRAYER

"I do my thing and you do your thing . . ."

Frederick S. Perls, *Gestalt Therapy Verbatim* (Gouldsboro, ME: Gestalt Journal Press, 1969).

REVOLUTIONARIES

"The true focus of revolutionary change is never merely the oppressive situations..."
   Audre Lorde, *Sister Outsider: Essays and Speeches* (Berkeley, CA: Crossing
   Press, 2007).

Divorce is such a common occurrence now, it's hard to remember the powerful
stigma it carried back in 1969 when my parents announced their split.
   W. Bradford Wilcox, "The Evolution of Divorce," *National Affairs*, Fall 2009,
   http://nationalaffairs.com/publications/detail/the-evolution-of-divorce.
   William A. Galston, "Divorce American Style, *National Affairs*, Summer 1996,
   https://www.nationalaffairs.com/public_interest/detail/divorce
   -american-style.
   "Network TV Schedules 1968–1969," *Rerun Century*, http://www
   .reruncentury.com/primetime/1968-1969/.
   "The Relationship between Television and Culture," *Culture and Media* 1.0,
   sec. 9.2, http://2012books.lardbucket.org/books/culture-and-media/s12-02
   -the-relationship-between-telev.html.

In 1970, the creators of The Mary Tyler Moore Show were forced to change the
backstory of hometown heroine Mary Richards.
   Amanda Robb, "Divorce-1981-Style," *AARP The Magazine* (Aug./Sept. 2016),
   https://www.aarp.org/home-family/friends-family/info-2016/divorce-1980s
   .html.

According to the National Jewish Population Study, 80 percent of adult American
Jews were married in 1970.
   "Vital Statistics: Select Indicators on World Jewry," *Jewish Virtual Library*
   (January 2012), https://www.jewishvirtuallibrary.org/jsource/Judaism
   /usjewfamily.html.

TERRA INCOGNITA

A current voluminous list of books recommended by UCLA children's therapists
includes only one book from that era:
   Richard A. Gardner, MD, *The Boys' and Girls' Book about Divorce* (New York:
   Bantam, 1970).
   Jason Steadman, Psy.D., Director, FELT for childhood anxiety, "Therapeutic
   Books for Children," *Center for Mental Health in Schools and Student Learning
   Supports at UCLA*, Bibliography, http://smhp.psych.ucla.edu/pdfdocs
   /childbiblio.pdf.

Studies show that in 1965, mothers spent an average of 12 hours and fathers only 4.5 hours each week on childcare activities.

> Claire Cain Miller, "The Relentlessness of Modern Parenting," *New York Times*, December 25, 2018, https://www.nytimes.com/2018/12/25/upshot/the -relentlessness-of-modern-parenting.html.

Given that between 1965 and 1975 the divorce rate went from 27 percent to 48 percent of all marriages, this off-ramp sounds more like a six-lane freeway.

> U.S. Census, *Vital and Health Statistics*, "Divorce and Divorce Rates, United States" ser. 21, no. 29, https://www.cdc.gov/nchs/data/series/sr_21/sr21 _029.pdf.
>
> U.S. Census Bureau, "Births, Deaths, Marriages, and Divorces," *Statistical Abstract of the United States: 2011*, https://www.census.gov/prod /2011pubs/11statab/vitstat.pdf.
>
> Vanessa Martins Lamb, "The 1950's and the 1960's and the American Woman: The Transition from the 'Housewife' to the Feminist," *History* (2011), dumas-00680821.

In her 1997 book *The Divorce Culture*, writer Barbara Dafoe Whitehead notes, "Nothing in the history of American childhood rivaled the scale or speed of this change in children's families."

> Barbara Dafoe Whitehead, *The Divorce Culture: Rethinking Our Commitments to Marriage and Family* (New York: Knopf, 1997), 82.

Ann Landers changed her story in 1972 when she said, "I no longer believe that marriage means forever no matter how lousy it is—or 'for the sake of the children.'"

The authors of the 1974 book *The Courage to Divorce* believed divorce could be a beneficial experience by "liberating children" and making them less dependent on their parents.

> W. Bradford Wilcox, "The Evolution of Divorce," *National Affairs*, Fall 2009, http://nationalaffairs.com/publications/detail/the-evolution-of-divorce.

Opinions about the effects of divorce on kids have seesawed over the years: (1) Kids are resilient and they'll be fine or (2) Divorce will damage them forever.

> David Masci, "Does Divorce Turn Children into Troubled Adults?," *CQ Press* 11, no. 2 (January 19, 2001), http://library.cqpress.com/cqresearcher /document.php?id=cqresrre2001011900.
>
> Maria Sciullo, "*Mad Men* Series Inaccurately Depicts Difficulties of Divorce for Women in '60s," *Pittsburgh Post-Gazette*, July 25, 2010, http://www.post -gazette.com/ae/tv-radio/2010/07/25/Mad-Men-series-inaccurately -depicts-difficulties-of-divorce-for-women-in-60s/stories/201007250142

J. S. Wallerstein, S. B. Corbin, and J. M. Lewis, "Children of Divorce: A 10-Year Study," in E. M. Hetherington and J. D. Arasteh (eds.), *Impact of Divorce, Single Parenting, and Stepparenting on Children* (New York: Lawrence Erlbaum, 1988), 197–214.
Judith S. Wallerstein, Julia M. Lewis, and Sandra Blakeslee, *The Unexpected Legacy of Divorce: The 25-Year Landmark Study* (New York: Hachette Books, 2001).

There is still little agreement about the effects of divorce on children, and recent studies continue to find conflicting results.
Alexa Dankowski, Suzanne Goode, Philip Greenspun, Chaconne Martin-Berkowicz, and Tina Tonnu, *Real World Divorce: Custody, Child Support, and Alimony in the 50 States* (Fifth Chance Media, 2017), http://www.realworlddivorce.com/History.
Gail Gross, "The Impact of Divorce on Children of Different Ages," *Huffington Post*, May 12, 2015, https://www.huffingtonpost.com/dr-gail-gross/the-impact-of-divorce-on-children-of-different-ages_b_6820636.html.
Shannon Marie Despain, "A Content Analysis of Family Structure in Newbery Medal and Honor Books, 1930–2010," *Theses and Dissertations* 3648 (2012), https://scholarsarchive.byu.edu/etd/3648/.

Despite the conflicting data, researchers universally agree on one thing: The way adults handle a divorce will affect its impact on their children.
Natasha Daniels, "The 10 Worst Mistakes Parents Make When Getting a Divorce," *Anxious Toddlers Parenting Survival*, https://www.anxioustoddlers.com/divorce-mistakes/.

GRIT

We are constantly rewiring our brains based on past experience and the expectation of how we need to use them in the future.
Richard A. Friedman, "How to Be More Resilient," *New York Times,* December 15, 2018, https://www.nytimes.com/2018/12/15/opinion/sunday/stress-anxiety-depression-research.html?action=click&module=Opinion&pgtype=Homepage.

Given that epigenetic memories are written into our very cells, with the potential to recall generations of adversity, is it possible that Jews and other victims of long-term trauma have a predisposition for resilience?
"Social Context," *National Human Genome Research Institute*, https://www.genome.gov/dna-day/15-ways/social-context.

Stephanie Hanel, "Epigenetics—How the Environment Influences Our Genes," *Lindau Nobel Laureate Meetings*, August 5, 2015, http://www
.lindau-nobel.org/epigenetics-how-the-environment-influences-our-genes/.
Nicole Creanza and Marcus W. Feldman, "Worldwide Genetic and Cultural Change in Human Evolution," *Current Opinion in Genetics and Development* 41 (December 2016), 85–92, http://www.sciencedirect.com/science/article/pii/S0959437X16301101.

As a recent *Discover* magazine article put it, "The mechanisms of behavioral epigenetics underlie not only deficits and weaknesses but strengths and resiliencies, too."
Dan Hurley, "Grandma's Experiences Leave a Mark on Your Genes," *Discover*, June 24, 2015, https://www.discovermagazine.com/health/grandmas
-experiences-leave-a-mark-on-your-genes.

Studies show that resilient children have certain things in common: a strong bond with a supportive caregiver, teacher, or mentor; a psychological makeup that allows them to meet the world on their own terms; and an internal locus of control.
Maria Konnikova, "How People Learn to Become Resilient," *The New Yorker*, February 11, 2016, https://www.newyorker.com/science/maria-konnikova/the
-secret-formula-for-resilience.
Tough, Paul, "How Kids Learn Resilience," *The Atlantic*, June 2016, https://
www.theatlantic.com/magazine/archive/2016/06/how-kids-really-
succeed/480744/.
Hampton, Debbie, "Heal Your Brain by Reversing Intergenerational Trauma," *Uplift*, April 10, 2018, https://upliftconnect.com/heal-your-brain-
by-reversing-generational-trauma/.

Locus of control is a personality trait that exists on a continuum.
Julian B. Rotter, "The Social Learning Theory of Julian B. Rotter," Department of Psychology, Cal State Fullerton, http://psych.fullerton.edu/jmearns/rotter
.htm.

She was also raised in a verbally abusive family, continually subjected to criticism, hostility, and "emotional over-involvement toward family members."
R. D. Freed and M. C. Tompson, Predictors of Parental Locus of Control in Mothers of Pre- and Early Adolescents, *Journal of Clinical Child and Adolescent Psychology* 40, no. 1 (2011): 100–110, https://doi.org/10.1080/15374416.2011.533
410.

LOOKING FOR THE EXITS

Gila Lyons wonders, "Is there some inherited resilience, or compulsion to keep surviving and thriving?"

Gila Lyons, "Jewish Trauma May Be Passed Down Through the Generations," *Medium*, June 27, 2016, https://medium.com/the-establishment/for-jewish -people-trauma-is-passed-down-across-generations-bf9aa503778b.

REMEMBERING AND FORGETTING

There's an interesting link between the way humans think about the past and the future: The same region of the brain is activated when we're asked to remember something, and when we're asked to imagine an event that hasn't happened yet. "The future is never a direct replica of the past," says psychology professor Jonathan Adler. "So, we need to be able to take pieces of things that have happened to us and reconfigure them into possible futures."

Julie Beck, "Life Stories," *The Atlantic*, August 10, 2015, https://www .theatlantic.com/health/archive/2015/08/life-stories-narrative-psychology -redemption-mental-health/400796/.

"For better or worse, stories are a very powerful source of self-persuasion," says psychology professor John Holmes. "Storytelling isn't just how we construct our identities, stories are our identities. Evidence that doesn't fit the story is going to be left behind."

Sadie F. Dingfelder, "Our Stories, Ourselves," *Monitor on Psychology* 42, no. 1 (January 2011): 42, https://www.apa.org/monitor/2011/01/stories.

In a 2014 TED Talk, author Judith Claybourne describes the negative self-image she'd constructed based on what she thought were "factual" childhood memories that turned out not to be true.

Judy Claybourne, "The Strange Relationship between Memory and Truth," filmed at TEDxBrixton, November 26, 2014, https://www.youtube.com /watch?v=ZuZrSqveOw4.

Not only does the human brain unconsciously remember what never happened, it can be intentionally trained to forget what really did. Forgetting is a protective device, a survival mechanism.

Benedict Carey, "Can We Get Better at Forgetting?," *New York Times*, March 22, 2019, https://www.nytimes.com/2019/03/22/health/memory-forgetting -psychology.html.

There is debate in the field of trauma recovery about whether revisiting traumatic memories is necessary for healing, or whether it may in fact be harmful.

Michaels, Carey, MPH, "Historical Trauma and Microaggressions: A Framework for Culturally-Based Practice," *University of Minnesota Extension Children, Youth & Family Consortium, Child Welfare Series*, October 2010, https:// drive.google.com/file/d/1sbxGiLMz95Sv4uPXOVsZqtTYhPbvpSTh/view.

"Post Traumatic Growth," *Manitoba Trauma Information & Education Centre*, 2013, http://trauma-recovery.ca/resiliency/post-traumatic-growth/.

Shawn Ginwright, "The Future of Healing: Shifting from Trauma-Informed Care to Healing Centered Engagement," *Medium*, May 31, 2018, https://ginwright.medium.com/the-future-of-healing-shifting-from-trauma-informed-care-to-healing-centered-engagement-634f557ce69c.

Erika Beras, "Traces of Genetic Trauma Can Be Tweaked," *Scientific American*, April 15, 2017, https://www.scientificamerican.com/podcast/episode/traces-of-genetic-trauma-can-be-tweaked/.

"There are places we need to fight. Absolutely. There's struggle, there's work, and there's fight. But if we're always in that state, the ideas that we generate will be fight ideas. They'll be struggle ideas. I don't want to live in a world with the DNA of fight and struggle. I want some of the visioning to happen from a settled, connected, and peaceful place."

Jennifer Brown, "Perspective Switch: Healing Trauma through Healthy Storytelling," *Medium*, November 25, 2018, https://medium.com/@jenniferbrown_97699/perspective-switch-healing-trauma-through-healthy-storytelling-dbd3c670343d.

Kenneth V. Hardy, "Healing the Hidden Wounds of Racial Trauma," *Reclaiming Children and Youth* 22, no. 1 (Spring 2013): 24–28, https://static1.squarespace.com/static/545cdfcce4b0a64725b9f65a/t/54da3451e4b0ac9bd1d1cd30/1423586385564/Healing.pdf.

"A Guide to Toxic Stress," *Center on the Developing Child, Harvard University*, https://developingchild.harvard.edu/guide/a-guide-to-toxic-stress/.

The way we remember and tell trauma stories varies widely across people and cultures, as do the ways communities and individuals interpret and respond to these narratives over time.

Nathaniel Vincent Mohatt et al., "Historical Trauma as Public Narrative: A Conceptual Review of How History Impacts Present-Day Health," *Social Science & Medicine* 106, (April 2014): 128–136, https://www.ncbi.nlm.nih.gov/pmc/articles/PMC4001826/.

Rignam Wangkhang, "Can Trauma Be Passed from Parent to Child?," *Ozy*, July 6, 2016, http://www.ozy.com/fast-forward/can-trauma-be-passed-from-parent-to-child/70261?utm_source=NH&utm_medium=pp&utm_campaign=pp.

Mary Annette Pember, "Trauma May Be Woven into DNA of Native Americans," *Indian Country Today*, September 13, 2018, https://indiancountrytoday.com/archive/trauma-may-be-woven-into-dna-of-native-americans#:~:text=The%20science%20of%20epigenetics%2C%20literally,react%20to%20trauma%20and%20stress.

M. Tirzah Firestone Friedman, "Transforming Jewish Historical Trauma: Tales of Choice and Redemption" (PhD diss., Pacifica Graduate Institute, 2015), https://www.pacifica.edu/dissertation-oral-defense/transforming-jewish -historical-trauma-tales-choice-redemption/.
Nancy Berns, "Why Remembering Matters for Healing," *The Conversation*, April 11, 2018, https://theconversation.com/why-remembering -matters-for-healing-94565.

For psychiatry and neuroscience professor Rachel Yehuda, what's interesting about this is that "these days occur on a specified time on the calendar. They start at a certain time. They end at a certain time, and then so too the effects end."

Rachel Yehuda, "How Trauma and Resilience Cross Generations," interview by Krista Tippett, *On Being with Krista Tippett*, American Public Media, July 30, 2015, https://onbeing.org/programs/rachel-yehuda-how-trauma-and -resilience-cross-generations/.

He wonders why some catastrophic events create lasting trauma that determine our trajectories while others seemingly don't. He points to his father who was a Holocaust survivor. "He experienced so much more trauma than I can even imagine, losing his entire family, losing his homeland, his language and culture, fleeing for his life. . . . He was marked by trauma, but it did not determine the shape of his life."

Dina Gilio-Whitaker, "Q&A: David Treuer on Uncovering the Untold Native American Histories of 'Heartbeat of Wounded Knee,'" *Los Angeles Times*, January 22, 2019, https://www.latimes.com/books/la-ca-jc-david-treuer -interview-20190122-htmlstory.html.

"A story can be a gift like Ariadne's thread; or the labyrinth, or the labyrinth's ravening Minotaur," says Rebecca Solnit. "We navigate by stories, but sometimes we only escape by abandoning them."

Rebecca Solnit, *A Field Guide to Getting Lost* (New York: Penguin, 2006), 181.

EPILOGUE: EVOLVING STORYLINES

"If I focus on the story of the history and not the story of what came out of it, which is a story of survival, triumph, and love, then I could miss out on the healing." Vanessa Jackson, president of Healing Circles

Jackson, Sha, "The Healing Power of Storytelling," *Coming to the Table*, https://comingtothetable.org/the-healing-power-of-storytelling/.

But when I researched this idea, I discovered that in Judaism, forgiveness is not designed to be easily given.

Sara Horowitz, "For Jews, Forgiveness Is Complicated," *The Canadian Jewish News*, October 7, 2016, https://www.cjnews.com/perspectives/opinions/jews-forgiveness-complicated.

The traditional Haggadah phrase, "He took us out from slavery to freedom . . . and from servitude to redemption," has been interpreted and reinterpreted over the centuries.
Rav Dovid Hofstedter, "The Meaning of Our Redemption," *Jewish Press*, March 20, 2013, https://www.jewishpress.com/indepth/front-page/the-meaning-of-our-redemption/2013/03/20/
Rabbi Michael Knopf, "Happiness in Slavery," *Haaretz*, March 23, 2016, https://www.haaretz.com/jewish/the-meaning-of-pesach-happiness-in-slavery-1.5235730

The Jewish tradition differentiates between fate (*yi'ud*), and destiny (*goral*).
Ephraim Mirvis, "What Passover Has to Tell Us about Freedom," *The Jewish Chronicle*, excerpted from radio interview, Channel 4 *Thought for a Day*, April 9, 2017, https://www.thejc.com/news/news-features/what-passover-has-to-tell-us-about-freedom-1.436049.

Jewish historian Yosef Hayim Yerushalmi says the entire history of Judaism is a history of interpretation. "But it is not only the interpretation of a text, or a set of texts, it is also an ongoing interpretation of experience."
For Yerushalmi, "history" is not only the story of what happened, but of how what happened was interpreted. "So long as there is a sense between the generations of continuity, then it doesn't really matter that the interpretations of one age, and the interpretations of another age will be very different. Jewish memory is at its heart an ongoing contest of interpretation, dialogue, and debate by Jews trying to define the law, the experience, the faith, which becomes the tradition."
Yosef Hayim Yerushalmi, "Heritage Conversations," interview by Bill Moyers for Public Affairs Television, February 15, 1986, https://billmoyers.com/content/yosef-yerushalmi/.

BIBLIOGRAPHY

Additional sources to which I am indebted for information, ideas, and inspiration:

Amram, Fred. *We're in America Now: A Survivor's Stories*. Duluth, MN: Holy Cow! Press, 2016.

Atkins, Annette. *Creating Minnesota: A History from the Inside Out*. St. Paul: Minnesota Historical Society Press, 2007.

Baack, Gita. *The Inheritors: Moving Forward from Generational Trauma*. Berkeley, CA: She Writes Press, 2017.

Berman, Hyman, and Linda Mack Schloff. *Jews in Minnesota*. St. Paul: Minnesota Historical Society Press, 2002.

Biss, Eula. *On Immunity: An Inoculation*. Minneapolis, MN: Graywolf Press, 2014.

Brodkin, Karen. *How Jews Became White Folks and What That Says About Race in America*. New Brunswick, NJ: Rutgers University Press, 1998.

Coates, Ta-Nehisi. *Between the World and Me*. New York: Spiegel & Grau, 2015.

Coontz, Stephanie. *The Way We Never Were: American Families and the Nostalgia Trap*. New York: Basic Books, 1992.

Didion, Joan. *The Year of Magical Thinking*. New York: Knopf, 2005.

Dregni, Eric. *Weird Minnesota*. Edited by Mark Moran and Mark Sceurman. New York: Sterling, 2006.

Ehrlick, Darrell. *It Happened in Minnesota*. Guilford, CT: TwoDot, 2008.

Frankel, Adam. *The Survivors: A Story of War, Inheritance and Healing*. New York: Harper, 2019.

Gottschall, Jonathan. *The Storytelling Animal: How Stories Make Us Human*. Boston: Mariner Books, 2013.

Hoffman, Eva. *After Such Knowledge: Memory, History and the Legacy of the Holocaust*. New York: Public Affairs, 2004.

Jackson, Kenneth T. *Crabgrass Frontier: The Suburbanization of the United States*. New York: Oxford University Press, 1985.

Johnson, Fenton. *Geography of the Heart*. New York: Scribner, 1996.

Karr, Mary. *The Art of Memoir*. New York: Harper Collins, 2015.

Lass, William E. *Minnesota: A History*. New York: W. W. Norton, 1983.

Latz, Robert. *Jews in Minnesota Politics: The Inside Stories*. Minneapolis, MN: Nodin Press, 2007.

Menakem, Resmaa. *My Grandmother's Hands: Racialized Trauma and the Pathway to Mending Our Hearts and Bodies*. Las Vegas, NV: Central Recovery Press, 2017.

Miller, Brenda, and Suzanne Paola. *Tell It Slant*. New York: McGraw Hill, 2012.

Nathanson, Iric. *Minneapolis in the Twentieth Century: The Growth of an American City*. St. Paul: Minnesota Historical Society Press, 2010.

Neidt, Jeff, and Lisa Wojna. *Minnesota Trivia: Weird, Wacky and Wild*. Charleston, SC: Blue Bike Books, 2008.

Orange, Tommy. *There There*. New York: Knopf, 2018.

Petrowskaja, Katja. *Maybe Esther: A Family Story*. New York: Harper, 2018.

Register, Cheri. *Beyond Good Intentions: A Mother Reflects on Raising Internationally Adopted Children*. St. Paul: Yeong & Yeong, 2005.

Rizzuto, Rahna Reiko. *Hiroshima in the Morning: A Mother's Search for Identity*. New York: The Feminist Press, 2010.

Rosenwasser, Penny. *Hope into Practice: Jewish Women Choosing Justice Despite Our Fears*. Penny Rosenwasser, 2013.

Rosner, Elizabeth. *Survivor Café: The Legacy of Trauma and the Labyrinth of Memory*. Berkeley, CA: Counterpoint Press, 2017.

Schloff, Linda Mack. *And Prairie Dogs Weren't Kosher*. St. Paul: Minnesota Historical Society Press, 1996.

Shin, Sun Yung, ed. *A Good Time for the Truth: Race in Minnesota*. St. Paul: Minnesota Historical Society Press, 2016.

Solnit, Rebecca. *A Field Guide to Getting Lost*. New York: Penguin, 2006.

Solnit, Rebecca. *Whose Story Is This*. Chicago: Haymarket Books, 2019.

Thomas, Abigail. *Thinking About Memoir*. New York: Sterling Publishing, 2008.

Treuer, David. *The Heartbeat of Wounded Knee*. New York: Penguin Random House, 2019.

University of Minnesota. "A Campus Divided: Progressives, Anti-Communists, Racism, and AntiSemitism at the University of Minnesota 1930–1942." University of Minnesota Exhibition on Antisemitism, 2017. http://acampusdivided.umn.edu/.

Verzemnieks, Inara. *Among the Living and the Dead: A Tale of Exile and Homecoming*. New York: W. W. Norton, 2017.

Wanderer Cohen, Emily. *From Generation to Generation: Healing Intergenerational Trauma Through Storytelling*. New York: Morgan James, 2018.

Whitehead, Barbara Dafoe. *The Divorce Culture: Rethinking Our Commitments to Marriage and Family*. New York: Knopf, 1997.
Wolynn, Mark. *It Didn't Start with You: How Inherited Family Trauma Shapes Who We Are and How to End the Cycle*. New York: Penguin, 2016.
Yerushalmi, Yosef Hayim. *Zakhor: Jewish History and Jewish Memory*. Seattle: University of Washington Press, 1996.

ADDITIONAL WEB SOURCES BY TOPIC

Suburban White Flight

https://www.ncbi.nlm.nih.gov/pmc/articles/PMC4887632/
https://www.nytimes.com/books/first/s/suarez-neighborhood.html
http://www.cliometrics.org/publications/flight.htm
http://www.soc.iastate.edu/sapp/WhiteFlight.pdf
http://citeseerx.ist.psu.edu/viewdoc/download?doi=10.1.1.540.3762&rep=rep1&type=pdf

Jews in Minnesota and the Upper Midwest

https://www.theatlantic.com/politics/archive/2016/12/are-jews-white/509453/
http://collections.mnhs.org/MNHistoryMagazine/articles/52/v52i05p166-182.pdf ("Gentiles Preferred: Minneapolis Jews and Employment 1920–1950," by Laura E. Weber)
http://www.irp.wisc.edu/publications/focus/pdfs/foc32a.pdf
http://www.jweekly.com/article/full/76950/its-no-myth-jews-storytelling-and-the-oral-tradition/
https://www.lib.umn.edu/umja (History: Upper Midwest Jewish Archives)
http://www.rchs.com/highland.htm (Ramsey County Historical Society)
http://www.mnopedia.org/exclusion-integration-story-jews-minnesota
http://collections.mnhs.org/MNHistoryMagazine/articles/52/v52i05p166-182.pdf
http://www.dailywritingtips.com/the-yiddish-handbook-40-words-you-should-know/
http://www.theatlantic.com/business/archive/2015/02/minneapoliss-white-lie/385702/

General Minnesota Suburban History

https://www.jewishvirtuallibrary.org/jsource/Judaism/usjewfamily.html
http://www.ci.new-hope.mn.us/about/duk_duk_daze.shtml
http://www.city-data.com/city/New-Hope-Minnesota.html#ixzz3ypWOWxk9

http://www.crystalmn.gov/docs/_A31ED2DD_DE04_4F3B
   _ADF1_27F624A8BB36_.pdf
http://www.stcloudstate.edu/graduatestudies/overview/documents
   /JoeRoshThesis.pdf

Jews in Minnesota Suburbia

https://www.minnpost.com/mnopedia/2014/11
   /north-sides-last-synagogue-beth-el
http://www.bethelsynagogue.org/about/history/
http://ir.stthomas.edu/cgi/viewcontent
   .cgi?article=1037&context=caps_ed_lead_docdiss
Blodgett, H. *Robbinsdale 1893–1983.* Robbinsdale, MN: Printing Arts, 1983.
http://forward.com/news/14189/spotlight-falls-on-minneapolis-suburb-that-bred
   -fr-02511/#ixzz48k1jTZtYSt. Louis Park History
http://slphistory.org/jewishmigration/
https://storymaps.arcgis.com/stories/695d1dcd10194addb331eebc5a21de73
   (*Exodus,* by Marguerite Mills, winner of the University of Minnesota's 2020
   Mapping Prize)
http://www.myjewishlearning.com/article/jews-in-the-suburbs/
http://jwa.org/encyclopedia/article/suburbanization-in-united-states
https://www.jewishvirtuallibrary.org/the-jewish-american-family

ABOUT THE AUTHOR

ELISA BERNICK is a writer and journalist in St. Paul, Minnesota. She is author of *The Family Sabbatical Handbook: The Budget Guide to Living Abroad with Your Family.*